Research in Social Sciences

Research in Social Sciences - A Survey

BY

Dr. K. L. NARASIMHA MURTY
Editor

GYAN

Published, 2020

Published by

Gyan Publishing House
5, Ansari Road
Daryaganj, New Delhi-110002
Phone: 011-47034999, 9811692060
www.gyanbooks.com
E-mail: books@gyanbooks.com

Printed at: G. Print Process, Delhi.

Cataloging in Publication Data—DK

Courtesy: D.K. Agencies (P) Ltd. <docinfo@dkagencies.com>
Research in social science : a survey / [edited] by Dr. K.L. Narasimha Murty.
pages cm
Contributed articles.
Cover title: Research in social sciences.
ISBN 9788121219464

1. Social sciences—Research. I. Narasimha Murthy, K. L. (Kalluri Lakshmi), 1949- editor. II. Title: Research in social sciences.
LCC H62.R47 2019 | DDC 300.72 23

Dedicated to

Research Scholars and

Practitioners of Social Sciences

Contents

Acknowledgement

Dr. K.L. Narasimha Murty is highly indebted to Professor P.V. Sarma, M.A. M.Sc., Ph.D., Department of Economics, Andhra University, Waltair for the continuous encouragement in the research activity and further to Professor R.B. Singh, Delhi School of Economics, University of Delhi. Delhi and Professor S. Galab, Director, Centre for Economics and Social Studies (CESS), has provided important material to Dr. K.L.N. Murty and he is highly indebted to him for the timely help.

Dr. K.L. Narashimha Murty expresses his gratitude to the contributors (Ph.D. Theses) who have made available for this structural preparation process of this volume in particular.

Hyderabad,

17th February, 2019 **K.L. Narasimha Murty**

List of Contributors

1. Professor Y.V. Ramanayya, Department of Geography, Srikrishna Devaraya University, Anantapur.'
2. Dr. K.L. Narasimha Murty, Department of Geography, Government College (Men), Srikakulam.
3. Professor S. Ramakrishna, Senior Fellow, ICSSR, Department of Geography, Osmania University, Hyderabad.
4. Smt. Kameswari, Varanasi Former Research Scholar, Centre for Economics & Social Studies, Begumpet, Hyderabad.
5. Dr. K. Anjaneyulu, Associate Professor, Department of Commerce, Vivekananda Government Degree College, Vidyanagar, Hyderabad, Telangana State, India.
6. Professor V. Madhava Rao, (R), NIRD, PR, Rajendranagar, Hyderabad.
7. Dr. CVSSRL Hamumantia Das, Department - of statistic, Matic Rajas College, Viziauagaram, Andhra pradesh, India.
8. Dr. S. Abdul Khadar, Principal (R), Government Degree College, Kurnool.
9. Professor R. Gangadhara Sastry, Director P.G. Courses, Sri Satyasai Institute of Higher Learning (Deemed University), Puttaparthi, Anantapur District, Andhra Pradesh.'
10. Dr. V. Gangaiah, Regional Centre of Urban & Environmental Studies, Osmania University, Hyderabad.
11. Prof. Kandimalla Bharathi, Department Library and Information Science, Osmania University, Hyderabad.
12. Dr. B.M.K. Mohan, Registrar (R), Barkatullah University, Bhopal, M.P.

Chapter - 1

Introduction

The Science of administration (Public and Private) and the art of administering policy implementation should go hand in hand. Administering Public Policies for welfare of the people in the country and the state is essential.[1] Business Organization, Business Administration, Business Management including commercial and innovative capabilities, capacities and Calibere are quite important and meritorious factors of both men and women. They create an easy 'landscape' for the origin, growth and development of a business environment and helps to sustainable development.[2] Appropriate economic policies suitable for agricultural and industrial development should be planned for developing Nation/State/District/Mandal/Village (Micro)[3] Human Resource Accounting and Management have been playing an important role in a state[4] Human skill and resources are important. Population growth, variations, spatial distribution, and environmental impact studies are important contributions to demography.[5] Geographical variations could also be identified and deciphered over a period of time, which are important factors for area specific development. Environmental and geographical factors play an important and pivotal role for human development.[6] Besides this, historical factors and local environmental conditions shape and sharpen the history of a given place/region. The art of presenting events in a chronological and sequential pattern is possible only to a historian.[7]

Human logical thinking about matter is most important for development and depend upon the acumen of a seasoned manager. Managerial capabilities significantly enhance and even with the environment and help to achieve developments.[8] It is understood that today's politics is tomorrow's history that is to say that political events submerge in a chronological way and these events lead to geopolitical environment and administration.[9] Bibliometric and Scientific methods play an important role in information science research.[10] In the context of urban development, geo-informatics play an important role.[11] In the context of rural development at the grassroots level, micro-level planning is a good tool and possible only through planning and development in a country or in a smaller (Micro Unit) in plan periods of years.[12]

Human efforts are unutilized used for observation, thinking and objective oriented matters, most important in real life scenario. Knowledge has been categorized into two major disciplines: (1) Earth Sciences Environmental Sciences and (2) Social knowledgeable Science. Social Sciences or 'Humanities are quite important for understanding the merit of 'men/women, gender and finally emerges out into societal use. 'Environment' is a bridge between the earth Sciences and Social Sciences.

The researched material has been classified broadly and consequently a distinction has been made from the three hierarchic words. They are (1) Project work, (2) Dissertation and (3) Thesis. This is further elucidated (presented) in the following lines. This distinction is most important for a candidate/scholar, who is at the threshold of research studies. At the same time the candidate cannot overtake/override and take 'U' turn without knowing the hierarchic pattern and the subject matter of the chosen topic.

Examples:

(1) **Project work:** Financial statement analysis - this is a part of study and has been submitted as a project work in commerce-faculty in (2001) for the award of M.Com degree from Dr. B.R.A, AU, P.G Centre Etcherla, Srikakulam (AP), under the jurisdiction of Andhra University, Waltair, A.P.

(2) **M.Litt dissertation:** Karimnagar District - A Geographic Study (I973), Department of Geography, Osmania University, Hyderabad, A.P., India.

(3) **Ph.D Thesis :** Micro-Level Planning - A case study of Nuzvidu Block, Krishna District, Andhra Pradesh, India (1982), Department of Geography, Andhra University, Visakhapatnam.

Thesis

The urimary importance in drafting a thesis goes to primary data collection and analysis. The researched material document (Thesis) leading to the award of Ph.D. is the outcome of the analysis of data and results wherein the candidate has arrived at good valid points. It is a result of the candidate's intensive structured efforts of both analytical and skill development who worked intensively and extensively in the field and in the laboratory over a stipulated period of time under an approved Supervisor/

Guide. 'Thesis' is the documentary evidence which stands as a support document/testimony to the candidate's work for the award of a research degree such as an M.Phil/M. Litt / Ph.D/D.Sc/D.Litt etc.

2. Present study, work and objective

Step One: Social Science research material has been presented in a document form, as a premier work because with this title so far no material has been presented and published till 28th June, 2018 by any Research Scholar or Social Scientist. Thesis enables the young researcher to search for a potential 'topic' for analysis in the process of seeking it for a Ph.D. Hence, this documentation has been selected and taken-up for analysis.

Step Two: To prepare the present work as a good research document on researched theses and also to identify and recognize the hitaerts to uncovered areas for future researchers study even for selecting, and designing the topic (should not be repetitive) to enable to help the society. In other words, Social Science research should be able to find solutions to the growing problems that are confronting the society.

Step Three: To identify and examine the central idea of Social Science Research (SSR) and pros and cons underlying problems of rural and urban inhabitants and suggest way of quality life by inducting inputs of infrastructural facilities for development selecting area and population as norms.

Step Four : To develop inquisitiveness and to accommodate themselves (researchers) with an understanding of society and societal needs.

Step Five: To find solutions for the mounting social problems through methodological research over a period of time (spatio-temporal base).

Step-Six: To create a sound database and also to gain a full understanding of the problems at the ground level as a step towards finding solutions throught planning for rural and urban development.

3. Backdrop of the work and the proposed (applicants) work has been submitted as a proposal for approval by Gyan Publishing House, New Delhi

The continuous research work of the author spanning around 45 years is the bedrock of the concept sought to be expounded in the current work. The author will also base his work on various similar studies taken-up by him in other journals and publications. Prominent among these are the following:

Editors previous work

I. International Geographical Research : A Survey (2018) Published by Gyan Publishing House, New Delhi.
2. Indian Geographical Research: A Survey (2017) Published by R.K. Books, New Delhi.
3. Urban Environment : Issues of Poverty (2015) Published by Concept Publication Co. Pvt. Ltd., New Delhi.
4. Research Methodology in Geography (2014) Published by Concept Publication Co. Pvt., Ltd ., New Delhi.
5. Indian Social Science Research - A Survey (2012), published by Teja Publishers, Hyderabad.
6. Geographical Research (1999), published by Concept Publication Co. Pvt. Ltd, New Delhi.
7. Research in Geography - A Survey (1992), published by Ashish Publication Com. Pvt. Ltd, New Delhi.
8. Applied Geo-environmental Studies - Two Volumes (2008 and 2009) Published by Mangal Deep Publications, Jaipur.
9. 'Planning for Integrated Area Development' (1986) Published by B.R. Publishing Company, New Delhi.

4. Material and Method

Step One: Critical assessment of the submitted and Ph.D. awarded theses by the scholars of different subjects covering the social sciences (reference 1-12 items).

Step Two: A total of 12 Ph.D. theses were selected as sample size and were covered to create and prepare the current document as a good database and reference work. It is expected to meet the needs of the future research scholars in social sciences and also to choose appropriate topic relevant to current and emerging social needs and also to help the urban planner to translate and include into the urban plan.

Step Three: Since 1970, academicians have stressed the importance of inter-disciplinary and multi-disciplinary research. This current study adopts the inter-disciplinary method which paves way for the adoption of this method and thereby its extensive use in the future.

Twelve Ph.D. theses were surveyed and tentative chapterisation is as follows:

Notes

1. Administration (Public)

2. Commerce
3. Economics
4. Management
5. Demography
6. Geography
7. History
8. Financial Management
9. Political Science
10. Library and Information
11. Urban geography/urban sociology/urban economics
12 Rural Development Through Integrated Area Development Planning Micro Level Planning and Development Planning Development Economics.

2.1 Regional Agricultural Geography of Andhra Pradesh;

The present study of the regional agricultural geography of Andhra Pradesh is conceptually designed in broad conformity with the views of Schaefer that "Regional Geography must become the laboratory side of an essentially theoretical subject" and the view of Bunge that "systematic geography must move into the theoretical spheres and regional geography into a search for generic and not unique studies" (Haggett, 1965, p. 4). It is hoped that this diagnostic study will help to evolve both prophylactic and curative measures ultimately to improve the agricultural economy of the State.

Obviously the state of Andhra Pradesh, with its diverse physical and socio-economic conditions as well as rich agricultural resources and development, has indeed provided an appropriate setting for the study. The economy of Andhra Pradesh is predominantly agricultural and consequently the development of agriculture is crucial to and forms the basis of the economic development of the State. The State has an enormous agricultural potential for developing a prosperous and opulent agriculture if some of the agricultural problems of the State are solved.

Andhra Pradesh is the only state in Southern India which produces surplus food production offsetting the deficit of the other Southern states. The State is the largest producer of paddy, tobacco and mesta in the country, the second largest producer of ragi, small millets and castor, the third largest producer of jowar and groundnut, the fifth largest producer of sugarcane, the sixth largest producer of bajra and the eighth largest producer of cotton. In addition, it produces large quantities of maize, pulses, grams, fruits, spices and condiments also.

About 42 per cent of the geographical area of the State is under cultivation. With 36 per cent of its cultivated area under irrigation, the State has the second largest Canal irrigated area in the country the first being Uttar Pradesh. It is the only State in India where three important rivers flow building two major deltas and one crypoto delta. The drainage basins of these three major river systems, namely the Godavari, the Krishna and the Pennar, cover 72.7 per cent of the total area of the State, In addition, there are another thirty and odd minor rivers which can be harnessed for developing irrigation. Agriculture contributes about 47 per cent of the Net Domestic Product of the State. As much as 70 per cent of the State's work force is engaged in agriculture.

Objectives of the Study; For providing a comprehensive plan to develop agriculture in Andhra Pradesh, it is imperative to gain insights in to the spatio-temporal aspects of landuse, crop farming and agricultural productivity in their ecological socio-economic and technological setting. It is also necessary to understand the main problems and constraints which hinder the development of agriculture in the State. Regionalisation of agriculture highlights the regional disparities and helps to pinpoint the regional problems peculiar to different regions of the State. The analysis in the study is made at taluk level and at five-year intervals spreading over a period of 15 years.

A Perspective and Setting: After highlighting the salient features of the theme and the importance of the region, an attempt is made to provide necessary geographical setting to the study. In this context, a brief discussion on the location and spatial aspects of the State, the topographical and climate characteristics, water balance, drought and floods, distribution and growth of population as well as the development of irrigation in the State is presented.

Landuse Classification, Dynamics of Landuse and Landuse Pattern

Any scientific and rational landuse planning must be envisaged within the framework of the ecological balance. The main problems of landuse include under-utilisation, over-utilisation and mis-utilisation. There is a physical limit for the horizontal expansion of arable land. Hence, the question arises as to how to gear up the agricultural economy to meet the ever-increasing pressure of population on land and the consequent decrease in the man-land ratio.

The present study of landuse classification in Andhra Pradesh is accomplished on the basis of the standard classification designed by the Technical Committee on Coordination of Agricultural Statistics in 1950 which suggested nine categories, namely (i) forest, (ii) area under non-agricultural use, (iii) barren lands, (iv) permanent pastures and other grazing lands, (v) area under miscellaneous tree crops etc., (vi) culturable wasteland, (vii) current fallows, (viii) other fallow lands, and (ix) net area sown. These nine categories are regrouped into four major landuse classes, namely (i) forest cover, (ii) land agriculturally not suitable or non-cultivable land, (iii) cultivable wasteland including fallows, and (iv) arable land or net area sown.

Forest: In Andhra Pradesh, the importance of forest landuse stands next only to arable land. In 1978-79, it accounted for 22.7 per cent of the total geographical area of the State. Conservation of the forest is of paramount importance not only to promote soil conservation in the catchment areas but also to regulate the run off and to maintain ecological balance. Forest wealth also provides considerable revenue to the State besides supplying raw materials for a number of forest-based industries.

The need for proper conservation and management of forest can not be overemphasised. Afforestation is as important as the 'green revolution' in agriculture.

The distribution of forest cover in the State is quite uneven. Chintapalle taluk of Visakhapatnam district accounts for 71.4 per cent of its geographical area under forest, while many coastal taluks do not have even a sembalance of forest. Much of the forest in the State is confined to hilly areas, valley sides and inaccessible areas of the plateaus and hills. Only 65 taluks of the 195 taluks of the State have moderate to high forest cover. The districts which have considerable forest cover are Khammam (47.7%), Adilabad (43.0%) and Warangal (28.9%) districts of Telangana, Visakhapatnam (36.5%), East Godavari (26.4%) and Prakasam (26.0%) districts of coastal Andhra and Cuddapah (32.3%) and Chittoor (30.0%) districts of Rayalaseema.

In the 15 year period between 1963-64 and 1978-79 there has been some spatial expansion in forest cover although it is rather marginal (only 0.4%). In terms of area, the net increase has been about 105,200 hectares, and this increase was achieved by the efforts of the State Government which launched schemes of afforestation, conservation and plantation of economically useful plants in the open scrub lands and the old forest areas. The highest increase of more than 7 per cent was recorded in 25 taluks while a decrease of equal magnitude in 18 taluks. Due to deforestation, overgrazing and lack of adequate rainfall in the semi-arid areas and the rain-shadow regions, the forest has considerably degenerated. About one-third of the total geographical area of the State must be under forest cover to maintain a proper ecological balance, whereas the present forest cover in the State falls too short of the optimum-level. Much has to be done not only to increase the forest cover in the State but also to improve the quality of it.

Non-cultivable Land: In 1978-79, the non-cultivable land in the State accounted for 16.4 per cent of the total geographical area. About 52 taluks of the State had more than 20 per cent of their area under non-cultivable landuse and these taluks are distributed in Cuddapah, Chittoor, Ananta-pur, Hyderabad, Nellore, Krishna, East Godavari, Visakhapatnam and Srikakulam districts. The low lying marshy areas and saline lands can be brought under cultivation by taking suitable measures for reclamation.

The non-cultivable land in the State has increased by 1.5 per cent in the 15-year period and much of the increase is due to mining, quarrying, erosion, dumping of industrial waste heaps etc. There has been more than 7 per cent increase in 28 taluks and a decrease of equal magnitude in

21 taluks. The decrease was due to reclamation of land and development of irrigation.

Cultivable Wasteland: The cultivable wasteland has the potential status for crop farming but it is not included under the net area sown. The area under cultivable wasteland in Andhra Pradesh in 1978-79 accounted for 19.5 per cent of the geographical area of the State. It is indeed a high proportion. The spatial variation in its distribution in the State is quite wide. Jangaon taluk of Warangal district has the highest percentage of cultivable waste of 52.5 per cent while Tenali taluk of Guntur district has the lowest percentage of cultivable waste of only 1.8 per cent. High and very high concentration of cultivable waste is noticed in 81 taluks of which 42 taluks are found in Telangana, 22 taluks in the Coastal Plain and 17 taluks in Rayalaseema. In Telangana and Rayalaseema a high proportion of cultivable waste is under fallow, whereas in the coastal plain large proportions of cultivable waste is under pasture. The study has shown that there is ample scope for horizontal expansion of agriculture in Telangana and Rayalaseema where there is high concentration of cultivable waste.

In the fifteen year period, this category of land has decreased by 1.8 per cent amounting to about 486,000 hectares. An increase in the percentage of wasteland is noticed in 10 districts while a decreasing trend in 11 districts. The decrease of cultivable wasteland has occurred in the areas where development of irrigation, extension of agriculture, reclamation of wastelands etc., have taken place. Much of the increase has taken place due to increase of fallow land on account of adverse climatic conditions and improper management of land. In fact, most of the development is rather vertical especially due to extension and modernisation of agriculture. It is a welcome sign. It is advisable to develop the agricultural wastelands by introducing farm forestry and animal husbandary. In fact some of the dry areas of the plateau are famous for breeding some of the best drought animals.

Arable Land: The area under arable land in Andhra Pradesh in 1978-79 accounts for 41.4 per cent of the geographical area of the State. There is wide variation in the distribution of arable land in the State. Alur taluk of Kurnool district has a maximum of arable land (88.6%), while Rampa-chodavaram taluk of East Godavari district has a minimum (6.5%). About 80 taluks in the State have more than 50 per cent of arable land and 50 taluks have low percentage of arable land. There is high concentration of arable land in the coastal districts due to favourable topographic, climatic and socio-economic conditions besides better irrigation facilities. Even in the Rayalaseema and Telangana regions the arable land is quite large.

It is intriguing to note that there has been marginal decrease of 0.1 percent in the proportion of arable land in the State during the 15 year period. It shows that practically there has been no horizontal expansion of agriculture in the last 15-year period. However, in about 100 taluks of the State there has been some increase in the proportion of arable land. Of them, 20 taluks have registered an increase of more than 10 percent.

Intensity of Cropping: The ratio between the gross sown area and the net sown area is termed intensity of cropping. The intensity of cropping in Andhra Pradesh is about 115.6 per cent on an average. But its spatial distribution shows a wide variation ranging between a maximum of 188 per cent and a minimum of 100 per cent. In 58 taluks the cropping intensity has been more than 120 per cent, while in the remaining taluks it has been less than 120 per cent. There has been a great leap forward in the intensity of cropping during the 15-year period. It is mostly due to the development of irrigation and cultivation of short period crops. The low intensity of cropping is generally found in the rainfed taluks of Telangana and Rayalaseema.

Landuse Orientation: The study of landuse orientation is based on the Kostrowicki's method. Each one of the four categories of landuse are classified into Predominant, Dominant, Semidominant and Accompanying on the basis of their magnitude. Combining these two aspects of landuse, various permutations and combinations of landuse orientation are worked out for all the taluks of the State. Predominant and dominant types of arable landuse (A4 and A3) are found in 23 taluks, mostly in the deltaic and river valley project areas. Dominant forest cover with accompanying agriculture (F3+A1) is found only in 3 taluks located in Adilabad, Karimnagar and Kurnool districts. There seems to be an inverse correlation between the net sown area and cultivable waste. It suggests that there is mutual transference of landuse between the two landuse types. The net sown area and the forest cover also are negatively correlated.

Changing Spatial Pattern of Landuse Efficiency

Agricultural landuse efficiency is a complex and dynamic attribute of land which provides a conceptual framework to understand the agricultural landuse and assess its overall performance. It is the product of natural, institutional technological and demographic factors.

The agricultural landuse concept is rather difficult to define and quantify. Kendall (1939) was the first to attempt to quantify and evaluate crop productivity by applying 'Rank Coefficient' method developed by himself. Stamp (1960), Shafi (1960), and Sapre and Deshpande (1964) employed the method to study agricultural efficiency which is nothing but crop productivity, Singh (1970) was the first to study agricultural landuse efficiency by taking five variables by employing the method.

Kendall's rank coefficient method is a rough method which does not bring to light the actual differences between the values of the variables of different areal units. To overcome this difficulty, a modified method called 'Standard Coefficient' method is employed in the present study. In this method, percentages of each variable are taken instead of ranks. The virtue of this method springs up from the fact that all the merits of the rank coefficient method are retained while its shortcomings are eliminated.

For evaluating the agricultural landuse efficiency in Andhra Pradesh, seven variables are considered i.e., (i) net sown area, (ii) intensity of cropping, (iii) irrigated land, (iv) area irrigated more than once, (v) area under high yielding variety, (vi) area under non-cultivable land and (vii) area under cultivable waste.

In 1978-79, about 15 taluks of the State were under very high landuse efficiency category, 14 taluks, under high efficiency category, 66 taluks under moderate efficiency category, while 100 taluks were under low and very low efficiency category. In the 15 year period, the State has shown an impressive progress in the landuse efficiency. The number of taluks under very high, high and moderate efficiency have increased more than two-fold. Of course, the number of taluks under moderate landuse efficiency have registered a three-fold increase. As many as 56 taluks of the category of low and very low efficiency have improved their landuse efficiency. There has been a wide spatial variation in the agricultural landuse efficiency in the State. For instance, Bhimavaram taluk in the Godavari delta with a mean standard coefficient of 72.2 and Rampachodavaram taluk with a mean standard coefficient of 9.4, present the maximum and minimum agricultural landuse efficiencies. The encouraging feature of the landuse efficiency is that much of the improvement has taken place in the upland areas because of (i) development of irrigation i.e., both surface and ground water, (ii) improvement of the socio-economic conditions, (iii) modernisation of agriculture, and (iv) application of better soil and water conservation and management methods. It is quite encouraging to note that as many as 150 taluks have improved their agricultural landuse efficiency in various degrees. The high increase of landuse efficiency is noticed in 44 taluks mostly distributed in the coastal plain and Telangana region.

A decrease in landuse efficiency is recorded in 38 taluks only. These taluks are mostly located in Rayalaseema, Srikakulam and Mahabubnagar districts. The impulses of landuse efficiency are diffusing and spreading in different parts of the State enhancing the level of landuse efficiency in the State as a whole.

Carrying Capacity of Land

The number of people that a unit area of land can support is said to be the carrying capacity of land. Of course, it is a complex and dynamic concept. In view of the physical limit of horizontal expansion of agriculture, the question whether it is possible to increase the carrying capacity of land to feed the ever-increasing population has assumed paramount importance.

To determine the carrying capacity of land, the total output in terms of Potential Production Units (PPU), and the consumption of daily food intake in terms of Standard Nutrition Units (SNU) are usually taken as the parameters. However, in the present study the SNU method is employed.

The average carrying capacity of land in Andhra Pradesh in 1979 was 3.77 persons/hectare. The highest carrying capacity of land is noticed in West Godavari district with a carrying capacity of 7.39 persons/hectare, while the lowest carrying capacity of land is noticed in Adilabad district with 2.14 persons/hectare. A wide regional disparity in the carrying capacity of land in the State is patently visible. Carrying capacity of land more than that of the State's average is found in 9 districts, namely West Godavari, East Godavari, Guntur, Krishna and Nellore districts of the Coastal plain, Nizamabad and Karimnagar districts of Telangana and Chittoor and Cuddapah districts of Rayalaseema. A high carrying capacity of land is mostly achieved due to the development of irrigation in these districts. Modernisation of agriculture also has an important role to play. In contrast, the region with low carrying capacity of land of less than 3 persons/hectare is observed in 7 districts, namely Anantapur and Kurnool districts of Rayalaseema, Mahabubnagar, Hyderabad, Medak and Adilabad districts of Telangana and Visakhapatnam district of the coastal plain. These districts are mostly drought-prone and less irrigated. They are essentially millet growing areas where crop farming is mostly rainfed. The agricultural prosperity of the State is very much linked up with the development and stabilisation of agriculture in these areas.

The most encouraging feature of the carrying capacity of land in Andhra Pradesh is that it has increased by more than one and a half times in the 18 years between 1961 and 1979. In 1961, the average carrying capacity of land was 2.35 persons/hectare and it increased to 3.77 persons/hectare in 1979. The highest carrying capacity also has increased from 4.07 persons/ hectare to 7.39 persons/hectare. Even the minimum carrying capacity has increased from 2.24 persons/ hectare to 2.77 persons/hectare. Spatially, the area under high carrying capacity of land has increased from 2 districts to 7 districts, the area under medium carrying capacity of land from 4 districts to 7 districts, while the area under low carrying capacity of land has decreased from 14 districts to 7 districts.

In 1978-79, the average per capita availability of arable land was 0.26 hectares as compared to 0.31 hectares in 1971 and 0.33 hectares in 1961. It shows the per capita gross arable land in the State is rapidly depleting due to the rapid increase of population. The per capita gross arable land available is relatively high both in Telangana and Rayalaseema than in the coastal districts. Presently, the available gross arable land in the State as a whole is short of the requirement and the problem will be more accute in future. In 1979, about 8 districts have a surplus of gross arable land, while 10 districts a deficit of arable land. West Godavari district followed by Nizamabad, Nalgonda, Krishna, Kurnool, Chittoor, Mahabubnagar and East Godavari districts have a surplus of gross arable land. Hyderabad and Visakhapatnam districts have a high deficit of arable land because of their large urban agglomerations. The study clearly point out that there is not much scope for horizontal expansion of the arable land and hence there is an immense need to improve the carrying capacity of land.

The Changing Distribution Pattern of Crop Farming

Cropping pattern represents the spatial crop sequence or association in a given area at a point of time. A systematic study of cropping pattern helps to regionalise agriculture which in turn forms the scientific basic for land resources allocation to various crops and planning for maximum productivity. For the purpose of the present anaysis, 17 crops which account for 97.7 per cent of the total cropped area in the state are considered. They include foodgrain crops like paddy, jowar, bajra, maize, ragi, minor millets and pulses and grams, commercial crops like sugarcane, cotton, tobacco, oil seeds and spices and condiments, fruit and vegetable crops, and fodder crops.

A detailed study of these crops at taluk level is attemped at 5 years interval periods separately for kharif, rabi and gross cropped areas.

Foodgrain crops play a major role in the cropland utilisation of Andhra Pradesh accounting for 73.5 percent of the gross sown area in the state. Paddy and jowar alone account for 66 percent of the total hectarage and 80 percent of the total foodgrain crops in the State.

Paddy: Paddy is the most important and widely grown crop in the state accounting for 30.3 percent of the total cropped area. Andhra Pradesh is the largest producer of paddy in the country. The crop is grown both in the kharif and rabi seasons under irrigation. About 40 taluks in the state have a concentration of more than 50 percent of the gross cropped area under paddy cultivation. Another 65 taluks have a concentration between 25 and 50 per cent. In another 85 taluks it has a low concentration since it is cultivated only in some parts. The Krishna, Godavari and Pennar deltas in particular and the coastal plain in general have the heaviest concentrations of paddy cultivation.

In the 15 years period, the area under paddy has increased by 4 per cent amounting to 0.616 million hectares. In the newly irrigated areas of Guntur, Nalgonda and Karimnagar districts, the increase has been more than 20 per cent. In Kurnool and Khammam districts also the increase has been quite significant. In some parts of Visakhapatnam, Nellore, Krishna, Chittoor and Anantapur districts, the area under paddy cultivation has decreased under pressure from other commercial crops.

It is advisable to take measures to improve the yields than going in for areal expansion of its cultivation. Demand for water by paddy crop is rather exacting. It is economical to grow other crops which require less water than paddy especially in the rabi season when the water is scarce. This is valid even in the case of deltaic areas. The cultivation of hybrid maize, hybrid jowar, hybrid bajra or cotton instead of rice in the rabi season will be more profitable. Both the intensity of cropping and production could be increase many fold by this. It also helps to improve even the soil condition. But in the low lying areas of the deltas and coastal plains paddy cultivation is ideal. Here, the soil moisture regime, the alkalinity of canal water, high returns of the crop and the ease of cultivation favour paddy cultivation.

Jowar: Jowar is the second most important cereal crop in the State. In contrast with paddy, it is basically a rainfed crop eminently suitable for cultivation in dry areas under low rainfall and drought-prone conditions. About 18 per cent of the total cropped area in the State is under jowar cultivation. Its concentration greatly varied from a maximum of about 60 per cent in Sirpur taluk of Adilabad district to total absence in some deltaic taluks. The concentration of this crop is mainly found in the plateau regions of both Telangana and Rayalaseema. In the fertile deep black soil regions, jowar has to face a keen competition from cotton, maize and tobacco. At the stable level, jowar is the first ranking crop in the rabi season.

The percentage of jowar area in the State has decreased by 2.6 percent in the 15 years period. The decrease is noticed in about 121 taluks. But the highest decrease is in Guntur district. The general decrease in jowar cultivation is due to (i) development of irrigation, and (ii) stiff competition from cotton, tobacco, maize and oil seeds. On the whole, jowar cultivation receive preferential treatment over other dry crops. Some of the dry farming techniques and introduction of high yielding hybrid variety and improvement in the jowar productivity under light irrigation have provided a boost to jowar cultivation in some parts of the State.

Bajra: Bajra is mainly cultivated as a Kharif crop under rainfed conditions on poorer and lighter soils. In contrast with jowar, bajra is wholly a Kharif crop. By virtue of low water requirement, it enjoys certain advantages. Bajra cultivation accounts for only 4.3 per cent of the gross cultivated area of the State. The greatest concentration of this crop is found in Visakhapatnam, Prakasam and Nalgonda districts which account for more than 40 per cent of the total area of the State under bajra cultivation. There has been a marginal decrease of 0.4 percent in its area in the 15 year period. It is facing a severe competition from groundnut. However, under light irrigation, hybrid bajra has become popular in many parts of the State.

Maise: It is the fourth important cereal crop in the State accounting for 2.5 percent of the total cultivated area in the State. More than 80 percent of this crop is grown in Kharif season. Although maize is cultivated in 91 taluks of the State, it is mainly concentrated in Telangana. Since it is a short commercial crop which could be cultivated both under rainfed and light irrigation conditions, it has shown a continuous increase in the areal extent. A high yielding maize crop must find a suitable place in the cropping pattern of the State as it will be a profitable venture.

Ragi: Ragi accounts for 2.4 per cent of the gross cropped area in the State. Although it is grown in Kharif and rabi seasons it is predominantly a Kharif crop. Srikakulam, Visakhapatnam, Anantapur, Chittoor and Mahabubnagar districts together accounted for 72 per cent of the ragi cultivated area of the State. Ragi cultivation has not shown much variation in the last 15 years, although there has been significant variation in its cultivation in some parts of the State.

Minor millets: A few minor millets like korra, varagu, samai etc., together account for 5,2 percent of the total cultivated area of the State. But many of them assume local importance. The rain-shadow areas of Kurnool, Anantapur, Mahabubnagar and Prakasam districts account for 76.6 per cent of the total area under these crops. The area under minor millets had shown a rapid decline in the 15 year period. It shows that minor millets are unable to stand competition from other crops.

Pulses and grams: The importance of pulses and grams lies in their high nutrition value both as a human diet and cattle feed. They are also cultivated as green manure crops to improve soil fertility especially for nitrogen fixation. The chief pulses and grams grown in the State are red gram, Bengal gram, green gram, black gram, horse gram, pearl bean and cow pea and due gram. Although they are cultivated both as Kharif and rabi crops, they are often cultivated as mixed crops with jowar, bajra, groundnut and other millets.

Pulses and grams accounted for 10.8 per cent of the total cultivated area in the State with wide spatial distribution. High concentration of this crop is found in Krishna, East Godavari, Guntur, Khammam, Warangal, Karimnagar, Adilabad, Hyderabad, Medak and Nalgonda districts.

Among the pulses and grams, the green gram has the largest area followed by horse gram, black gram, red gram and Bengal gram. Krishna, Nalgonda, Warangal, Khammam and Karimnagar districts account for nearly 70 per cent of the total area under green gram. Red gram is prevalent in Kurnool, Anantapur, Hyderabad, Mahabubnagar and Adilabad districts, Bengal gram is prevalent in Adilabad, Medak and Nizamabad districts and black gram in Krishna and Guntur districts. There has been an areal increase of 0.1 per cent under the cultivation of pulses and grams in the 15 year period. Concerted efforts must be made to increase both the cultivated area and production of pulses and grams as they form an important part of the diet.

Sugarcane: Sugarcane area accounts for 1.2 per cent of the gross sown area in the State. Although it is cultivated in 114 taluks of the State in various concentrations, about 25 taluks show significant concentration of this crop. Nizamabad, Chittoor, East Godavari, Krishna, Visakhapatnam, Medak, West Godavari and Srikakulam districts account for 90 per cent of the total sugarcane cultivated area of the State. The area under sugarcane has recorded only a marginal increase in the 15 year period. The high fluctuation of its price has greatly hindered the expansion of sugarcane area.

Oil Seeds : The oil seed cultivation in the State accounted for 13.8 percent of the gross sown area. Oil seeds play a significant role in the agro-industrial economy of the State. Groundnut, castor and sesamum together account for 94.3 per cent of the total area under the cultivation of oil seeds.

Groundnut is an important cash crop and accounts for 9.7 per cent of the gross sown area of the State. It is essentially a Kharif crop although it is cultivated both in the Kharif and rabi seasons both under irrigation and rainfed conditions. Groundnut is essentially the characteristic Rayalaseema crop in the State. High concentrations of its cultivation are found in many taluks of Chittoor, Anantapur and Cuddapah districts. It is also cultivated in Kurnool, Mahabubnagar, Nalgonda, Warangal, Karimnagar and Khammam districts. In the 15 year period, groundnut cultivation has increased by 2 per cent. A two-fold increase of its cultivation is recorded in the rabi season. Groundnut cultivation is favoured by the farmers especially in the upland areas for the following reasons: (i) it fetches a good income, (ii) it is a short growing crop, (iii) the cost of cultivation is less, (iv) it requires less water, and (v) it can be cultivated under rainfed conditions.

Castor is the second most important oil seed in the State accounting for 14 percent of the total area under oil seeds. Overwhelmingly it is a Kharif crop and cultivated under rainfed conditions often as an intermixed crop. If groundnut is the characteristic crop of Rayalaseema, Castor is the characteristic crop of Telangana. Mahabubnagar, Nalgonda, Hyderabad and Prakasam districts account for 97 percent of the total castor cultivated area in the State. In the 15 year period, the extent of castor cultivation has decreased by 0.5 percent. This declining trend is partly due to low yields besides competition from groundnut.

Sesamum is the third important oil seed in the State which accounts for 1.3 percent of the gross sown area. Its share among oil seeds is 9.6 percent. As a rainfed crop, it is cultivated mostly in the humid areas. Although it is widely cultivated in the State, it shows a high concentration in some taluks of Adilabad, Cuddapah, Visakhapatnam, East Godavari, West Godavari and Guntur districts. There has been a considerable decline in its cultivation in the 15 year period.

In conclusion it may be stated that the cultivation of all the oil seeds together in the State has shown a net gain. Most of them are mainly grown in the upland and semi-arid areas of Rayalaseema and Telangana. It is an important commercial-industrial crop in these regions.

Cotton: The cultivation of cotton accounted for 2.9 percent of the cultivated area of the State. More than 90 percent of it is cultivated in the Kharif season. The introduction of hybrid variety and the application of better farming technology and high productivity under light irrigation have favoured cotton cultivation in many areas. Adilabad, Guntur, Prakasam and Kurnool districts together account for 80 percent of the total area of cotton cultivation. Although the production of cotton has increased, the hectarage under cotton cultivation has decreased in the 15 year period. This is due to the shift of its cultivation from the low yielding non-irrigated areas to the high yielding irrigated areas.

Mesta is another fibre crop which is highly localised in its cultivation. More than 90 percent of its cultivation is confined to Srikakulam and Visakhapatnam districts.

Tobacco: Andhra Pradesh is famous for tobacco cultivation. Its cultivation accounted for 1.5 percent of the gross cropped area in the State, Prakasam district alone accounted nearly 30 percent of the tobacco cultivated area in the State. Prakasam, West Godavari, Krishna, Guntur, Nellore and Khammam districts together accounted for 80 percent of the total tobacco cultivated area in the State. Due to price fluctuations, tobacco cultivation has decreased in its area by 0.2 percent. It is interesting to note that the traditional tobacco growing areas have shown a decrease in its cultivation, while new areas have started growing tobacco.

Spices and condiments: The important spices and condiments grown in the State are chillies, coriander, turmeric, tamarind, garlic and ginger. These crops together account for 2.5 percent of the gross sown area in the State. All these crops are cash crops and important in different regions of the State. Since they are high value crops which fetch good income there has been a significant increase in their hectarage during the 15 year period.

Fruit crops like mangoes, oranges, lemon, plantains, grapes, guava and cashewnut are important cash crops in the State which have regional preponderance. The area under fruit crops has also increased in the last 15 year period.

High Yielding Varieties: The cultivation of high yielding variety crops account for about 25 percent of the gross sown area in the State. Much of the cultivation under high yielding variety is confined to the irrigated hybrid paddy, hybrid jowar, hybrid bajra, hybrid maize, hybrid cotton and hybrid groundnut. Assured water supply is a must for successful cultivation of high yielding varieties. The high concentration of HYV is found in West Godavari, East Godavari, Guntur and Krishna districts. The outcome of the cultivation of HYV is the 'green revolution, The HYV of paddy, jowar, bajra and maize together accounted for 96 percent of the total area under HYV. Paddy is the main beneficially followed by bajra, maize and jowar. There is a great scope for extending HYV in the State to increase the productivity atleast by two times. Development of HYV to the dry crops will bring about agricultural revolution in the drought-prone areas and the semi-arid tracts in Andhra Pradesh.

Crop Combinations and Crop Regions

Crops are generally grown in combination or association as a response to physical, socio-economic, demographic and technological factors. A study of crop combinations immensely helps regional agricultural planning and to optimise crop farming. The present study is based on Doi's method. In all, as many as eight crop combinations are identified in the State. A careful analysis of the crop combinations in Kharif and rabi seasons individually and together has revealed the following:

1. The number and spatial extent of each one of the crop combinations has tended to decrease from 1963-64 to 1978-79 partly due to the development of more and more irrigation facilities and partly due to the preference of the farmers to cultivate more remunerative and superior varieties of crops.

2. The tendency to specialise rather than diversify the cropping pattern is patently noticeable e.g., paddy, groundnut and maize have gradually tended to replace minor crops. Some of the inferior crops like millets are getting eliminated from the cropping pattern in this process of transformation.
3. Crop combinations with a fewer crops i.e., one-crop, two-crop and three-crop combinations, are far more prevalent than too much multiple crop combinations.
4. Crop combinations with a lesser number of crops are found in much larger number of taluks as well as in spatial contiguity. In contrast, the crop combinations with larger number of crops are not only limited in their areal spread but also highly scattered in their distribution and isolated in location. This tendency has shown an increase with the increase in the number of crops in the combinations.
5. The crop combinations with less number of crops as well as specialisation of crops are mostly found in the high rainfall regions, irrigated areas, coastal plains and river valleys. In contrast, more diversification and combinations with more number of crops are mostly prevalent in the dry uplands, rainfed areas and unirrigated or scantily irrigated regions of the State.
6. As the process of change in the cropping pattern has progressed, a greater degree of uniformity and stability are brought about in the crop farming economy of the State.
7. In the irrigated areas, crop rotation, especially in the rabi season, seems to be increasing.
8. There is more diversification of crops in the Kharif season since it is the main cropping season throughout the State. In contrast, the cropping pattern is less diversified in the rabi season because crop farming is practiced in this season only in selected favourable areas.

Thirteen crops are identified as primary crops out of which paddy, jowar and groundnut are overwhelmingly predominant. On the basis of the spatial distribution of primary crops (first rank crops) the crop regions are delimited. Fourteen crops are identified as secondary crops (second rank crops). Many of the crops which figure in the primary category are identified as secondary crops also in other regions. As many as 19 crops are recognised as tertiary crops. Here also many of the primary and secondary crops figure as tertiary crops in other regions.

Regionalisation of Agricultural Productivity

On the basis of agricultural productivity and agricultural efficiency an attempt is made to develop regionalisation. Such a study highlights (i) the spatio-temporal yield levels of important crops, (ii) the spatial variation in agricultural productivity, (ii) the decrease or increase in the level of agricultural productivity in the 15 year period in its spatial context, (iv) the hierarchy of agricultural productivity regions, and (v) the magnitude of variations between high productive and low productive areas. Taking the intensity and spread indices of yield, caloric equivalent and cropping system as variables, the aggregate agricultural productivity indices are calculated.

A detailed and in depth study is made of the yield levels of different crops in the State. On the basis of the analysis, five agricultural productivity regions are identified. They are (i) the region with very high agricultural productivity (category A), (ii) the region with high agri-cultural productivity (categories B_1 & B_2, (iii) the region with moderate agricultural productivity (categories C_1, C_2 C_2), (iv) the region with low agricultural productivity (ca-tegories D_1 and D_2), and (v) the region with very low agricultural productivity (category E).

The region with very high agricultural productivity comprises the two deltaic districts of West Godavari and East Godavari and Chittoor district. They are characterized conditions, the high level of development of canal irrigation, a well developed communication system, a high density of population and modernisation of agriculture have contributed to the agricultural development of the first two districts. In the case of Chittoor district, the eastern part receives higher rainfall. The soils, especially in the valleys are fertile. Both well irrigation and tank irrigation have helped intensive cultivation. Cultivation of commercial crops with groundnut, paddy and sugarcane combination have yielded encouraging results.

No district in the State can be classified as the region with high agricultural productivity.

The region with moderate agricultural productivity comprises six districts, namely Guntur, Nizamabad, Visakhapatnam, Warangal, Karimnagar and Krishna. Krishna and Guntur districts which are served by the Krishna irrigation system have a high density of population and highly developed transport and communication system. Visakhapatnam receives high rainfall. Nizamabad, Warangal and Karimnagar districts have fertile soils and recently developed irrigation system.

The region with low agricultural productivity includes three coastal districts of Srikakulam, Prakasam and Nellore, Rayalaseema districts of

Anantapur and Kurnool and Telangana district of Nalgonda. Different factors are responsible in different districts for the present agricultural situation in this region. The cropping pattern is also highly diversified. With the exception of Anantapur district, the region has a high potential for further improvement in its agricultural productivity.

The region with very low agricultural productivity is obviously least developed. It comprises five Telangana districts of Khammam, Medak, Adilabad, Mahabubnagar and Hyderabad and the Rayalaseema district of Cuddapah. The region is handicapped by low and erratic rainfall. The socio-economic conditions also have inhibiting influence on the agricultural development. However, the soils in this region are fertile. By improving the irrigation facilities and applying improved farming techniques and by evolving proper cropping pattern, the agricultural productivity of this region can be greatly improved.

The study of agricultural productivity in terms of money value coefficients have provided a different perspective. Here the value of a crop is taken into consideration. These two perspectives of study are mutually complimentary and help to cover up the gaps of each other.

In conclusion, it may be stated that the further success of agriculture in the State will depend upon (i) stabilisation of the agricultural economy in the drought-prone and semi-arid areas, (ii) extension of irrigation by conjunctive use of both surface and ground water, (iii) optimisation of cropping pattern, (iv) application of better soil and water conservation methods, (v) improvement in farming techniques especially dry farming techniques, and (vi) modernisation of agriculture. Improvement of institutional factors such as financial assistance, education and improvement of agrarian relations are no way less important for agricultural development. The State has an immense potential for developing itself into a prosperous agricultural State.

2.2 Planning for Integrated Areas Development – A study from Andhra Pradesh State, India.

'Regional Planning' is an important branch of Geography and has created new vistas in the field of research. It deals with the principles of delineation of hierarchy of regions both for physical and human resource appraisal, and helps to plan for a balanced and integrated development of a region. Regional approach and regional problems were marked in the First and Second Five Year Plans of India. In the Second Five Year Plan, emphasis was made on planning at districts level but not much was done in this context. Block Development programmes included in the Third Five Year Plan for rural development are some of the attempts of area approach to planning at lower level. In the Fifth Five Year Plan document, the planning commission has emphasised the need for the location of specific district plans for an integrated and balanced development of the rural areas in India. It is felt that if the Micro Level units are properly planned, they promote the maximum utilisation of resources. Further, these potential units will support the rural poor at the village level. This in turn curtails rural-urban migration and congestion in urban areas. It is important that the formulation of spatial frame-worn of development should include plans for land use, human settlements, social service and amenities required by the people. In order to bring development at the grass roots, planning will have to start necessarily from the bottom instead of from the top. In this context it is feasible to study the Micro Regions and their problems at the taluka level. An attempt is made in this thesis, to study the aspects of Micro Level Planning and its problems of Tamuku Taluka of West Godavary district of Andhra Pradesh, India.

Data Base

The study is based on the primary as well as secondary data. Secondary dat were collected from different offices located in the taluka and also at the districts headquarters i.e., Eluru. Primary data were collected through questionnaires and schedules exclusively designed for this study. The other relevant data were also obtained from the local leaders, Karnams, Mansiffs and village Development Officers through personal interviews.

Plan Period

The plan period proposed in this study spreads over a 10 years from 1981.

Objective of the Study Area

The salient objectives of the study are:

1. To identify and rank central places of various orders.
2. To delineate the tributary areas or complementary zones of the central places.
3. To identify the existing functional gaps in the study area and to make substantive recommendations for their removal and for more efficient functional integration.
4. To assess and appraise the potentialities of human, agricultural and industrial aspects of the study area for recommending suitable development programmes.

5. To integrate all sectoral development programmes into a spatial frame-work so as to plan for Integrated Area Development of the study area.

Methodology

Christaller's Central Place Theory is used as a major theoretical frame of reference.'

Data Analysis and Maps

Data collected from the survey and secondary sources are analyzed and tabulated for the purposes of this study. Several working Maps were prepared to facilitate data analysis. Data analysis is done with the help of statistical techniques and cartographic methods.

Design of the Thesis

Chapter I deals with the introduction, (a) the nature of Micro Level Planning, (b) Central Place Theory, (c) Methodological issues in Central Place Theory, (d) Central Place Theory, (e) Concept of integrated area development, (f) Review of some important aspects regarding Micro Level Planning and (g) Integrated Area Development, (h) Problem, Objectives and design of the study.

In Chapter II, an attempt is made to present the general characteristics of the study area.

In Chapter III, Appraisal of Agricultural Industrial, Transport, Demographic and Poultry resources and development of the study area are discussed.

In Chapter IV, Identification of Central Places and their complementary regions are presented. Central place methodology is adopted for identifying the Central place hierarchy in the study regions. First, Second and Third order Central places and their complementary regions are identified and presented in the maps. In the Central place hierarchy, at the first level, and their complementary regions, eight Central villages were identified in their spatial distribution.

At the second level of centres and their complementary regions, six central villages were identified in their spatial distribution. On an average each centre is serving 35.71 square miles of area and nearly 73,700 population. Their individual pattern is an important factor in detecting the spread of population and their interaction.

At the third level centres and their complementary regions, four centres were identified in their spatial distribution. On the average, each centre is serving 53.57 square miles of area and 1,10,542 population. The whole of the Tanuku Taluka is shared by four growth centres, namely Tanuku, Attili, Penugonda and Penumantra.

Chapter V is divided into two sections. In the first section, an attempt is made to study the standard of service offered by the service centres to their dependent territories. Norm Population and Norm Area are considered as standards in order to find out the adequacy or inadequacy of a service within the complementary region. In the second section, an attempt is made to plan for social facilities in the study area for providing adequate frame-work for socio-economic and institutional development. This part deals with the identification of locational gaps on the basis of population thresholds and range of a function and to identify new locations (Service Centres). Keeping in view the two aspects, and with the hypothesis that if the locational priorities are identified on scientific basis, the maximum gap (by functions and areas) can be reduced and the socio-economic spheres of life in a long way be improved, has attempted to study the problems with a view to suggestions solutions. Given the criteria, nine Service Centres are proposed in the study area for the balanced socio-economic and institutional development.

Chapter VI is divided broadly into there sections. In the First section, an attempt has been made to study the land utilization and cropping pattern in order to propose the necessary infrastructural facilities and to propose suitable agro-based industries for the development of the study area. In the Second section, detailed proposals pertaining to the total number of birds, daily output, demand and consumption input-output ratios, and net income to be generated to the farmer in poultry farming have been worked out. Keeping in view the resource appraisal in the field of biotic resources, the author proposed popultry units for the teeming population in the study area. Further the author has proposed milch cattle programme to make available the nutritious food item like milk, for the future population in the study area. A detailed programme of outlay is given with the cost-benefit analysis for the development of milch cattle programme.

In Chapter VII, detailed project appraisal for socio-economic and Institutional facilities with a Cost-Benefit analysis is also presented. Six important functions have been considered for decentralisation over the space. Education, Health, Communication, Credit, Transport and Extension services and their segmented patterns are presented in a detailed manner.

In Chapter VIII, an Integrated Area Development Plan for Tanuku Taluka has been presented.

Policy Measures

The following are the salient features of the study area:

1. Even in the agriculturally developed region, out-migration is noticed as an important factor. Many of the people in about 10 percent of the villages have migrated to the Gulf Countries as semi-skilled labourers. The income recipients of the dependent families are investing the in flow of money mainly on Agriculture. Hence the income flow is just helping to transfer the resource ownership but not to generate any additional income and employment. Had they been inested in agro-industries or in trade and commerce, much more development could have been taken place in the study area. Hence attempts should be made to industrialise the region with agricultural surplus and from the inflow of money.
2. As agriculture has already reached a peak in development, there is every need for investing surpluses on agro-based industries and to concentrate on the development of allied activities especially in livestock.
3. At present, Six centres have been identified as service centres of the study area. The analysis of travel patterns, and accessibility of the socio-economic institutions have revealed that there is every need to develop nine more potential centres as service centres for the development of the study area. On the basis of adequacy or inadequacy of the service facilities, proposals for the development of the centres have been made. Hence, priority should be given for the identified centres and the services for the balanced development of the region.
4. Since many of the settlements in the study area are not linked up properly with the nodal centres transportation has become a serious problem. Hence efforts should be made to link-up the peripheries with the nodal centres.
5. To meet the demand for agricultural inputs and services, the central places identified should be strengthened as service centres.
6. To achieve integrated area development, efforts have been made to integrate spatial, functional and developmental activities in the study area. Cost-Benefit ratios have also been worked out and a number of proposals have been made for the development of the region. This should be taken up by the newly constituted Planning Boards for the development of the region.

7. Peravali and Panumantra are the two blocks in Tanuku Tuluka. 'Peravali' Block headquarters is not located in Peravali, but is located in Tanuku due to political reasons. As Tanuka has already been well developed even though it is located 8 kms away from the Narasapur-Nidadavole Bus route, disclosing an active process of urbanisation. There is every need to shift the Block headquarters from Tanuku to Peravali. As this problem has already been realised by the new Government, efforts should be made to shift the headquarters so as to develop the region on scientific lines.
8. Recently, Tanuku Taluka has been reorganised into (1) Tanuku Taluka and (2) Penugonda Taluka with Tanuku and Penugonda as headquarters respectively. But formerly these talukas formed part of Peravali and Penumantra blocks with Peravali and penamantra as headquarters respectively. As Tanuku and Penugonda have already developed and are classified as towns even by 1961 Census, there should be some decentralisation in the urban process. The present centrifugal forces may act more on Penugonda and Tanuku urban nodes. But there is every need for diversification of the urban process of development. Penumantra is centrally located between At tili and Penugonda as per the viable norms. As a growth promoting factor, Penumantra should be developed. Penugonda taluka may be renamed as Penumantra Taluka; as noted earlier, Block headquarters of Peravali may be shifted from Tanuku town to Peravali. In this process we can maintain Tanuku and Penugonda as urban centres and promote Penumantra as Taluka headquarters. This makes the Taluka boundary to coincide with the Block boundary.

2.3 Location, structure, problems and prospects of Small Scale Industries in Telangana.

Industrial sector plays a vital role in the economic development of any Nation. Small Scale Industry, which is one of the sub-species of the genus of the industrial sector, is important for a nation to provide employment, to ensure more equitable distribution of income, to facilitate effective mobilisation of resources of capital and skills and to help in reducing regional imbalances. There role is also of great significant in regional resources of both human and material. They are used for the development of enterpreneurial skill for further industries.

The Small Scale Industrial sector in our country is recognised as a dynamic and progressive one. During the last two decades the progress achieved in this sector testifies its valuable contribution to our economic growth and the promise that it holds for the future.

Studies in industrial geography by Indian geographers since 1940 were systematically analysed the special distribution of industries, and geographical factors operating in their location and features of industrial landscape. The present study considers the small scale industries as a solution to enhanced comprehensive development to overcome the short-comings of regional disparities, unbalanced growth and development. This is an investigation into the "Location, Structure, Problems and Prospects of Small Scale Industries in Telangana". This study also highlights nature of the Small Scale Industrial Development in Telangana Region.

Study Area

Telangana is a region in Andhra Pradesh State which extended to 2.74 lakh sq.km. with a population of 2.02 crores (1981 census). This region encomposes the districts of Adilabad, Hyderabad, Karimnagar, Khammam, Mahaboobnagar, Medak, Nalgonda, Nizamabad, Ranga Reddy and Warangal districts in Andhra Pradesh. In spite of the abundant resources available for the development, the study region continues to be lagging behind economically. This is one of the important reasons for selecting this region for the present study. To fight against backwardness, Small Scale Industrialisation is an important strategy. Though the importance of small scale industries was recognised by the planners, they viewed the Small Scale Industries as employment generation, but not as output generation.

The Small Scale Industries requires protection from modern factory industries with respect to production. This will enable the Small Scale Industries to meet the two requirements viz., output generation and employment generation. The present study attempts a geographical assessment of the possibilities of multiple issues of available resources at minimum cost for economic development with a view to uplift the region from the economic backwardness.

Objectives of Study

The following objectives are considered in making the present research:

1. To appraise the existing industrial resources in Telangana.
2. To analyse the structure and growth of Small Scale Industries in Telangana region over a period of time (1957-85).
3. To assess the employment growth rate of Small Scale Industries in Telangana.

4. To find out the magnitude of the investment in Small Scale Indust-ries in Telangana region.
5. To examine the different levels of Industrialisation in Small Scale Industrial Sector in Telangana.

Hypothesis

The study proposed to test the following hypotheses:

1. Industrial development has not been commensurate in relation to the available resources in Telangana.
2. Rapid agricultural growth can change the structure of Small Scale Industries.
3. Unemployment due to sickness of units is caused by a large number of Small Scale Units.
4. Urban population growth and demand for industrial products are directly related.

Data Base

Present research based on both Secondary and Primary data. The data is drawn from such sources as number of Small Scale Industrial Units, Employment and investment were collected from the officers of the Commissioner of Industry, District Industrial Centres, Industrial Estates, Industrial Entrepreneurs, Bureau of Economics, Hyderabad, Books, Technical Reports etc.

Primary data was collected by means of a questionnaire from the randomly selected Small Scale Industrial Units in the study area.

The method of analysis of the data acquired is essentially a composite one.

Tools of Analysis

The following tools were adopted to analyse the growth, structure and location of Small Scale Industries in Telangana region. These are index numbers, annual composed rate of growth and location coefficient. Percentages for the number of units, employment and capital investment, were also calculated to present the structure of Small Scale Industries for the Telangana region as well as for Andhra Pradesh State.

Index Numbers are employed to know the magnitude of number of units, employment and investment in Small Scale Industries.

To determine the level of Small Scale Industrialisation the equation of manufacturing industry has been used.

Spearman's Rank Correlation Method (Location Factor) has been adopted to calculate the relationship between size of Small Scale Industrial units in the region and size of the work force employed by the units. The localisation of Small Scale Industries for each district over the time period is analysed through the of location coefficient for every district in Telangana region and for every region of Andhra Pradesh.

Super Imposed Technique is used in order to identify the development and deviation of Small Scale Industrial Units, workers and capital investment in Small Scale Industries in Telangana region.

Organisation of the Thesis

The present thesis includes the analysis of Location, Structure, Problems and Prospects of Small Scale Industries in Telangana. It also includes the growth and development of Small Scale Industries in Telangana region. The study is organised into five chapters. Chapter one deals with introduction and methodology of study. Chapter two is devoted for an appraisal of industrial resources in the region. Chapter three is concerned with the location structure of Small Scale Industries in Telangana in terms of units, workers, capital, investment. Chapter four is about the growth and development of Small Scale Industries in Telangana for the period 1957-85. The fifth Chapter consists of the problems, prospects and conclusion of Small Scale industries in Telangana Region.

Findings of the Study

1. Telangana is an underdeveloped region, for, its economy is mainly dependent on agriculture and partly on minerals and forests and industry.
2. Telangana is in dearth of capital resources. Lack of technical know-how is one of the factors for its slow development.
3. Power supply has been always a problem and hindrance for the development of Small Scale Industrial Sector in the region.
4. Inadequate supply of raw materials is another constraint for the growth of Small Scale Industries in Telangana.
5. Lack of proper transport facilities in rural Telangana is one of the major hindrances for the development of Small Scale Industrial sector in the region. The Transport problem affects the marketing facilities and supply of raw material.
6. Inadequate planning of production, longstanding shortage of raw materials and power, lack of interest in modernising the units, lack of preventive maintenance etc., are leading to spreading the industrial sickness in leaps and bounds.

7. The prospects for the development of Small Scale Industries in Telangana are currently not very bright, in view of its industrial backwardness and absence of a strong enterpreneurial base. However, there is an immediate need to create the necessary environment for its development to evolve the balanced structure and sustained growth of the industrial sector.

Chapter - 2

Agro Economic Studies

Impact of Cyclone on Development: A Case Study of Yanam

Planning for Integrated development deals with the study of physical and human resources of an area and the prevailing environmental conditions. Resource utilisation on scientific basis and the equitable distribution and utilisation at the regional level are very much essential for an integrated development. Regional approach to the problems were started from the First and Second Five Year Plans.[1] But due to the enormous stress on attaining self-sufficiency in food production, too much importance was not given for regional development programmes. The Third Five Year Plan included the preparation of Station plan and Block Development programme for rural development. This was perhaps the first step towards planning from grass roots.

1. Regionalisation in India

Regional differentiation of a country can be done in three ways.[2] Depending on the similarities and differences of areas, like mountains, plateaus, plains etc. (2) Depending on the administrative purposes. (3) Regions delimited by resource development, Stamp(1922)[2] divided India into three macro regions, and 22 sub natural regions, Bhat (1964)[3] suggested a scheme of seven macro economic regions based on the distribution of resources and possibilities of developing regional production complexes. Based on the work done by Indian Statistical Institute and earlier Census Regions, Nath (1967)[4] prepared a scheme of resource development regions and division, which was published by the Planning Commission. Singh (1971)[5] and others made a detailed study on regionalisation of India and presented a micro level regional picture in each micro region.

In 1962, Regional Survey of Unit of ISI prepared a scheme of planning regions of India[6]. Distribution of resources, physical complexes, cropping pattern, distribution of urban centre, natural resources, and industries were the main indicators used in differentiating different regions. Nath divided India into fifteen regions and sixty-one sub-regions based on an analysis of data and topography, geographical formation, soils, rainfall, agricultural land use, cropping pattern, population density and occupancy of mineral resources. The scheme of regionalisation which was adopted by the Planning Commission of India, was presented by Sen Gupta. (1966).[7] She divided India into six macro regions and forty-two meso regions.

Depending on the area under which the major development programmes are to be implemented, the regions are classified into macro, meso and micro regions. The macro planning regions are larger areas of diversified natural conditions and resources. The meso planning regions have been divided on the basis of potentialities of the region.

Micro regions should satisfy some of the basic needs and desires of the people. Structural, functional and organisational aspects, should be viable for direct interaction which determine the main issues of area development The heterogeneous composition of people and regions and wide regional and local variations in their development indicate that a plan should be based on local resource potential. The necessity of area-based micro level plans for correcting this situation was recognised in the Fourth Five Year Plan.[8] If the micro level plans are properly formulated they help in maximum utilisation of resources. The assessment of these resources can be accurate only if the past experience, present structure, and the forthcoming problems of the region are considered simultaneously. It is important that the formation of spatial framework of development should include study of land use, human settlements, social services, industrial output and the requirement by the people to bring development from the grass roots. The strategies for development should be laid down keeping in view the growing population and the expected higher demand for resources, any contingencies etc., due to natural disasters. To achieve integrated development at the national level, the cumulative effect of the success of micro plans help the macro plans prepared at the national level. Thus, micro planning contributes to development at national level.

The study of resource base may include:

(1) the geographical location of the area,

(2) the climatic conditions of the area,

(3) the quality of human resources, i.e., the composition of occupational structure,

(4) the area under irrigation, cropping pattern, agricultural productivity,

(5) number of industries and their composition, whether they are agro-based, heavy, cottage industries, etc.,

(6) the service sectors,

(7) mines and minerals,

(8) fishing,

(9) financial institutions,

(10) Educational institutions and

(11) the institutions that promote trade and commerce, etc.

An area has to be studied, taking into consideration all the above factors. Telangana Development Prospects and Problems' by Satyanarayana.B (1973) is a work in this direction.[9] Another study by Sundaram (1977) deals with some of the problems of Urban Village in India'[10]. According to Guner Myrdal economic geography sets the stage for development[11]. In the words of Friedman "Resource endowment is a changing concept closely associated with dynamics of economic growth".[12]

This analysis has to take into consideration the increase in income and also population and analyse the relation between them. A macro study of fifteen major states by Mahajan (1982) analyses the growth performance for the subperiods in the year 1951-61 to 1962-71.[14] The resource potentials of different areas were analysed in terms of land, labour and machine. This type of comparative study in micro level planning is essential to find out the development strategy keeping in view the growing population.

2. Micro level planning

Efforts were made by many in micro level studies. The contributions made by Roy, B. K., Burman and Chandrasekhar[15] are worth mentioning on the aspects of integrated regional approach and the frame of balanced regional development. Chakravarthy expressed the need for the adoption of all techniques at micro level and in turn help integrated area development.[16] Patel (1975) has made an attempt to point out the economic fallacies of balanced regional development in Indian conditions with special reference to tribal region of Madhya Pradesh.[17] He states that the emphasis should be at micro level. According to Murthy (1986) it is necessary to study micro areas to identify focal points and their hinterlands to assist the planners in planning for all sectors relevant to the area.[18]

3. Cyclones as Natural Disasters

Reports indicate that between 1891 and 1977 nearly four hundred cyclones were born in Bay of Bengal and about 90 cyclones in the Arabian Sea.[19] A study of cyclone of 1977' by P. Cohen, C.V. Raghavulu (1979) gives the causes and physical and social impact of cyclones.[20] According to Aqueil Ahmed, " to identify disaster preparedness and response as separate but interdependent analytical and empirical categories, to distinguish structural preparedness from behavioural readiness and systematic response from individual action; and to delineate interdependent primary and secondary systems of preparedness and response; and to introduce economic infrastructure as an important variable in disaster management are some of the novel features of the framework with far reaching policy implications for disaster management and mitigation.[21] Natural disasters cause hindrance in implementation of economic plans.

United Nations declared 1990s as the International Decade for Natural Disaster Reduction.[22] It has alerted all the National Governments to detect, warn and help people of the areas to take minimum precautions for safety and to mitigate all the ill effects caused by disasters. According to their recommendations, flood management is more appropriate than flood control. According to Clark (1989) density of population has a direct relationship to the magnitude of disaster.[23] Depending on the physical and human characteristics every natural disaster has a particular way to be dealt with. The evolving interaction of the people and the environment effects the opportunities and the costs that the forces of nature may reap. This provides the scope for the study for disasters, their characteristics, mitigation and management.[24]

In a study of tropical cyclones, Anjaneyulu (1973) observed that it was possible to avoid loss of life and minimize damages by taking precautionary measures well in advance.[25] Kayasta (1996) states that natural disasters compel interests because of their dramatic violence and human suffering[26] (26).

The most severely affected areas are also the backward areas. The developing countries with their problem economies and large growing population are faced with increasing disasters; sometimes not without their political repercussions. For example, in 1970, a tropical cyclone and storm devastated the then East Pakistan, killing nearly 5,00,000 persons. Inadequate response to disaster and relief to alleviate the suffering by the national leadership a thousand miles away in West Pakistan, led to civil war and to the eventual independence of East Pakistan, now known as Bangladesh.[27]

4. Cyclones and Disaster Management

According to Nick Carter[28] the cyclone can be well predicted well in advance by systematic international meteorological observations. It usually tends to confirm to seasonal pattem and is slow in the beginning. The effects of cyclone are usually caused due to the destructive forces of winds, storm-surge and flooding from intense rainfall, landslides rnay follow flooding and heavy rainfall. It is expected that during a cyclone usually severe damage to buildings and other structures, roads, essential services, and crops is caused.

It is observed that the Coromondal Coast is often affected by cyclones. The affected areas are most of the time in Krishna, Prakasam, East and West Godavari districts.[29]

On 6th November, 1996, the Coromondal Coast was hit by a severe cyclone. Yanam was one of the severely affected areas. In 1994, also floods had damaged the settlements of this region and the agricultural production was severely affected. The area of Yanam though consists of same villages and a small town area, for administration purposes it is treated as a single unit. The uniqueness of its administration relating to surrounding area facilitates the study of this micro region. The study undertaken in this region is the impact of cyclone of 1996 on the development process of this region and whether the region could withstand the calamity and recover quickly.

5. Objectives

The objectives of the present study are:

1. To analyse the development pattern of the region over some years.
2. To examine the impact of November 1996 cyclone on the economy of Yanam.
3. To analyse the future prospects for the development of the region in the light of the resource base of the region and the impact of the cyclone.
4. Methodology

A comparative study of population growth among different regions of Union Territory of Pondicherry has been done. The characteristics like the working population, sex, density, literacy and the occupational structure of the population have been analysed over a period of forty years. The resource base of the region is discussed in terms of land resources, water resources, livestock and the role of co-operatives for agricultural development of the region are studied.

The study of cyclones on the East Coast over a period of time has been done with special reference to the cyclone of 1996 on Yanam. The production in agriculture from 1990 to 1998, the marine production and the industrial scenario in the nineties, are analysed to examine the effect of cyclone.

7. Conclusion

The study of this region reveals some salient features about the economy. Agriculture plays an important role in the economy of the region. It is observed that the pressure on land is constantly increasing because there is very little chance of shift of work force from agricultural to non-agricultural activities. The production in agriculture shows high variations because of the unforeseen weather conditions. The area being nearer to the sea is prone to frequent cyclones. Fishing is an important occupation which can be continued along with agriculture and can be further improved in order to relieve pressure on agricultural land. Though the percentage of population dependant on fishing is almost the same for the last one decade, there is an increase of fish catch even with the primitive mode of fishing. Therefore, stress should be given on the development of fishing using more sophisticated methods. Though there was comparatively heavy loss incurred in agriculture, fisheries and industries during the cycles, the authorities were successful to elevate these sectors of the region to the normal level through cyclone relief measures. The precautions taken before and after the cyclone were appreciable and helped the poor to come back to normal life very quickly. The Government has to take permanent measures to overcome the impending threats of future cyclones. There is large scope for further development of fishing through modernisation of fishing boats and by adopting modern techniques in fishing. A compressive plan is to be evolved and implemented by taking into consideration the agricultural, biotic and industrial resources in order to achieve the overall development of the region. Any plan prepared on scientific lines and with the complete Geonomic knowledge about the problems and prospects of the region, if implemented, will definitely be a success.

References

1. Cyril Antony, F. (1982), *Gazetter of India.* Administration of the Union Territory of Pondicherry. Pondicherry, Vol. 1.
2. Stamp, L.D (1954), *Asia: A Regional and General Geography* Methuen, London, pp. 274-278.
3. Bhatt, L S (1964), *Liverpool Essays in Geography,* Aspects of Regional Planning in India, London.
4. Spate, O H K. (1967), *India and Pakistan: A General and Regional Geography,* Methuen, London, pp. 351-354.
5. Singh, R L et.al, (1971), *India: A Regional Geography,* N. G. S. I., Varanasi.
6. Nath, V (1964), "A Resource Development Regions and Divisions of India". Planning Commission of India, New Delhi, Prakasa Rao., V.S. L and Bhat L.S.(1962), A Regional Framework for Resource Development, Bombay *Geographical Magazine* Vol. pp. 35-38.

7. Sen Gupta, P (1966) 'Planning Regions for Resource Development in India' *National Geographic Journal of India,* Vol. XII, No. 1, pp. 1-2.
8. Fourth Five Year Plan, Planning Commission, op, cit., pp. 229-230.
9. Satyanarayana, B. (1973), *Telangana Development Prospects and Problems.*
10. Sundaram, K. V. (1977), *Urban and Regional Planning in India,* Vikas Publishing House.
11. Guner Myrdal (1957), *Economic Theory and Underdeveloped Regions,* pp. 38.
12. John Friedman and William Alonsoled. Regional Development and Planning, p. 216.
13. John Friedman and William Alonsoled, *Regional Development and Planning,* p. 216.
14. Mahajan, OP (1982), *Economic Planning and Regional Development in India.* Sheel Sethi, Ms Ess Ess Publications.
15. Vasudeva Rao, D "Identification of Potential Growth Centres An Alternative Method," *Indian Journal of Regional Science,* Vol. IX No. 1, 1977.
16. Satyesh, C. Chakroborty, Some Consideration on the Research Objectives of Rural Area Development" *Indian Journal of Regional Science* IV, (1), pp. 1-50.
17. Patel, M L (1975), *Dilemma of Balance Regional Development in India,* Bhopal, pp. 33-34.
18. Murthy, K.L.N. (1986) *Planning for Integrated Area Development,* B. R. Publishing Corporation, Delhi.
19. Centre for Science and Environment - *Floods, Flood Plains and Environments, Myths,* State of Indian Environment. A citizens Report.
20. Stephen, P. Cohen and Raghavulu, C. V. (1979), *The Andhra Cyclone of 1977*, Vikas Publishing House.
21. Aqueil Ahmed, e.d. (1981), *Disaster Management Preparedness and Response*, Workshop proceedings Pb. AS C 17 A RTIC.
22. R.B. Singh (1996), *Disaster Environment and Development,* Oxford & IBH Publishing.
23. Clark, John. I.P. Curson, Kayasta S.L., and Nag. P (1989), *Population and Disaster.* Basil Backwell Oxford. p. 173.
24. Kayasta, S. L. *Disaster Environment and Development* Ed. R. B. Singh (1996) Oxford & IBH Publishings, p. 63.
25. Anjaneyulu, T.S.S. (1973), Cyclones – The havoc caused by them and the planning required. Vayumandal, pp. 71-78.
26. Kayasta, S. L. op.cit, p. 70.
27. Melham, Tom (1986), Acts of God, Acts of Man, *Nature on the Rampage.* The National Geographic Society, Washington D.C. 17.
28. Carter, W. Nick. (1991), *Disaster Management: a disaster manager's handbook.* W. Nick Carter. Manila ADB.
29. Stephen, P. Cohen and Raghavulu, C.V. (1979), *The Andhra Cyclone of 1977,* Vikas Publishing House.

Chapter - 3

Commerce

3.1. Human Resource Accounting

Renade has looked at the issue of HRD from the viewpoint of human resource accounting. His proposition of human resource accounting is directed to the organised sector, and may be relevant to the issue of employer-employee relationship.

Adam Smith has described the contribution made by human capital as one of the major factors of production in the economic world. More than half a century ago, Alfred Marshall remarked that the most valuable of capital is that invested in human beings. Ardent support for the concept that labour was an element of capital was forthcoming from Jean-Baptise Say. In his efforts to extend the theory, Say interrelated the effect of education on the productive ability of highly trained labour.

Still there exists a continued disagreement in economic literature regarding human capital.

In its micro-aspect human resources is certainly the most important asset in a particular undertaking. It is also agreed that the practising accountants have not been able to develop adequate criteria to measure the value of this asset, and show it in a balance sheet. Small items like furniture are valued and put on the balance sheet, but the acquisition, training and development cost of the manpower is not at all properly projected in financial statements.

Conventional accounting is inadequate for recognising human resources as assets. Probably the reason for not treating, or the reluctance to consider human resources as capital arises from the fact that while other assets are owned by an organisation, human resources are not so owned. The organisation pays only wages or salaries to its employees, which are of a revenue nature, and as such are treated as current costs. It was never thought that investment in human resources could be treated as capital.

The American Accounting Association has described it as a process of identifying and measuring data about human resource and communicating this information to the interested parties. Others have defined it as a process of developing financial assessments of people and groups of people within organisation.

The importance of human resource development, and its accounting has been receiving increased importance for the last two decades.

Theodore W. Schults said in his presidential address to the American Economic Association:

The failure to treat human resources explicitly as a form of capital .. as a product of investment, has fostered the retention of the classical notion of labour as a capacity to do manual work requiring little knowledge and skill, a capacity with which, according to this notion, labourers are endowed about equally. This notion of labour was wrong in the classical period and it is patently wrong now.

Investment in human beings has accordingly seldom been incorporated in the formal core of economics, even though many economists, including Marshall, have seen its relevance at one point or another in what they have written.

A number of business houses in the US have since up accounting systems for human resource costs. HRD may be defined as a process of measurement and reporting of the cost and value of people as organisational resources. It involves accounting for investment in people and their replacement cost, in addition to accounting for the economic value of people to an organisation.

The following are reasons for using HRD:

(a) Human labour plays a vital role in the production process, as the success of other factors mainly depend on the extent of efficiency of human resources.

(b) Day by day, the amount of investment made in human resources by any concern has been increasing substantially, e.g. expenditure on recruitment training and orientation of the technical staff, skilled labour, accountants, managers, etc. The degree of such expenditure can't be ascertained without proper accounting.

(c) In service-oriented industries, human resources play a pivotal role. Again, in labour-based production processes, human resources are the real resources.

(d) Managerial decisions, regarding human resources would be more accurate and prompt if PRA is adopted, e.g., internal promotion vs. direct recruitment, transfer vs. retention.

(e) Labour unrest and its outcomes like strikes and lockouts could be efficiently monitored and judged with the help of HRA.

Before we proceed with the models and methods of HRA, let us scrutinise the special features of human resources, which differentiate them from other resources:

(a) The use of physical resources depreciates their efficiency, while it is likely that due to ageing and experience human resources efficiency appreciates.

(b) Life of human resources are uncertain, form the viewpoint of the organisation as well.

(c) Their value depends on how they are used by the organisation, as the value can be increased, reduced or conserved by various the value can be increased, reduced or conserved by various management actions like training, ill-treatment, technological obsolescence, etc.

(d) Human resources are not owned by the organisation unlike other physical resources.

The models of HRA which have so far been developed can be classified into three groups, viz, cost models, economic models and behavioural models. We will analyse the cost models only.

Introduction

A firm having incompetent management will soon, run through the physical resources available to it. There have been generals who have got defeated - on the verge of victory just as there have been others who turned almost certain defeat into victory. Fayol, the noted French Management writer, was given charge of an almost bankrupt company but he made it into a very successful concern. It is, however, unfortunate that so far there is no agreed and generally accepted method of putting a value on this vital asset and showing it as part of or along with financial statements. However, work has been done in the western countries to evolve a suitable method.

Man plays the most important part in an enterprise. There may be good materials, good machines, good buildings and the like, but if the man who has to work is not good, results will not be upto the mark. Human beings are considered as the most important organ of an enterprise. It is the human ability which makes the mare go. Human resource is the best asset which an enterprise possesses, hence amount invested in human beings can give better result to the industry.

In the balance sheet human resource is not indicated as an asset while machinery, plant and furniture etc. are shown. Though it is the board of directors on whose policy, planning and management, the company progresses, but this board does not appear in the asset side of the balance sheet.

According to Caplan, E.H. and Landekich, "People are the most important asset of an organisation and yet, the value of this asset does not appear in tbe financial statements. This information has not even been included as a part of internal accounting and reporting for management purpose."

Trading practice in Accounting

The expenditure incurred on the services of persons working in an organisation is charged to Profit and Loss Account as an item of revenue expenditure. It is in the form of wages and salaries. As it is of revenue nature, it is taken to profit and loss account. However, during these days companies are investing huge amount of money to acquire their employees for the training and development and also for developing the human organisation. It is also hoped that these trained persons will continue to work in the organisation as organisation is a going concern, thus the training will be of great use to the organisation in future years. Certain future benefits will accrue to the organisation due to human resource expenditure, yet it is not treated as an asset.

It is a fact that success of an organisation depends on its managerial, scientific and commercial personnel. The results of application of physical resources are reported in various financial statements under conventional or traditional system of accounting, but this system of accounting fails to incorporate the value of human resources.

Shortcomings of Traditional Accounting or Conventional Accounting regarding Human Resources

1. Management wants to know the total amount invested in Human Resources. This information is not available in conventional accounting.
2. Capacities, abilities and potentialities of human resources are not recognised in traditional accounting.
3. Expenses incurred in wages, salaries and training etc. are treated as revenue expenses in conventional accounting. It is desirable that the expenditure incurred in development and training of the employees should be capitalised because the benefits of this training etc. will be utilised in the years to come.

4. There is no separate record in conventional accounting about the amount spent in acquisition of human resources. This information is of very great use to the management in the field of planning.
5. Human resource is the most important asset in an enterprise but it is not shown as an asset in conventional accounting.

The inability of the traditional accounting system to report on human resources led to the development of human resource accounting.

History of Human Resource Accounting

1. Origin of human resource accounting is found in the work of Rensis Likert, social psychologist, who was the first person to use the term 'human asset' in the late 1950s. Scholars replaced this term of 'human asset' hy the term 'human resources'.
2. Conventional accounting practice was criticised by behavioural scientists during early and mid-1960s for its failure to value the human resources.
3. According to the report of American Accounting Association Committee (AAAC) on accounting for human resources "The obvious importance of people in organisations and as productive resources was largely ignored by the accounting profession until approximately 1965. Now there appears to be widespread interest for human resource accounting ."
4. Real work on HRA (human resource accounting) started from 1960. Following prominent persons have done work on HRA. They are of the opinion that there is need of HRA and hence they have pointed out the methods of valuation of HR (Human Resources):
   a. Schulty (1960)
   b. Hermanson (1964)
   c. Hekiman and Jones (1967) Rensis Liket (1967)
   d. Brumnet, Flamholtz and Pyle (1969)
   e. Lev and Schwartz (1971)
   f. Flamholtz (1972)
   g. Morse (1973) Likert and Bowers (1973)
   h. Jaggi and Lev (1974)
   i. Flamholtz (1975)
   j. Pekin Ogan (1976)
   k. Kenneth Senedier (1978)

5. R. C. Bany Corporation, Ohio, (USA) is the first in the world, which introduced HRA in 1967. Now many countries of the world are using HRA.
6. In India, since 1978-79 tend of valuation of HR has started on minor scale. Following companies and corporations are reporting valuation of Human Assets in India:

(A) Companies

(i) BHEL, (Bharat Heavy Electricals Ltd.); (ii) Electronics India Ltd.; and (iii) Engineers India Ltd.

(B) Corporations

(i) CCI (Cement Corporation of India Ltd.); (ii) MMTC (The Minerals and Metals Trading Corporation of India Ltd.; and (iii) PEC (Projects and Equipment's Corporation of India Ltd.,

Meaning and Definition of Human Resource Accounting

1. According to Woodruff Jr., Vice-President of R.G. Bany Corporation of U.S.A., "Human Resource Accounting is an attempt to identify and report investment made in human resources of an organisation that are not presently accounted for under conventional accounting practices. Basically, it is an information system that tells the management what changes over time are occurring to the human resources of business."
2. According to American Accounting Association Committee (AAAC)

   "Human resource accounting is the process of identification and measuring data about human resources and communicating this information to interested parties."
3. According to Eric Flamholtz, "Human resource accounting is the measurement of the cost and value of people for the organisation."
4. According to Stephen Knauf, "Human resource accounting is the measurement and qualification of human organisational inputs, such as recruiting, training, experience and commitment."

Ideal meaning of HRA

Human resource accounting is recording (i) the process of identifying the data about human resources, (ii) investments made in human resources and (iii) measurement of cost and value of human resources of the organisation. It also records the changes which occurs in the human resources of the organisation over a period of time and communicates this information in the financial statements for the use of all those who are interested in this information.

Characteristics of HRA

1. It is a system of accounting in which identification of human resources i.e., employees of the organisation is made. Employees here refer to all categories of the people of the organisation from the top management to the bottom.
2. Investment made in human resources is recorded.
3. Measurement of cost and value is made.
4. Changes occurring in human resources over a period of time are also recorded.
5. The information about human resources is communicated through financial statements to the interested parties.
6. HRA helps the management in having knowledge about various aspects of the employees, which is of great use for the progress of the organisation.
7. HRA is a part of the management information system.
8. Joint efforts of behavioural scientists, accountants and managements are needed for the working and development of HRA.

Objects of Human Resource Accounting

1. The main object of HRA is to have best management of human resources, because the progress of organisation is fundamentally based on human resource.
2. Improvement of human resources is possible on the basis of information submitted by HRA.
3. Correct value of the organisation can be found out because in conventional accounting human resource is not recognised as an asset.
4. HRA makes quantitative information about human resources available.
5. Worth of Human Resources is found out.
6. Whatever investment on human resources is made, its return can be evaluated.

Merits of HRA

I. *Improvement in Internal Management Decisions.* HRA helps in making internal management decisions better. For instance, the transfer of an employee from one department to another or promotion of an employee to higher position. If these acts increase the value of HRA, it is good and profitable otherwise not. R.G. Barr Corporation was the first corporation to adopt HRA for improvement of internal management.

2. *Motivation of Employees for Production Purposes.* HRA helps in finding out the time cost of human asset. If hourly time cost of this asset is brought to the knowledge of various classes of employees, it is hoped that they may devote there every second for productive purpose only.
3. *Saving of time in Meetings of the Executive.* The executives of an enterprise have a daily engagement cards in which the times of various meetings, to be attended by them during the day, is mentioned. If the value of time of executives is known to them, they may devote the most reasonable time in the meetings and some of the meetings may be avoided also. This value of time can be quantitatively expressed on the basis of HRA.
4. *Indicator of the Health of the Enterprise.* On the basis of HRA, value of human resource to the enterprise can he found out and the knowledge about this type of value helps in assessing the health of the enterprise, i.e., whether the enterprise will make profit in future or not.
5. *Impact on Investors Decisions.* HRA helps in finding out rate of return on investment. Though rate of return on investment can be found out under traditional system of accounting also but this rate under HRA is better than the rate of traditional accounting system because under traditional accounting system all expenses on human resources are treated as revenue while under HRA some of these expenses are treated as revenue and others as deferred revenue and these are written off over a certain period of time.
6. *Knowledge of value of employees on the basis of training etc.* HRA helps in finding out the addition made in the value of employees due to training etc.
7. *Knowledge about economic value of the Personnel.* HRA helps in having knowledge about the economic value of the personnel of an enterprise.
8. *Improvement in decision-making process.* If human resource data are included in financial reporting, the management gets information about the value of human resources and this information given by HRA improves the decision-making process.

9. *Decision about further recruitment.* Whether further recruitment of personnel be made or not is decided on the basis of HRA information.
10. *Judgement of negative effects of the programmes.* HRA helps in judging the negative effects of various programmes.
11. *Assistance in planning.* HRA is of very great use in planning for the management.
12. *Success and Progress of the Enterprise.* The success and progress of the enterprise can be judged on the basis of HRA because it gives information about human resources and human resource is the nerve centre of the enterprise.

Limitations of HRA

I. *Non-availability of Standard.* Certain standards are needed to measure the human resources. At present adequate standards are not available for such measure. Institute of Chartered Accountants of India should devise certain standard in this respect.

2. *Opposition of Trade Unions.* It is feared that valuation of human resources may be opposed by trade unions. These unions represent various classes of employees. These leaders may be convinced about the utilities of HRA for employees before introduction of HRA in an enterprise.
3. *Expenditure on HRA.* When HRA is adopted, it is certain that additional expenditure will be incurred on it and this additional expenditure will reduce is desirable to assess the cost-benefit ratio of introduction of HRA.
4. *Objection about treating employees as assets.* Some persons are against the view that employees are assets. They say that if employees are bracketed as assets, they will come in the category of slaves, but such arguments are wrong because it is the investment on employees which is shown in the asset side and not the employees.
5. *Variety of approaches.* For valuation of human resources there are various approaches, hence they create confusion so far as adoption of a particular model is concerned.
6. *Category of Asset.* There is no certainty about the category to which this asset of human resources should belong. Various authors have grouped it according to their conscience to various heads. Some regard HRA as fixed assets while others as investment etc.

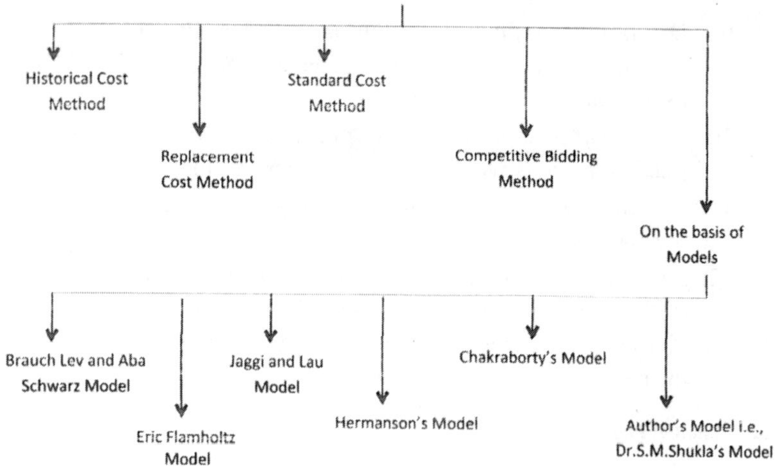

Valuation of HR Accounting

7. *Uncertainty about continuance of employees.* Machinery and building etc., can remain in the business as long as the proprietor needs them, hut there is a lot of uncertainty in the continuance of this asset namely, HR, because employee is free to leave the organisation whenever he likes and thus enterprise may suffer abruptly due to sudden vacancy of the employee and valuation concept of human resource is disturbed.

Before we proceed with the models and methods of HRA, let us scrutinise the special features of human resources. which differentiate them from other resources:

(a) The use of physical resources depreciates their efficiency, while it is likely that due to ageing and experience human resources efficiency appreciates.

(b) Life of human resources are uncertain, form the viewpoint of the organisation as well.

(c) Their value depends on how they are used by the organisation, as the value can be increased, reduced or conserved by various management actions like training, illtreatment, technological obsolescence, etc.

(d) Human resources are not owned by the organisation unlike other physical resources.

The models of HRA which have so far been developed can be classified into three groups, viz., cost models, economic models and behavioural models. We will analyse the cost models only.

Cost Models

(1) The first historical cost model was developed by the Institute of Social Research, University of Michigan. Brummet, Pyle and Flamholtz were involved in the process of valuating the human resources of R. G. Barry company's employees. They used conventional accounting procedures to combine recruitment, training and orientation costs. The training costs under this models are amortized over a shorter period than recruitment costs, since training becomes out-dated as new skills are developed to meet the technological changes.

The researchers proposed that acquisition cost alone should be used for human assets valuation. These costs include hiring and training expenses. Since these costs are easily quantifiable, the method is consistent with standard accounting practices. But the model ignores changes in values. Promotions and job-received skills.

(2) Lee and Rosenbloom used a replacement cost model. Values are assigned on the assumptions that employees would have to be replaced if they leave the organisation. Replacement costing relates to the current cost accounting, which has not been adopted by most of the organisations.

(3) Flamholtz's replacement cost model includes factors for productivity within rank and a likelihood of a worker's termination. A 'condition value' is computed representing the present value of future services.

Flamholtz states: The model accounts for one's value as an independent phenomenon. Variables included are the nature of the organisation and the extent of interdependence on organisational roles. The model does not fully recognise dynamic aspects of organisational phenomena.

(4) Hekimian and Jones advocate using either net present value determinations, or opportunity cost to arrive at emplyees' worth. They have a preference for opportunity costs ad would permit managers to bid for employees so that the highest bidder wins. Hekimian and Jones favour the bidding system for 'more optional allocation of personnel', and a 'quantitative base for planning evaluating and developing human assets.' They have also proposed the capitalisation of acquisition, training and development costs.

Thus, human resources accounting may be classified into (i) human resources, cost accounting (HRCA) and (ii) human resources value accounting (HRVA).

The HRCA system is like accounting for any other asset as such, it involves (a) capitalisation of investments made in human resources. (b) recording the normal and usual expiration on the basis of amortisation, (c) recording losses due to labour turnover or outdated skills, and (d) recording the value of human resource within the organisation after such adjustments.

Thus, HRCA fits naturally into the long-standing conventional accounting system. This concept is generated from the usual concept of cost. Thus, there is cost in order to acquire or replace people, having both an expense and asset component. The costs of recruitment, training and orientation are historical costs while replacement costs are represented by the expenditure on the fresh recruits, and the loss of profit till the fresher's attain the efficiency of those whom they replace.

Historical costs can be classified into two groups as acquisition costs and development costs. The former includes various expenses incurred on recruitment, selection, hiring etc. While the development costs would be those which are incurred on training and orientation. For each group mentioned expenses incurred have to be identified and classified as human resources cost.

Once the costs are identified, they have to be accounted for through some new subsidiary ledgers. Again the imputed costs which are associated with the sacrifice of certain benefits in acquiring the human resources should be identified, quantified and accounted.

The replacement costs of human resources consist of acquisition, development and termination. While the first two types of cost are self-explanatory, the termination costs are those that arise due to payment of compensation in different forms, as also the imputed costs due to the position being vacant.

The determination of the amortisation procedure is the next hurdle to HRA, since each part of the investment may require a different amortisation period. It depends on the nature of the organisation, as well as on the length of the benefit periods, the physical and mental condition of the employees, etc. The amortisation period should be reviewed continuously, and the significant health changes in individuals and the changes in their position should be taken into account.

As HRCA is a new concept, an organisation should arrive at a satisfactory procedure by the trial and error method.

As far as the value concept of HRA is concerned, it can be stated that, since it has not yet been used, by and large, for other assets to start with, HRCA may he adopted to give proper representation to human resources in the accounting structure.

In India, few companies have noticed the importance of HRA. For the last few years BHEL has been adding a note on HR in its annual reports. More and more private sector companies should come forward to support this neglected but vitally important sphere of accounting.

Historical Cost Method of Valuation

(1) Historical cost is also known as acquisition cost. The amount spent on recruitment, hiring, selecting, placing, training and developing of human resources is capitalised.

(2) The period of service of human resources is estimated and on the basis of this period the amount capitalised above is written off.

(3) If the service period of human resources increases then the estimated working life period, the written off process is revised. On the other hand if the working life period of human resources ends earlier than the estimated period, the amount of unwritten off cost of human resources is written off in that year.

(4) In this historical cost method human resources are more or less treated like fixed assets.

Critical appraisal of this Method

(1) Exact estimate regarding the working period of human resources cannot be made as is done in the case of plant and machinery etc.

(2) Human resources are trained and efforts are made to develop them, so the value of human resources increases to the organisation in future years, this appreciation in value is not taken into consideration under this system, on the other hand due to writing off certain amount every year, under this method, value of human resources appears decreased.

(3) It is very difficult to select the method of depreciation for this asset of human resources. There are many methods of depreciation, it is difficult to find out the best method for this asset. The common practice is to charge constant amount of depreciation every year in this method.

(4) This method does not provide any information to the investor, though it may be of some use to the management.

(5) The main purpose of HRA is to assist management in decision making, but according to this method historical costs can be of very little use to the management due to changing values of human beings.

Replacement Cost Method

I. Under this method, the cost, at which existing human resources can be replaced, is estimated.

2. This estimated cost of replacement may be: (a) positional cost and (b) personal replacement cost.

Positional Cost. Under this cost, the cost of recruitment, electing, hiring, placing, development and training etc. are included. Here position or status of the employee is considered i.e., if a secretary is to be replaced, what amount will be made to recruit, to select, to train and to develop the recruitee for occupying the position of secretary.

These days some amount is often paid as compensation for terminating the services of an employee. This amount is also included in the positional replacement cost. An estimate of the total amount needed for the above mentioned purposes is called positional replacement cost.

Personal Replacement Cost. (1) The amount needed to replace a person is known as personal replacement cost. In the positional replacement, position is considered while in the personal only person is considered, but person without position has no meaning, therefore replacement cost really means the cost required to replace the existing employee by an identical employee who should be as competent in all respect as the previous one who is to be replaced.

(2) Current value of human resources to the enterprise is considered at the time of estimating replacement cost.

(3) Changes in price level are considered in making an estimate of replacement cost.

Ments of this Method

1. This method helps in assessing the economic value of the employee.
2. National Association of Accountants (NAA) regards replacement eost as 'present oriented', i.e., this method takes into consideration the resent value of the employee. It helps in finding out the correct value of the organisation.

3. It helps the management in decision-making to a very great extent.

Demerits of this Method

1. It is very difficult to find out an individual who is as competent as one to be replaced.

   Even by training and development etc., an individual may not replace the existing one in all respects because human beings have some natural gifts which under no circumstances can be acquired by training etc. Therefore, replacement cost is not real one and does not indicate the advantage of 'present-oriented' as has been pointed out by some persons.
2. Estimated of replacement cost may differ from person to person. It is not possible to assess the correct replacement cost of each individual of the organisation. This view is also supported by Likert, R. and Bowers.

Standard Cost Method

Under this method standard costs of human resources are found out, e.g., standard cost of recruitment, training and development etc. These standard costs are compared with actual costs. On the basis of variations management tries to make improvement in various process of human resources.

Opportunity Cost Method

An interesting method advocated by Hekimian and Jones, called opportunity cost method, is that divisional heads may bid for the services to various people whose services they may require and then include the bid price in the investment base. The method roughly works as shown below. Suppose a division's target ROI is 15 percent, it has capital base of Rs. I ,00,00,000 but its profit is only Rs. I3,00,000 i.e., Rs. 2,00,000 short of the target. It is felt that if it can acquire the services of a particular executive, its profits can improve by Rs.90,000 i.e., the profit will be Rs.15,90,000. Rs. 90,000 more than Rs.15,00,000. Rs. 90,000 capitalised at 15percent comes to Rs. 6,00,000. The division certainly may bid up to Rs. 6,00,000 for the services of the executive. Actually, the maximum bid may even be the capitalised value of Rs. 2,90,000, the extra profit likely to be generated by the executive's availability.

The method can work for some of the people but, surely, quite a few people, specially those at the top, will not be available for the auction. It also ignores people that are not scarce.

Competitive Bidding Method

I. This method is applied only in the case of scarce employees. Here human assets mean only scarce employees.
2. Increase in profit on account of the acquisition of the services of an employee is found out.
3. This increase in profit is capitalised at the rate of normal return of profit which is known as Return on Investment (ROI).
4. The above mentioned capitalised value of increased profit is added in the capital base of the enterprise and then profit is found out on this new capital base, i.e., the old capital plus capitalised value of increased profit.
5. Excess of the profit calculated in (4) above over the profit earned on original capital base is capitalised. The maximum bid is made upto the limit of this capitalised value of excess profit.
6. This method is also called Opportunity Cost Method. Hekimian, J.C. and Jones. C.H. are in favour of opportunity cost in human resource.
7. Opportunity cost is found out by making competitive bidding. This bidding is done by various departments and investment centre managers who want to recruit scarce employees.
8. Under this method such employees are not included who are not scarce.

Merits of this Method

1. This method is of very good use to the management because it helps in the revaluation of human resources.
2. This method helps the management in planning for human resource.
3. Development in human resource can easily be made on the basis of the information of this method.
4. It is most suitable for that organisation in which services of scarce employees are needed.
5. Shortcomings of replacement of cost method are overcome by this method.

Demerits of this Method

1. The greatest shortcoming of this method is that those employees who are not scarce, are not treated as human asset. Under this method true cost of full human resource of an enterprise cannot be found out because only scarce employees are considered in this method.

2. Wherever this method is adopted, the moral of employees goes down because a discrimination is made in this method between scarce employees and ordinary employees.
3. Bidding of top management is not made, hence this method does not apply in case of such management.
4. Bidding is mostly a costly affair. In competitive bidding prices go up, hence such divisions which are not making more profits find it difficult to make use of this method. If they bid, it may not be in their favour from profit making point of view.
5. It is difficult to estimate accurately the future benefit which will be made due to the recruitment of scarce employee.

Brauch Lev and Aba Schwartz Model Present Value of Future Earning

Present value of future earnings is a model which is known as Brauch Lev and Aha Schawrtz model or in short Lev and Schwartz model. This model recognises an individual's expected economic value to the enterprise during his remaining service period. An estimate about future earning is made. These earnings relate to the period which extends to the date of retirement of the employees. Such earnings are discounted by an appropriate rate to get the present value.

Formula for this model is as under:

$V_r =$

T= X

V_r=human capital value or a person *r* years old

E *(t)* = retirement person's expected annual earnings upto

r = a discount rate

t = retirement age

Lev and Schwartz have divided all the employees into homogenous classes such as unskilled, skilled, semi-skilled and managerial staff etc. Average earnings of different age groups are found out taking their classes into consideration and then the present value of human resources capital is ascertained. There is an assumption in this model that employees will not make role changes during their service in the enterprise.

Bharat Heavy Electrical Ltd. uses the Lev and Shwartz model. Stating that the value of human capital embodied in an individual is the present value of his remaining future earnings from employment, the promotion policy and pay scales being assumed as constant, the company reported the under the following categories:

Executives	XXX
Supervisors	XXX
Artisans	XXX
Supporting Technical Staff	XXX
Clerical and Office Supporting Staff	XXX
Unskilled and Semi-Skilled Staff	XXX
Total	XXX

Objections. One can easily spot the main difficulty with the so-called value approaches based on future earnings. Further earnings of employees will be the costs to the firm; how can they be the value to the firm? The assumption, of course, is that the benefits from the services of the employees will be the same as their remuneration. If this valid, how will the firm survive? The fact is that human beings yield, specially because of their team work, much more than they are paid. Even for individuals as Economic Theory points out, the pay is based on marginal productivity and that naturally leaves a large surplus for the employer. One would think that it is the human resources as a whole, or all employees as a team, that has to be valued; otherwise the result is likely to be unsatisfactory. Also, the value must be based on the benefit likely to be derived by the firm.

Merits of this Model

I. This model has introduced economic value concept to HRA.
2. Human capital value is found out after considering the remaining period of service of the employees, thus due weightage is given to working life span of the employees.

Demerits of this Model

1. If some employees leave the organisation before their retirement, the result shown by the model will not be upto the mark, because it ignores such employees.
2. The assumption in this model that employees will not change their role is not correct, because employees are often transferred from one department to another and from one post to another on promotion.
3. In this model it is assumed that the person's value to the enterprise is due to his abilities and qualities but the fact is that his value may increase or decrease due to the role of the organisation also to which he belongs, this fact has not been considered in this model.

Eric Flamholtz's Model

An estimate of expected future services of the employees is made in this model. This model points out the value of an employee to the enterprise to which he belongs. Every employee provides service to the enterprise and generates value to it. The expected realisable value of an employee is the ultimate measure of his value to the enterprise.

Whatever period an employee is expected to remain in the organisation, same services will be provided during this period by him, the present worth of these future services is found out and this present worth is the expected realisable value of an employee. Just as all other assets provide services in future in the same way human beings also provide services in future.

A person is valued in the enterprise according to the post which he occupies. If he occupies a high post or senior technical post, his value is more. Value is also found out on the basis of the role which an employee will play in future in the enterprise.

Following stages are used in measuring the value of an employee for the enterprise in this model:

I. The period during which the employee is expected to remain in the enterprise in future is estimated.

II. The position which the employee will occupy in future is also estimated. It is also estimated that at what time he may leave the enterprise.

III. The value which the enterprise will get from the position of the employee is estimated.

IV. An estimate is also made about the possibility of occupying a certain position at specified future period.

V. Finally, the present value of future service reward is found out at discount rate.

Jaggi and Lau's Model

Under this model group valuation in made. Group here refers to homogenous group of employees of an enterprise. The employees belonging to one homogenous group may belong to different departments.

It is not easy to predict about the promotion or staying of an employee in a department or quiting the department by an employee, but it is possible to make above prediction on a group basis.

In this model it is assumed that over a period of time the pattern of movement of employees is likely to remain constant, hence, whatever probabilities are for one period they are expected to be extended for the period to come.

Hermanson's Model

It is a common belief that normally there is relation between the salary of an individual and his value to the enterprise and it is on this belief that this Hermanson's Model is based. Under this model present value of future salary of employees is found out.

An efficiency ratio is used to adjust the discounted future value. For the purpose of this ratio weighted average is found out and highest weight is given to the current year and less weight is given to the previous year.

Adjusted present value of future wages and salaries is found out in the following way:

I. Annual wages and salaries for next some years are estimated. Mostly this period is five years.
2. Discounter factor, is applied to determine the present value of the estimated future wages and salaries of the employees of the enterprise.
3. Above mentioned present values of the wages and salaries of all the employees are totalled and then this total is multiplied by the efficiency ratio and this efficiency ratio is found out by weighted average. Thus, the present value of human resource is found out.

S.K. Chakraborty's Model

Prof S.K. Chakraborty has made one model for the valuation of human resources. The essentials of this model are:

1. He is in favour of valuing human resources in aggregate, opinion that there may be made two groups for such aggregate managerial group and non-managerial group.
2. In one group average salaries of the employees of a group are… Average tenure of employment of employees of that group is also and then the above calculated average salaries are multiplied calculated average tenure. The result of this multiplication is the above human resources.
3. Expenditure on recruitment, hiring, training and development etc. employees should be calculated on individual basis and then this expenditure should be treated as deferred revenue expenditure.
4. The above mentioned deferred revenue expenditure should be written during the period during which the employee is expected to remain in the organisation on an average.
5. That portion of the above deferred expenditure, which has not been written off, should be shown in the asset side.

6. If an employee dies or due to retrenchment, he has to leave the enterprise, then the underwritten off balance of the deferred expenditure is transferred to the profit and loss account of that year in which the employeedies or is retrenched.
7. The present value of estimated payments to be made to the employee in future is found out by discount rate. This discount rate should be the expected average rate of return over capital employed over the average period of tenure of the employee, but tax should be deducted from the above return before finding out the average rate.
8. According to the view of Prof. Chakraborty human resource should be treated as an asset but it should be included in 'Investment' and not in fixed assets or current assets in the asset side of Balance Sheet.

Dr. S.M. Shukla's Model

According to Dr. S. M. Shukla, expenses incurred by the employer over employee are grouped under four categories for treatment in Human Resource Accounting.

Recruitment. A human being is recruited for increasing the utility of existing inputs and equipment. It is certain that the returns from this recruited employee will be more than the amount spent on him at various stages. The amount spend in recruiting and placement of an employee should be treated as deferred revenue expenditure.

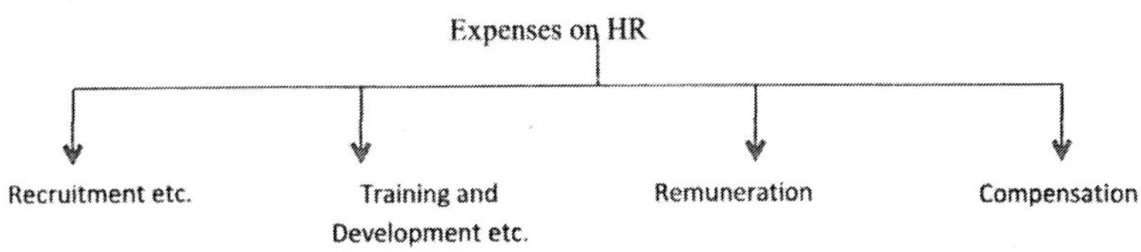

Training and Development. Human beings are trained and expenditures are also incurred in making various types of development in them, because all this increases the human value of an organisation. Just as value of fixed assets is increased by overhauling and making additions etc., in them, in the same value of human being becomes of greater use for the organisation when he is trained. Expenditure made on training and development of human resources should be treated as deferred revenue expenditure.

Remuneration. The remuneration paid to an employee is of a recurring nature hence it should be treated as revenue expenditure and be recorded in the Trading and Profit and Loss Account.

Compensation. When some accident takes place and the employees is injured, compensation is paid to him according to Workmen's Compensation Act. Payment of such compensation increases the morality of other employees. They don't hesitate in doing work sincerely and with faithfulness, thus output increases. If this amount of compensation is a huge amount, it should be spread over a number of years for writing it off. The remuneration of years over which it should be written off will differ from case to case.

Premature Exit. If on account of retrenchment or death or an employee becoming completely incapable of doing work, vacancy has been caused, the unwritten off amount of deferred revenue account related to such employee should be written off against the profit and loss account of the year of exit of such employee.

Calculation of Deferred Revenue Amount

(i) Average tenure of employment of an employee should be found out.

(ii) Average salary of an employee should be found out.

(iii) Above two should be multiplied.

(iv) The above process should be adopted in case of all the employees who belong to middle and lower level and then all multiplied amounts should be totalled. This total should be divided by the total of average tenure of employment of all the middle and lower level of employees and the amount thus arrived is written off to profit and loss account and the balance should recorded in the asset side.

(v) In the case of top management, valuation of human beings may be made on individual basis.

Human Resources as an Asset

At present there are four groups in the asset side of a registered company's balance sheet, namely, Fixed Assets, Investments, Current Assets, Loans and Advances, and lastly miscellaneous expenditure. According to the author (or Shukla) Valuation of Human Resource should not be included in any of the groups mentioned above, because it is the human being who operates all the activities of an organisation, his position is superb. He cannot be grouped anywhere, hence it is suggested that there should be a separate head of asset for HR. This head should be known as HRV (Human Resources Valuation) and its place should be first in the order of assets in the asset side of balance sheet.

Conclusion

Human resource occupies the key position in the organisation. All the process is of the organisation are operated by HR, hence valuation of this resource is very necessary and information about human resource valuation should be given to the investors and management etc. through financial statements. HRA should be treated as a part of Management Information System (MIS). Institute of Chartered Accountants of India must take a lead in this respect in prescribing various standards in this connection and in acquainting the entrepreneurs about the utility of HRA. Government should also give recognition to HR as an asset and Part I of Schedule VI of the Companies Act, 1956 should be amended so as to include human resource as an independent asset rather than including it in any of the existing groups of assets.

3.2 Economics

3.3 Planning and Management of Rural Electrification: A Case Study of Medak Region of Andhra Pradesh

Abstract

A Research Study was conducted on the Planning and Management of Rural Electrification in Medak Region of Andhra Pradesh, to study the rural electrification scene in Medak region, activities of Rural Electrification Corporation, State Electricity Board and Rural Electric Cooperatives operating in the region, assess problems faced and associated factors in the promotion of rural electrification, and to suggest technological alternative light of the problems being faced in the region and growing need of electricity for various potential activities in Medak region.

The operational methodology adopted for this study was to collect data from all available sources from Secondary Sources and also to investigate situation through Primary Survey of the actual beneficiaries of the Schemes and the Grassroot Panchayat Raj Institutions. Detail data pertaining to the operation of various implementing agencies which are involved in promoting rural electrification namely REC, APSEB, Rural Electricity Cooperatives etc were collected through intense interaction with various Officials and Non-Officials and the People's Representatives. The Primary Survey was conducted with a structured Questionnaire from among the Farmers/ Beneficiaries and from the Panchayat Raj Institutions, who were the bulk users of the rural electric power supply, with in depth study and to enhance the quality of data.

The prime-mover functions of rural electrification and selected-improvements can be made balancing for social justice and equitable distribution of electric power and rational tariff structure. In addition, other non-conventional power generation sources have to be augmented with the present sources for adequate power supply and meeting the growing demands. Eventually energy planning and audit should be an integral part of any sectoral planning or area planning and rural electrification to be reflected prominently, as base infrastructure for development.

The Study on Rural Electrification in Medak Region of Andhra Pradesh has thrown new insights in the implementation and operational aspects of rural electrification. The response of farmers/beneficiaries and Panchayat Institutions had surprisingly indicated that the local people are aware of the issues and dimensions of rural electrification in their locality and had an urge to look for more efficient and smooth functioning, bringing in greater benefits to the people of the region.

The Study clearly revealed the seriousness and commitment of local farmers/Villagers in the management of rural electrification programmes. As R.E programmes are handled by Panchayats henceforth under the new Constitutional Amendment (73rd), the participation of people from the conceptual stage to the implementation stage and further operation and maintenance, to ensure success of these projects.

Retrospect

The Rural Electricity Act 2003 mentions rural electrification in a Law, with the Section 6 of the Act mandates UniversalService Obligation by the Government to supply electricity to all areas including villages and hamlets. The Section 5 requires the formulation of National Policy on RE focusing specially on management of local distribution networks through local institutions, which frees stand-alone generation and distribution networks from licensing requirements, under the Section 4. According to electrified village, a village will be deemed to be electrified if electricity is used in the inhabited locality within the revenue boundary of the village for any purpose whatsoever.

The basic infrastructure such as distribution transformers and or distribution lines is made available in the inhabited locality within the revenue boundary of the village including at least one hamlet/ Dalit Basti as applicable. Any of the public places like schools, Panchayat office, Health centre, Dispensaries, Community Centres, etc avail power supply on demand and the rating of distribution transformer and LT lines to be provided in the village would be finalised as per the anticipated number of connections decided in consultation with the Panchayat/ Zilla Prishad/ District Administration, who will issue the necessary certificate of village electrification on completion of works and the number of households electrified should be minimum 10 percent for villages which are unelectrified, before a village is declared electrified.

The main sources of funding for current rural electrification programmes are the Rural Electrification Corporation (REC), Plan allocation to the States, Funds support from Government as loan and grant, Institutional financing bodies like commercial banks, and International financing agencies like OECF, World Bank etc.

The Government of India has been promoting the rural electrification under various Rural Electrification Schemes and some of the significant schemes are Pradhan Mantri Gramodaya Yojna (PMGY), Kutir Jyoti Programme (KJP), Minimum Needs Programme (MNP), Accelerated Rural Electrification Programme (AREP), Rural Electricity Supply Technology Mission (REST), Rajiv Gandhi Grameen VidyutikaranYojna, Deendayal Upadhyaya Gram Jyoti Yojana for rural electrification, and the Pradhan Mantri Sahaj Bijli Har Ghar Yojana, (Saubhagya).

Pradhan Mantri Gramodaya Yojna (PMGY)

The PMGY launched in 2000-2001 provided additional financial assistance for minimum services by the central government to all states on a 90 percent loan and 10 percent grant basis. These included rural health, education, drinking water and rural electrification. The PMGY, with an outlay of about ₹ 1600 crores during the 10 Plan Period, was being coordinated and monitored by the Rural Development Division of the Planning Commission. More importantly, under PMGY states had the flexibility to decide on the inter-reallocation of funds amongst the basic services, to enhance allocations to expedite the pace of rural electrification.

Kutir Jyoti Programme (KJP)

KJP was initiated in 1988-89 to provide single point light connection (60 W) to all Below Poverty Line (BPL) households in the country. KJP provides 100 percent grant for one time cost of internal wiring and service connection charges and builds in a proviso for 100 percent metering for release of grants. Nearly 5.1 million households have been covered under the scheme to date. The scheme was merged into the Accelerated Electrification of One Lakh Villages and One Crore Households in May 2004 and latter into the Rajiv Gandhi Grameen Vidyutikaran Yojana (RGGVY).

Minimum Needs Programme (MNP)

The MNP, exclusively targeted states with less than 65 percent rural electrification and provides 100 percent loans for last mile connectivity. The programme resources were drawn from the Central Plan Assistance. Rs. 775 crore was released during 2001-03 for rural electrification under the MNP. The scheme was discontinued in 2004-05 on account of difficulties in implementation.

Accelerated Rural Electrification Programme (AREP)

The AREP, was operational in 2002, provides an interest subsidy of 4 percent to states for RE programmes. The AREP covers electrification of un-electrified villages and household electrification and has an outlay of ₹ 560 crore under the 10th Plan. The interest subsidy was available to state governments and electricity utilities on loans availed from approved financial institutions like the REC (Rural Electrification Corporation), PFC (Power Finance Corporation) and from NABARD under the Rural Infrastructure Development Fund (RIDF).

Rural Electricity Supply Technology Mission (REST)

The REST was initiated on 11 September 2002, with an objective of electrification of all villages and households progressively through local renewable energy sources and decentralised technologies, along with the conventional grid connection. REST aimed to identify and adopt technological solutions, review the current legal and institutional framework and make changes when necessary, promote, fund, finance and facilitate alternative approaches in rural electrification, and to coordinate with various ministries, apex institutions and research organisations to facilitate meeting national objectives.

Rajiv Gandhi Grameen Vidyutikaran Yojna

The Accelerated Electrification of One Lakh Villages and One Crore Households, MNP and Kutir Jyoti were latter merged with the RGGVY, launched by the Ministry of Power to execute the vision for rural electrification with an objective of cent percentage of electrification of all villages and habitations in the country, electricity access to all households, and free of cost electricity connection to BPL (Below Poverty Line) house-holds.

Deendayal Upadhyaya Gram Jyoti Yojana for rural electrification (DDUGJY)

Government of India has launched the scheme Deendayal Upadhyaya Gram Jyoti Yojana for rural electrification, with erstwhile Rajiv Gandhi

Grameen Vidyutikaran Yojana (RGGVY) scheme, subsumed in the DDUGJY, for village electrification and providing electricity distribution infrastructure in the rural areas scheme. The Rural Electrification Corporation is the Nodal Agency for implementation of DDUGJY.Under DDUGJY-RE, Ministry of Power has sanctioned 921 projects to electrify 1,21,225 un-electrified villages, intensive electrification of 5,92,979 partially electrified villages and provide free electricity connections to 397.45 lakh BPL rural households. As on 30th June 2015, works in 1,10,146 un-electrified villages and intensive electrification of 3,20,185 partially electrified villages have been completed and 220.63 lakh free electricity connections have been released to BPL households.

Pradhan Mantri Sahaj Bijli Har Ghar Yojana (Saubhagya)

Despite the many rural electrification schemes that India has launched since 2005, there are about 3.21 crore households in India still without electricity. The Pradhan Mantri Sahaj Bijli Har Ghar Yojana, shortened into Saubhagya, was flagged off in September 2017, with the objective of electrifying all left-out Indian households. The scheme covers both urban and rural households. Under it, free electricity connections are provided to below poverty line (BPL) households, while other households have to pay ₹ 500 for the connection.

This is recoverable by the power distribution company in 10 instalments along with the electricity bills.The total cost of the Saubhagya project is pegged at ₹ 16,320 crore, of which, 60 percent is funded by the Centre, 30 percent by bank loans and the remaining 10 percent by State governments. Of the total outlay, a chunk of ₹ 14,025 crore is proposed for rural areas.The scheme envisages electricity connection for each household by drawing a service cable from the nearest electricity pole to the home, installing an energy meter, and wiring for a single light point with an LED bulb and a mobile charging point. In case a pole is not available, a new one is erected with a conductor and associated accessories. For remote and inaccessible areas, electricity is provided through solar panels and five LED lights, one DC fan and one DC power plug can be used. Repair and maintenance for five years is also part of the scheme.

It is a great achievement for India that the last unconnected Indian village of Leisang in Manipur had been connected to the grid, with last-mile infrastructure and affordability. Saubhagya aims at improving education, fuel economic activity and create more job opportunities across villages. Power generating and distributing companies, currently saddled with excess capacity, are expected to benefit through an increase in the demand for power. Power distribution companies who are in financial distress may be able to recover some of their costs through the new household connections and added demand.

Research Methodology

The operational methodology adopted for this study was to collect data from all available sources from Secondary Sources and also to investigate situation through Primary Survey of the actual beneficiaries of the Schemes and the Grassroot Panchayat Raj Institutions. Detail data pertaining to the operation of various implementing agencies which are involved in promoting rural electrification namely REC, APSEB, Rural Electricity Cooperatives etc were collected through intense interaction with various Officials and NonOfficials and the People's Representatives. The Primary Survey was conducted with a structured Questionnaire from among the Farmers/ Beneficiaries and from the Panchayat Raj Institutions, who were the bulk users of the rural electric power supply, with in-depth study and to enhance the quality of data. Stratified Random Sampling method is followed for collecting Primary Data on rural electrification in Medak region. The sample collected has two dimensions viz. from Agricultural Farmers/ Beneficiaries and that from Panchayati Raj Institutions. The basic reason for choosing only these two aspects was that majority of rural electrification activities primarily fall under these catagories, the most prominent being for energisation of agricultural pumpsets, street lighting, rural domestic and light industrial power supply, and meeting the power requirements of social infrastructural needs. The sample has been selected from among wide cross-section of users spread over in the entire region of Medak.

Findings and Observations

The Summary of the Findings and Observations of both Agricultural Farmers/Beneficiaries and Panchayat Institutions are presented below:

Agricultural Farmers/Beneficiaries Ownership Status

Among the status of agricultural farmers/ beneficiaries, the owners of enerqgi sed pumpsets/ diesel pumpsets represent about 70 percent followed by lease diesel pumpsets users 30 percent. This trend indicate that either farmers own the energised facilities or obtain the facilities through lease rentals.

Average Land Holding

The average land holding of beneficiaries/ farmers were between 5 to 50 acres. This constitute small and large farmers among users.

Type of Irrigation Wells

Among the type of wells used for energised pumpsets, old open wells constituted 30 percent and open wells comprise of 20 percent, while the renovated wells share the major chunk with 50 percent. This indicates that most of the wells after energisation had been renovated.

Water Level Status

The water level indicates that there was no sufficient water available for irrigation purpose in the wells. About 64 percent of the farmer users expressed concern over low level of water in their wells while balance 36 percent expressed satisfaction over present levels of water. While the present position indicate 80 percent inadequate water, the expected trend in future also seems to be almost similar with 86 percent. This trend indicate that general water level in the area is in declining trend.

Ground Water Potential and Locating Source

It had been opined that the ground water potential of the Medak region seem to be moderate (64 percent) and poor (16 percent). The water sources were mostly located by private agencies (54 percent). The Water Diviners and Self locating water sources stand at 22 percent and 24 percent respectively.This situation signify that private agencies were intensely engaged in locating the sources of water, which was of moderate nature.

Agency Drilling the Wells

Among the Agencies drilling the tube wells for irrigation purposes, Private Agencies stood at 36 percent, followed by Irrigation Department at 34 percent and Panchayati Raj Engineering (PRE) Department at 30 percent.This indicates that the drilling work for tube wells were almost equally shared by Private Agencies, Irrigation Departments and PRE Department.

Trial Boring Status

While one trial boring were performed in 86 percent cases, the rest of the 14 percent cases had the track record of trial drilling for two times, for drilling tube wells for irrigation purpose. No State subsidy were given for failed borings for the sample cases surveyed.This situation reflect the risk and uncertainity involved in trial borings, which adds to the cost. This has also called for scientific source identification and drilling activity to minimise failure cases.

Pump Status

The Survey data revealed that 82 percent of the respondents had electric pumps for agricultural purpose and all respondents had purchased pumps both electric and diesel from private sources.This situation indicates that Private Suppliers have a major role in the rural electrification efforts in agricultural promotion.

Time-lag in Power Connection

The time lag between boring a well and getting power connections had variations. In 38 percent cases, the time lag was 4 months and in 30 percent cases, it was 2 months. Only in 10 percent cases, the power connection was given in about a month.The situation indicates that there is a time lag between availability of water source and obtaining a power connection for energisation. The time lag was between 2 to 4 months.

Period of Energisation

It was observed that 68 percent of the respondents had one pump while 32 percent had more than one pump. Further it was observed that about 76 percent pumps were energised.The data revealed that the energisation movement had taken momentum during last decade than the present decade. This may be due to fall in water levels and incentives like subsidied power tariff, easy and soft credit, priority in power connections etc.

Irrigation Practices before Energisation

It was found that before farmers adopted well energisation, they were mostly dependent on bucket lift irrigation (46 percent) and rainfed agriculture (30 percent). This indicate that people had strong conviction about probable benefits from energization, which made them to shift from traditional irrigation methods to modern irrigation methods by energization of wells.

Preference of Pumpsets with reasons

The 70 percent of the user farmer respondent's favoured electric pumpsets and the main reasons cited for favouring electric pumpsets were power availability at subsidised rates, smooth flow of water through electric pumps, less operational problems and credit availability. In spite of diesel pumpsets had been cited to have the advantage of portability, hire rental possibilities, use by maximum people and use in different land areas, 70 percent of the respondents prefer electric pumps over diesel ones. This indicate strong preference and importance attached to rural electrification in light of weightage given to energisation of pumps.

Sources of Funds

While funding energisation programmes were taken lead by Banks with 46 percent cases, about 23 percent cases had invested Own Funds and 26 percent cases had taken funds from Private Sources for incorporating the energisation of pumpsets. Bank loan was preferred for soft interest and easy credit while it had inherent problems of security obligations.

Time-lag in Bank Loans

For the loan amount, the Bank had a timelag of three (32 percent) to four (24 percent) months for release.The whole scenario looks discouraging and incentives of Bank Loan do not give an edge over Private Borrowing.

Type of Power Connection

It was observed that 86 percent of the power connections among the respondents were agricultural energisation in nature, while the domestic coverage was 14 percent under rural electrification activities.

Time taken for power connection

The power connection took about 4 months (44.80 percent) in maximum cases while about 17.60 percent cases experienced a timelag of 2 months and in 15.2 percent cases, the lag was 3 months.

Visits to Departments for Power Connection

In ensuring source finding, construction of well, loan arrangements from the Bank, and the energisation of wells, the respondents had visited on an average about 4 times to the Bank and SEB Office, while that to Ground Water Department was practically nil. A number of visits were made to the Bank and the SEB Offices in connection with the loan arrangements and getting power connections.The field conditions reveal that agriculture energisation is the major activity under rural electrification. Further there was prolong timelag between application and actual connections of power. In connection with energisation of agricultural pumpsets, number of visits were required to Bank and SEB Office, indicating bureaucratic procedures, red-tapism, and delays in those organisations, which needs improvements for better rural electrification results.

Official and Non-Official Help

Among the Agencies helping the farmers/beneficiaries to energise their pumpsets, the Mandal Development Officer/Block Development Officer/ Village Development Officer play a significant role (32 percent). The local leaders (28 percent) also equally render their helping hand. But, the fact remains that about 40 percent of the farmers/beneficiaries surveyed were not given any help from either grassroot level Government Officials nor from the local leaders.This fact signifies that farmers nonage their own energisation programme largely by themselves while some help is given by local level Government Officers and local leaders.

Causes for delay in Power Connection

The causes for the delay of power connection was cited to be due to red tapism, corruption, security stand-by by the Bankers, apathy of officials, procedural problems, lack of dynamic leadership, lack of organised efforts and low level of awareness about Institutional arrangements, among the farmers/beneficiaries.

Water Potential Certificate

It was opined that in about 94 percent cases, no Water Potential Certificates were submitted while obtaining Bank loans, indicating no objective assessment of technical aspects by the Banks for loan approvals and dispersal.This is obvious because the Banks only insist on security obligations, without bothering about the technical feasibilities. In 6 percent cases who obtained Water Potential Certificates for obtaining Bank loans, these were obtained mainly from Private Sources and Ground Water Departments.The time lag to get Water Potential Certificates vary from one month to two months.

Status of Minimum Distance Maintenance

Scientifically for getting better water levels in the wells, a minimum distance is recommended based on the soil conditions, water levels, climatic conditions, vegetation, water bodies in the region, slope, drainage pattern etc.The respondents (66 percent) maintained minimum distance criteria, which is logical and a sustainable and viable proposition.

Status of Bank Loans

About 74 percent cases among the respondents had no arrears in Bank loans.This may basically because most of the farmers/ beneficiaries had not taken Bank loans for the reasons cited earlier. And even if the loan was taken, the impact of energisation might have had greater achievements of returns, which would have helped the borrower to repay the Bank loans in time.

Measures to Improve Bank Loan System

The respondents suggested measures like simplification of Bank procedures, Govt standing as Bank Security, availability of adequate credit, more period for repayment and Panchayat role as the decider, for loan disbursements to the farmers/ beneficiaries.These suggestions have great significance and meaningful propositions for developing the overall performance of rural electrification in general and energisation of pumpsets in particular.

Daily Power Supply Position

The situation of power supply was not smooth in the field condition with frequent interruptions. In about 28 percent cases only, there was 6 hours power supply.

Voltage Fluctuations and Power Cuts

Further there was widescale power fluactions (74 percent), which disrupts the working of the energisation of systems which can cause frequent breakdowns.There was practically no prior intimation about the power cuts (86 percent), which jeopardasises therural electrification programmes.The dimensions of power supply situation in Medak Region seems to be not very promising. However such trends and situations are not uncommon in other parts of the country as well.The major impediments in energising pumpsets include schemes which were not counted as rural electrification schemes, small and fragmented land, lack of finance, long distance from power lines etc. Among other reasons, power availability, lack of repair and maintenance, spare parts availability, diesel availability, irregular power supply and delay in obtaining finance from Bank etc were prominent.

Impediments in Energising Pumpsets

The opinions of respondents give new insights into the energisation programmes in agriculture, Lack of finance, small and fragmented land, distance from power lines signify sensitive parameters for overall impact and growth of rural electrification. Among other reasons, the problems of spare parts, repair and maintenance, irregular power supply and delay in obtaining finance from banks were the major reasons for unsteady growth of rural electrification programme in the study area. Under the Panchayati Raj Institutions Nature of Schemes, the agricultural energisation of pumpsets stand for maximum coverage in the Medak region with 73 percent cases falling in this category. Other Schemes like social infrastructural requirements, street lighting, domestic power supply etc under rural electrification were at the low ebb in the study area.This figure indicates significant contribution of rural electrification towards agricultural development. Other activities had a great bearing with the rural social economic, cultural and emotional life of people.

Problems in Rural Electrification

The overall situation of rural electrification in the study area was not very promising with 45 percent responded as frequent breakdowns, 43 percent responded as delay in maintenance and 9 percent responded as delay in installation and commissioning.The study result indicate need for greater improvement in the rural electrification situation with proper monitoring and evaluation, preventive maintenance and with proper project management.

Causes of Problems in Rural Electrification

The reasons attributed for frequent breakdowns, delay in maintenance and installation and commissioning, were stated to be cumbersome procedural problems, redtapism, corruption, improper supply of required installation materials from headquarters, credit problems, budgetary problems, unreliable and impractical planning, political influence, lack of coordination among various rural electrification programme agencies and apathy of Government Officials.The feedback given by the Panchayati Raj Institutions covered the total dimensions and issues of the rural electrification problems domain, which urgently acquire the attention of the Government, Private Cooperative General Public, Local Leaders and Implementing Agencies to streamline systems and instill proper management of rural electrification programmes. In about 25 percent cases, the timelag for getting power connection was three months. About 18 percent cases, the delay was about two and four months.The field data reveals that there was a timelag between application to intsallation, which has been a regular practice everywhere. This needs implementing agencies to adopt proper project management techniques and through utilisation of various resources, the Panchayati Raj Institutions can impress the State Electricity Boards, to release connections 'at the earliest time'.

Institutional Help in Rural Electrification Programmes

It was found that the Institutional help in rural electrification programmes was rendered mainly by the State Electricity Boards (SEBs) (74 percent). Rural Electrification Corporation (REC) (14 percent) also helped in the rural electrification programmes in the region. Other Agencies who were promoting the rural electrification programmes were the Electricity Cooperatives, (12 percent), Non-Governmental Organisations (4 percent) and the Panchayat Bodies (6 percent). In the financial/funding aspects, it was reported to be NABARD (82 percent), District Lead Bank, State Bank of India in case of Medak District (14 percent) and the Commercial Banks (4 percent), who support actively the rural electrification programmes.The above situation re-emphasise the critical role played by SEB, REC, NABARD and Lead Industries opted for promotion in the region. Banks in the promotion of rural electrification programmes in the region. Baiscally REC is a Re-financing Agency and SEB is Implementing Agency. Hence the SEB was popularly known in the region than the REC. NABARD as an apex organisation for promoting agriculture and rural development, has been playing a keyrole in the agricultural energisation of pumpsets.

Voltage Fluctuations and Advance Notice in Power Cuts

There was wide scale power fluctuations (74 percent), which disrupts the working of the energisation of systems which can cause frequent breakdowns. There was practically no prior intimation about the power cuts (86 percent), which jeopardies the rural electrification programmes. The dimensions of power supply situation in Medak Region seems to be not very promising. However such trends and situations are not uncommon in other parts of the country as well.

Reasons for Industrial Backwardness

The main reasons attributed for industrial backwardness was cited by the Panchayats as improper power supply, lack of good road networks, lack of adequate finance, lack of entrepreneurship, lack of business opportunities, lack of forward and backward linkages, lack of proper local leadership etc.The development of industrial base in the rural areas can change the scenario of power utilities, economic development, employment opportunities and overall development of the area. And thus industrial development in the rural areas has a great bearing on the rural electrification aspect. The reasons identified by the Panchayats on industrial backwardness have far reaching implications and proper national and regional policy framework need to be evolved to address to these issues and dimensions.

Industries Opted for Promotion in the Region

The Panchayats visioned potential for ancillary industries, service and commercial activities, repair and maintenance services, agro-based industries and building materials industries in the Medak region.

Reasons for Industrial Backwardness

The main reasons attributed for industrial backwardness was cited by the Panchayats as improper power supply, lack of good road networks, lack of adequate finance, lack of entrepreneurship, lack of business opportunities, lack of forward and backward linkages, lack of proper local leadership etc.The development of industrial base in the rural areas can change the scenario of power utiliti es, economic development, employment opportunities and overall development of the area. And thus industrial development in the rural areas has a great bearing on the rural electrification aspect. The reasons identified by the Panchayats on industrial backwardness have far reaching implications and proper national and regional policy framework need to be evolved to address to these issues and dimensions.

Panchayat Suggestions to Improve Rural Electrification Programmes

The Panchayats suggested preventive maintenance, elimination of procedural bottlenecks in proposal clearance and financing, coordination among implementing agencies, responsive role of local leaders, proper monitoring of progress, grievance handling, adequate supply of installation materials, advance intimation of power cuts, participation of government officials in the programmes and extension education, as vital measures for promotion and expansion of rural electrification programmes. The above measures have great significance and pragmatic rationality for promotion of rural electrification in the country and to enhance the quality of life of rural people and their environment.

Policy Recommendations and Strategies

The following Policy Recommendations and Strategies are suggested based on the Research Study findings and observations, which are summarised below:

Integrated Approach

Rural Electrification alone may not be able to meet all the rural energy requirements for development, it should conjunctively act with other sources of energy.

Local Need-based R.E Strategies

Variations in agro-climatic and socioeconomic situations require local need based rural electrification strategies suitable for a particular region, rather than introducing an uniform system althroughout.

Contract System

Contract system in implementation of rural electrification programmes will help in the speedier progress of R. E. works People's Participation. System of introducing private and cooperative tube wells will have greater involvement of people in rural electrification programmes.

Subsidy for trial borings

There should be an element of subsidy for the failed trial borings for the Small and Marginal Farmers. Energy conservation measures should be propagated extensively in rural areas and alternative energy sources should be tapped, with less dependency on conventional energy sources.

Insurance for IP Sets

An insurance scheme may be introduced for IP sets for operational and functional availability, at the time of breakdowns.

Institutional Building

Institutional building at local level through people's participation and Panchayat involvement through Multi-Level Committees, can facilitate convergent efforts to promote rural electrification, energy conservation methods, functional and operational advantages and implementation of RE programmes effectively with people's involvement.

Scientific Methods

Qualitative efforts are required for ground water investigation and exploitation, on scientific methods, like remote sensing, GIS, ground water surveys etc, for helping the farmers in locating the correct sources for drilling bore wells. Prior information on service connection may be given to users, for initial preparations and planning their activities, without elements of uncertainities.

Extension Education and Training

Extension education and training may be imparted to the village level mechanic, presently available for hand pump maintenance, on maintaining street lights and also supervise proper functioning of electrical meters.

Concessional Tariff for Drinking Water

There should be concessional tariff for drinking water pumping in rural areas and this subsidy may be recovered from energisation of pumpsets from large farmers and medium and heavy industries.

Participatory Management

At each level of electricity planning, expansion and growth and demand, local leaders, people, consumers, etc one side and suppliers i. e. SEB or Electric Cooperatives at the other, need to be involved and objectives made clear to all, for the sustenance of the project.

Average time for Power Connection

Department of Non-Conventional Energy Sources, GOI have been promoting the same, vigorous propaganda and social advertising is required to tune the peoples mind to direct towards these sources.

Rational Planning

The present practice of rural electricity projects on the basis of people's representation need to be oriented towards rational planning, as to assessing resource endowments, agricultural and industrial loads as well as rural electrification requirements, at present and for coming five years.

Relevant Database

R E Projects based on detailed information on ground water potential, resource endowment, social infrastructure etc are more successful than mere extension of R E to an area. There is an urgent need for a Database on the ground water potential, rainfall pattern, resource endowment, social and industrial infrastructure etc at District level through Discoms.

Priority to high potential areas

As RE is a capital intensive decision, areas of high potentiality should get priority over areas of low potentiality and extraneous considerations should not be allowed in the decision process.

Structured Format for Data Collection

Though each agency and department whether implementor, financer or maintainer/promoter, have been gathering information in their own way without any standardised practice. It is suggested that a "well structure format, may be used by concerned with R E Projects, so that decisions based on these data will be more reliable.

Consideration of Multiprong Factors

For agricultural load forecasting, rather than taking a fixed percentage of energisation in an year, factors like depth of water table, seasonal fluctuations of waterlevel, landholding, cropping pattern and water requirements etc also influence significantly for deciding for installation of pump set for the well.

Availability of Local Resources

While assessing the R E requirements for industries, the availability of local resources namely agricultural products, minerals, forests, horticulture and livestock etc. which has a direct bearing on the location of industry, are often not considered, thus forecasting industrial loads will not reflect real field situation.

Proper stock of houses for domestic load

Even the domestic load is assessed with number of houses in each village reported by District Census Hand Book. New houses likely to be constructed and dwelling units to be demolished due to deterioration and houses of poor people, who do not have the paying capability, are also to be considered for assessing the R E requirements for domestic sector in an area.

Provision for material price escalation

The cost of materials to be procured for R E Projects is worked out based on prevailing market rates, while because of market fluctuations, the prices too escalate. It is suggested that suitable provisions may be made in the Project Outlay for future price hikes.

R E as an integral part of Total Development Plan

Rural electrification should form an integral part of the total development and hence it is necessary to formulate the rural electrification programme within the framework of an integrated area development plan for a taluk or a district.

Project Management Techniques

In most of the R E projects, there are delays and time and cost overruns. This is basically because of non-availability and delays in the supply of materials and the centralised system of SEBs in the procurement and supply of materials. PERT and CPM analysis may help in optimising the construction and monitoring.

Improving the performance of Agricultural Projects

The performance of R E projects in agricultural projects are very poor because of reasons Iike non-consideration of ground water potential, soil fertility and land holding, cumbersome procedures in gett ing loans for this purpose, lack of promotional efforts by SEBs and absence of special staff for operation and maintenance in R E Projects. Simplificatlon of loan procedures, consideration of water potential, soil fertility and land holding, promotional efforts and provision of technical personnel for operation and maintenance of R E projects can substantially improve the performance of agricultural projects.

Improving the industrial sector

In industrial sector, the achievement of R E efforts fall short of targets because of sickness of industries and stock pile-up, delay in getting capital loans from financial institutions, lack of proper conservation methods, and impact of structural adjustment and new economic reforms; Revamping sick industries and bringing overall improvements in the industrial scene in the region, needs energy conservation methods, adjusting to new economic policies, and proper financial support from lending institutions.

Streamlining SEB Procedures

The procedures followed by SEBs in sanctioning of work and staff in respect of R E Projects appear to be quite laborious and some of the formalities can be easily dropped. The administrative, financial and technical approval and sanctions of the SEBs take substantial time which needs to be streamlined.

Location Specific Projects and Priority on Merits

The release of different instalments from REC needs certain pre-conditions to be fulfilled, by submission of ground water certificate and other pre-conditions such as construction of transmission line and distribution transformers, financial expenditure and release of service connections. It is suggested that REC should consider the R E Projects on location specific merits and case wise and should relax norms, wherever it finds viable.

Promotional Efforts

The success of R E projects will depend on promotional efforts, which are missing from the various projects undertaken. Promotional measures can give the prospective users all information on importance of power, it's utilisation, maintenance of equipment; trouble shooting; productive use of power; and help the implementing agencies and functionaries to exert right support in time.

Inter-Departmental Committee

Power is the nerve centre of all development and hence it requires coordinated efforts of all departments like agriculture, industry, social infrastructure-health, education drinking water, etc, irrigation, power etc to work in this direction for proper planning, implementation, budgeting and monitoring of R E projects. A Committee in this regards should comprise of members from all user departments at various levels, including members from financial institutions and promoting organisations in Government and in Non-Government to take policy decisions, take stock of resource position and priorities of various departments and provide guidelines towards formulation of R E projects.

Alternative Sources of Electrical Energy

Alternative sources of electrical energy are being promoted all the world over, as the energy costs have gone up steeply. Alternative energy models like solar, wind, bio-gas, etc has great relevance to rural development. Though Department of Non-Conventional Energy Sources, GOI have been promoting the same, vigorous propaganda and social advertising is required to tune the peoples mind to direct towards these sources.

Rational Planning

The present practice of rural electricity projects on the basis of people's representation need to be oriented towards rational planning, as to assessing resource endowments, agricultural and industrial loads as well as rural electrification requirements, at present and for coming five years.

Power support to Social Infrastructure

Rise in domestic power tariffs and cost of domestic appliances have led to non proportionate rise in agriculture, priority need to be given for social sector.

Street Lighting

In case of street lighting, the achievements of R E projects are comparatively better. Panchayats should promote street lighting and maintain and operate the same, with proper payments of power tariffs. The Street lighting fixtures are decided presently on population criteria, i.e. settlement, habitations, street wise etc., rather they should be planned and provided based on Local Body/ Gram Panchayat allocation.

Standardisation in wage payments for R E Works

The wages for different items of piece work in terms of quality and quantity in R E projects needs to be standardised, within the norms of productivity.

Post R E impact on agriculture

The broad indicators of electrification impact in agricultural sector include factors like net shown area, cropping pattern, irrigated area, agricultural yield, agricultural inputs, agricultural implements, returns on agricultural investment and sale of agricultural produces. Success in R E projects reflect in the form of increase in cultivated area, predominance of crops of high economic returns, increase in the extent of irrigated land. higher yield and production, increased demand of improved seeds and fertilisers, improvements of agricultural implements higher return on agricultural investment and increased marketed surplus. Rural electrification impact on agricultural should be assessed on these parameters.

Impact of RF on Industrial Sector

The broad indicators of industry sector on the impact of RE projects on the post electrification phase are growth, capital investment in plant and machinery, employment, operational costs, expansion programmes, economic and social change, changes in income, changes in food consumption, possession of livestock, materials and housing etc. Electrification really brings in a transformation of the area and the people towards better amenities of life and thus improves the quality of life of rural people. Power is the prime-mover but finance, technology and entrepreneurship along with power availability can generate an economic base for a growing economy and strengthen the rural economy.

Major structural and policy changes are taking place in the Indian economy. These changes that began in 1991 are still continuing and can have a significant impact on the energy sector. Government has thrown open the doors for private participation in development of power sector. The pervasive and critically important role of power in national economies and the complexity of power-energy-economy interactions involved indicate that energy sector investment planning, pricing and management should be carried out on an integrated basis, e.g within an integrated national energy planning framework, which may help analyse the whole range of energy policy options over a long period of time. Access to electricity affords the rural population an obviously better quality of life. Costs on rural electrification are sensitive to distance, population density, consumption level and the shape of the load curves. Planning for rural electrification has to be judicious to serve remote, low-population density regions, in rural areas, at greater distances and at lower consumption level.The standard of life and improvement of environments in rural areas, conducive to integrated rural development, shall be possible only when the amenities of modern life which are very much linked with the availability of continuous and reliable power supply is ensured.

As rural electrification, is intended to spread the benefits of modern civilisation and to help the development of the country-side culturally, socially, economically, it has to be an integral part of any development planning and policy framework.The Study Area of Medak Region of Andhra Pradesh, which has an agrarian economy and economic backwardness, has thrown light on the pros and cons of rural electrification and identified real issues and factors, affecting the promotion of R.E. The situation, it is hoped, to be similar with other parts of the country and thus it is expected that measures suggested based on the findings and observations of the present study would have far reaching policy implications on the national front, towards evolvinq a rational and appropriate R E strategy and action plan, for reaching electricity productively to all villages in the country. India, a country where about 70 percent of people live in the rural areas and depend on agriculture as change in the attitude of people, local level leaders and policy-makers to stand on a common platform to think in terms of spatial development, with a comparative advantage to the local situation and area. Rural electrification with twin objectives of removing poverty and reducing rural disparity is the base for rural development. Agriculture production has greatly increased; healthcare at grassroot level has become timely and efficient such immunization programmes, cottage, rural and agro-processing industries got a boost, literacy nd information flows booms with satellite communications, basic repair and maintenance as a support function to various agriculture and allied activities etc are just a few cases where the results are just coming in and development visible.

With scientific approaches and with technological options available, rural electrification can be very well managed economically and efficiently, with optimum conservations and maximum productive use.

The prime-mover functions of rural electrification and selected-improvements can be made balancing for social justice and equitable distribution of electric power and rational tariff structure. In addition, other non-conventional power generation sources have to be augmented with the present sources for adequate power supply and meeting the growing demands. Eventually energy planning and audit should be an integral part of any sectoral planning or area planning and rural electrification to be reflected prominently, as base infrastructure for development.

The Study on Rural Electrification in Medak Region of Andhra Pradesh has thrown new insights in the implementation and operational aspects of rural electrification. The response of farmers/beneficiaries and Panchayat Institutions had surprisingly indicated that the local people are aware of the issues and dimensions of rural electrification in their locality and had an urge to look for more efficient and smooth functioning, bringing in greater benefits to the people of the region. The Study clearly revealed the serious-ness and commitment of local farmers Villagers in the management of rural electrification programmes. As R E programmes are handled by Panchayats henceforth under the new Constitutional Amendment (73rd), the participation of people from the conceptual stage to the implementation stage and further operation and maintenance, to ensure success of these projects.

Conclusion

India, with about 70 percent of people live in the rural areas and depend on agriculture as their main avocations, rural electrification gives the edifice of economic strength to the unproductive and low-return agriculture practices and brings in a sea-change in the attitude of people, local level leaders and policy-makers to stand on a common platform to think in terms of spatial development, with a comparative advantage to the local situation and area.

Rural electrification is the prime mover for the development of thc rural economy, agricultural productivity, communication and social development in India. The National Solar Mission is playing an important role in the work towards renewable energy, and interventions in rural electrification and new ultra-mega power projects are moving India towards achieving universal energy access.

The Government of India (GoI) gives priority in the adoption of RE into the country's energy mix and promotes policy supporting RE diffusion in the country, by targeting about 20,000 MW of solar energy by 2022. The Wind Energy and Small Hydro Energy Projects could revolutionise the rural electrification scenario in India. The Global Wind Energy Council (GWEC) estimates conservatively that the wind energy capacity in India could be 24 GW by 2020 and 30.5 GW by 2030. The small hydro (up to 25 MW) has capacity of over 15,000 M Win India And Private Sector has established 2,700 MW capacity.

The study of Medak district rural electrification gives insights in understanding how RE can be effectively used, promoted and upscaled for wider applications for the economic and social sector development of the rural areas in the country and also developing compatibility with SDG 2030 and integrating renewable modes of energy sources, for Indian economy to evolve as a developed country.

3.4 Statistics

Queueing models create a lot of interest due to their ready applicability in wide varieties of situations prevailing at places like, transportation and communication network, biological and population growth, inventory control, machine repairing, reliability analysis and computer performance evaluation studies etc. A queue is a waiting line of units demanding service at a service facility. A great deal of research has been carried out in queueing theory for the last eight decades. Starting from the pioneering work by A.K. Erlnag (1909), several queueing models have been developed with various assumptions. One of the potential string in developing these models is replacing some of the assumptions where a more realistic nature can be employed.

The major constituent processes of the queueing model are arrival and service processes. It is customery in many of the queueing models to consider that the arrival and service processes are independent and homogeneous. But this assumption is meaningful only, when we develop and analyse the models in a single environment. However, in some processes like, production process, machine repairing, reliability analysis, biological process etc., where the environment for the input source is not uniform. The arrival and service processes are considered to be interdependent and non-homogenous in order to have some operational conveniance or to induce more realistic nature. In this thesis an effort is made to bridge the gap in this area of research by developing and analysing some queueing models for these sort of situations, where arrival and service processes are interdependent and non-homogeneous.

1.2 Review on Heterogeneous Queueing Models

In this section we briefly review some of the heterogeneous queueing models in chronological order. A queueing model is said to be hetergeneous if any more of its constituent processes is non-homogeneous. In queueing model the homogeneity may prevail either in arrival process or in service process or in both arrival and service processes.

Morse, P.M. (1958) pioneered the heterogeneity in service to illustrate the situation of hyper-exponential distributions for service times with parallel channels. He considered a service facility consisting of two independent branches. An arrival enter one or the other branch, when the customer in service departs from the occupied branch. The steady-state results are obtained. Harold Gumbel (1960) investigated a multiple server system with non-homogeneous service. He analysed under the assumption of Poisson distributed arrivals and exponential service times with different individual, mean service rates for each server and obtained the explicit expressions for the state probabilities under steady-state conditions. Krisna Moorthi, B. (1962) studied a Poisson queue with two heterogeneous servers, and two alternative queue disciplines, one with a slight and the other with a greater modification of the classical one. Eisten, M. and Tainiter. M. (1963) considered a queueing problem in which there are two mean arrival and service rates. Not only does the system randomly changing from one mode of service to the other, but unit arrive at random and require varying amounts of service. They obtained the analytic expressions for generating functions, the mean queue length, and the waiting time.

Godini, G. (1965) developed a queueing system with K service stations with different service rates. The system had a modified service discipline i.e. if a service station with a smaller rate is available, then the customer might prefer to wait until a service station with a more rapid service is available, if the total time spent in the system was shorter. For such a system the probability to have *n* customers in the system at time *t* was calculated. Yadin, M. and Naor, P. (1967) studied a queueing system in which the total service capacity utilised at any given time was a variable under the control of a decision maker. Steady-state probabilities, expected queue lengths and frequencies of change in capacity were evaluated for a wide class of possible control schemes and the optimisation procedures were outlined. Harris, C. M. (1967) developed queues with stochastic service rate. The generating function of the queue size distribution and the Laplace transform of the waiting time distribution of the steady-state were obtained. To explore the steady state behaviour of an MM/ I queue, the service time parameter was considered as a random variable. Vijendr, Singh, P. (1970) analysed a Markovian queueing system with balking and two heterogeneous servers to determine the capacity of the slower server and obtained the optimal service rates that minimise the average. The heterogeneous system is compared with a homogeneous system and a condition showing the efficiency of the heterogeneous system was obtained, this condition involves only the traffic intensity and the service rates. Yechiace and Naor, P. (1971) analysed a two level modification of the M/M/I queueing model where the rate of arrival and service capacity are subject to Poisson alternations. The two dimensional problem was analysed by using a partial generating function technique. The steady-state probabilities and the expected queue sizes are evaluated.

1.4 Focus of the Thesis

With brief review of the above models given in sections 1.2 we can understand that the assumptions on the constituent processes like, arrival process and service process, number of channels play a vital role in developing the queueing models. Simple variation in the assumptions of these processes gives a broad spectra of queueing models which serves as close models in approximating some of the realistic situations. For example, in production process, when we are developing a queueing model for the inventory control of goods produced, the output process of the production is the arrival processes. In general this process is having two types of environments at the source namely, operative and non-operative. In these two different situations the production process is not uniform, particularly when there is a strike, the production will be halted for a period of time and after some period it may be resumed for production. In this process the input is non-homogeneous having different rates of input source. To analyse this situation, we relax the homogeneity of the process which forms the heterogeneous queueing models. Even in this heterogeneous queueing models it is also important to consider that the arrival and service processes are correlated in order to have some optimal (feasible) policies and to have efficient control. These queueing models with correlated arrival and service processes are known as interdependent queueing models. However, very little work is reported in literature, regarding heterogeneous interdependent queueing models, which are much useful for analysing the situations arising at places like, manufacturing, reliability analysis, machine repairing, manpower planning and biological studies etc.

In this thesis we develop and analyse some heterogeneous interdependent queueing models by assuming that the arrival and service processes are correlated and follows a bivariate Poisson process and having two states of the input source namely, operative and non-operative. First we develop a state dependent heterogeneous interdependent queueing model with finite capacity. Here we assume that the duration of stay of the arrival process in the operative state is exponential and a general distribution for duration of stay in non-operative state. Using the supplementary variable technique, the difference-differential equations are developed and the Laplace transformations of the system size in both states of the input source are derived. Assuming that the system is in steady state the equilibrium behaviour of the model is also investigated. By considering that the parameters are linear dependent on system size, the state dependent model is also studied.

Another variation in these models is also studied by considering that the source size is finite and equal to the system capacity. Here we develop the single server finite source heterogeneous interdependent queueing model by using the supplementary variable technique. The system behaviour of this model is analysed by deriving explicit expressions for the system size distribution for both states of the input source. This model is also extended to multiple server finite source heterogeneous in the dependent queueing model. The system behaviour of this model is also analysed by deriving the Laplace transformations of the system size distributions under transient and steady state conditions. The sensitivity of the models with respect to the dependence parameter [the covariance between the arrival and service processes] is also investigated. These models also include some of the earlier models as particular cases for specific or limiting values of the parameter.

1.5 Basic Methodology of the Models

Supplementary Variable Technique: Whenever the arrival process or the service process or both are other than exponentially distributed, then the queue length process is a non-Markovian process. To analyse such process one of the important technique is to reduce non-Markovian queueing process into a Markovian one in continuous time. This can be achieved by the addition of one or more random variables. This method was first named as the Augmentation technique by Kendall (1953). He used this method for solving a general process GI/G/S/ by introducing (S+1) variables. The first S variables representing the elapsed service time of each of the S servers and $(S+1)^{th}$ variable representing the elapsed time since the lost arrival. The method is also known as "supplementary variable technique". Cox (1955) obtained the steady state solutions of M/G/1 system by using this method. Cox defined Pn *(t, x) dx, n*>0 as the first order probability that at time *t*, the queue length is *n* and elapsed service time of the unit under service lies between *x* and *x*+*dx*. Probability that at time *t* the server is idle is defined by $P_0(t)$. The equations governing the queueing models given by Cox are.

$$\frac{\partial}{\partial x} P_n(t, x) + \frac{\partial}{\partial t} P_n(t,x) + [\lambda + \eta(x)] P_n(t,x) = \lambda P_{n-1}(t,x), \qquad n > 1$$

$$\frac{\partial}{\partial x} P_1(t, x) + \frac{\partial}{\partial t} P_1(t,x) + [\lambda + \eta(x)] P_1(t,x) = 0$$

$$\frac{\partial}{\partial x} P_0(t) + \lambda P_0(t) = \int_0^\infty P_1(t,x)\, \eta(x) dx,$$

where, λ is mean arrival rate and η *(x) dx* is the probability that the service will be completed in the time interval *x* and *x*+*dx*, it has not completed till time *x*.

The equations are solved using the boundary conditions,

$$P_n(0,t) = \int_0^\infty P_{n+1}(t,x)\, \eta(x) dx$$

$$P_1(0,t) = \lambda P_o(t) + \int_0^\infty P_2(t,x)\, dx$$

If the probability density function of the service time is denoted by *f(x)* and F(x) represents the distribution function of the service time U, then the distribution of η *(x)* lead to

$$f(x) = \eta(x) \exp\left[-\int_0^x \eta(u)du\right].$$

This method has extensively used in analysing non-Markovian queues by several researchers.

Bivariate Poisson Process: We briefly present the dependence structure used by Rao, K.S. (1986). Consider a single server queueing system, where arrivals (input) and services are interdependent and having a bivariate poisson distribution of the form

$$P[X_1 = x_1, \quad X_2 = x_2, t] =$$

$$e^{-(\lambda+\mu-\varepsilon)t} \sum_{j=0}^{\min(x_1,x_2)} \frac{(\varepsilon t)^j [(\lambda-\varepsilon)t]^{x_1-j} [\ (\mu-\varepsilon)t]^{x_2-j}}{j\,!\,(x_1-j)\,!\,(x_2-j)\,!}$$

$$x_1, x_2 = 0, 1, 2, \ldots \infty$$

$0 < \lambda$, μ and $\varepsilon < \min(\lambda, \mu)$ (Johnson and Kotz (1974)

P ($X_1 = x_1$, $X_2 = x_2$, *t*) is the joint probability of X_1 arrivals and X_2 Services during time *t*. The marginal distribution of arrivals and services are Poisson with parameters λt and μt. Thus the inter-arrival times and service times follows negative exponential distributions with λ as the mean arrival rate and μ as the mean service rate. *"εt"* is the co-variance between the number of arrivals and services at time *t*. This dependence structure turns out to be independent if ε equals to 0. Further for given values of λ, μ the covariance ε *equals to rλμ,* where *'r'* is the correlation coefficient between arrivals and services, since 'ε' is a function of *r* throughout this thesis 'ε' is treated as dependent parameter.

Postulates of the model: The postulates of the model with the dependence structure discussed above are,

(i) The occurrence of the events in non-overlapping time intervals are statistically independent, (ii) The probability that no arrivals and no service completions occur in an infinitesimal time interval of length δt is $=1-[(\lambda+\mu-\varepsilon)\delta t] + 0(\delta t)$, (iii) The probability that no arrival and one service completion occurs in small interval of time $\delta t = (\mu - \varepsilon)\,\delta t + 0\,(\delta t)$, (iv) The probability that one arrival and no service completion occurs in small interval of time $\delta t = \varepsilon\ (\delta t) + 0\ (\delta t)$.

This postulate is due to the dependence structure between the arrivals and service completions and (vi) the probability that the occurrence of an event other than the above events during a small interval of time δt is $0(\delta t)$.

There is an equivalence between these postulates and the process. The queueing mode is developed with this dependence structure are termed as Interdependent queueing models.

1.6 Organisation of the Thesis

This thesis is divided into five chapters. The chapterwise outline of the thesis is given below.

Chapter I of the thesis gives a brief review of the literature on heterogeneous queues and queues with interdependent arrival and service processes. A brief introduction of the problem, the basic structure of the model are also included. The brief description on the organisation of the thesis is presented.

Chapter II deals with single server finite capacity state dependent heterogeneous interdependent queueing system with FIFO queue discipline having two states of input source with the duration of one state as exponential and other as general distribution. The transient and steady state system behaviour is analysed. This model is also used to analyse the single server heterogeneou s interdependent queueing model, when the parameters are linearly dependent on system size. As a particular case the duration of time the input remains in the non-operative state is assumed as exponential and explicit expressions are obtained.

Chapter III deals with single server finite source heterogeneous queueing model having interdependent arrival and service processes with the two state of the input source in which the duration of one state is exponential and the other as a general distribution. The transient and steady state system behaviour is analysed as a particular case the duration of the time the input source remain in the non-operative state is assumed as exponential and explicit expressions for the system characteristics are derived.

Chapter IV is devoted to study the multiple server finite source heterogeneous queueing model with interdependent arrival and service processes having two states of input source. The transient and steady state behaviour of the system is analysed by deriving explicit expressions of the system characteristics. By assuming the duration of the steady state as exponential another model is also developed and analysed as a particular case.

Chapter V of the thesis is devoted to the summary and conclusions of the ideas and results discussed in the earlier chapters. Some interesting topics for further research in this area are also pointed.

Summary and Conclusions are presented in the following paragraphs.

This thesis contributes the descriptive modeling of queueing systems having interdependent arrival and service processes with heterogeneous arrivals. The queueing models gain lot of importance in operations research and statistics due to their wide applicability in transportation, business datavoice transmission, Neuropsychological systems, manufacturing, machine repairing and reliability analysis etc. These models are useful for efficient analysis and design of many realistic situations with close approximations. Along with several other assumptions it is also customary to assume that the arrival and service processes are independent. However, this assumption is meaningful only when these two processes are analysed independently. In many practical situations the arrival and service processes are correlated in order to have some optimal (feasible) considerations. The queueing models with correlated arrival and service processes are known as interdependent queueing models. The dependent queueing models have been classified by U.N. Bhat (1969) into five categories namely, (1) Models with correlated arrivals, (2) Models with dependent service times (3) Models with state dependent arrivals, (4) Models with state dependent service times, (5) Models with interdependent arrival and service processes. This fifth class of models gain lot of momentum during last decade, even though the roots goes back to 1952 of Lindley. In these interdependent models there are some situations like, manufacturing, inventory and maintenance problems and biological studies the arrival process is heterogeneous having two states of input source namely, operative and non-operative. Due to some unforeseen factors the input source remains in operative state for a random duration of time, which has a negative exponential distribution. The input remains in non-operative state for a random period which has a general distribution. The system capacity may be finite. For these sort of situations, the finite capacity interdependent queueing models with heterogeneous arrivals are needed to have efficient design of the systems.

In this thesis we developed and analysed some interdependent heterogeneous queueing models with finite capacity. Using the supplementary variable technique the difference-differential equations of the model are developed and solved through Laplace transformations. These models also include some of the earlier models as particular cases for specific or limiting values of the parameter. The system characteristics are developed explicitly for specific distribution of the duration of input source in non-operative state.

The first chapter of this thesis briefly introduces the motivation of present research work. The review on some of the heterogeneous queueing models and interdependent queueing is also given in order to highlight the present work in its right perspective. A queue is said to be heterogeneous if any of one or both of its constituent processes namely, arrival and service processes are having non-homogeneous nature. The heterogeneity prevails if the input source is having different environments depending upon the nature of the heterogeneity. The heterogeneous queueing models can be classified as (1) Queueing models with heterogeneous arrival process (2) Queueing models with heterogeneous service process and (3) Queueing models with heterogeneous arrival and service processes. A queue is said to be interdepedent if its arrival and service processes are correlated and follows some distribution. Lindley (1952) pioneered the interdependent queueing models. Then after several authors (Conelly, Conolly and Hadidi, Hadidi, Conolly and Choo, Mitchal Paulson, Bhasker SenGupta, K.S. Rao, K.S.S. Rao, R.P. Rao, L.V. Rao, Vijay Kumar, etc.) have developed some interdependent queueing models during the last few decades. But no serious attempt has been made to develop and analyse heterogeneous interdependent queueing models with two states of input source. This concept has motivated to investigate the models presented in this thesis. The basic methodology on supplementary variable technique and interdependent queueing model with bivariate Poisson process is briefly included as a ready reference. The chapterwise outline of the thesis is also presented.

In Chapter II the finite capacity single server FIFO service discipline queueing system with state dependent heterogeneous arrivals with the assumption that the arrival and service processes are correlated and follows a bivariate Poisson processes, is developed. A queue is said to be state dependent if its parameters are dependent on system size. Here we assume that the input source has two states namely, operative and non-operative. It remains in the operative state for a random time with exponential distribution. It remains in non-operative state for a random time which follows a general distribution. There are two service rates corresponding to the two states of the input source. Using the supplementary variable technique the non-Markovian process is converted into Markovian process. The difference-differential equations of the models are obtained and solved recursively. The Laplace transformations of the system size distributions, when the input is in operative and non-operative states, are obtained for the transient case. Assuming the steady state of the system the explicit expressions are obtained for system characteristics. Using these results the queueing system is analysed when the parameters are linearly dependent on the system size. This model is more realistic in situations like, machine repairing and reliability analysis. The system behaviour is also analysed by considering the time that the input source in non-operative state is also exponentially distributed. The probability of the system emptiness, the mean number of customers in the system etc., are also derived. This model includes the finite capacity heterogeneous arrivals with independent arrivals and service processes, when the dependence parameter is zero. This model also includes the infinite capacity model, when 'K' tends to infinite.

In Chapter III the finite source single server, FIFO discipline interdependent heterogeneous queueing model is developed. A queue is said to have finite source if its calling population is finite. Here we assumed that the arrival process is generated from an input source, which is having two states namely, operative and non-operative. If the input source is active in generating the arrivals then we say that it is in operative state. If the input source is not in a position to generate arrivals for a period of time like, strike period of an industrial concern of production processes, medically controlled period in the spread of recurrent communicable disease etc., then we say that it is in non-operative state. Here we further assumed that the arrival and service processes are correlated and follows a bivariate-Poisson process. The input remains in operative state for a random time with exponential distribution and in the non-operative state for a random time which follows a general distribution. In both the states of the input source, the service completions are correlated with the arrivals. The non-Markovian queue is converted into a Markovian process by using the supplementary variable technique given by Kendall (1953) and Cox (1955). The difference differential equations of the model are derived and solved through Laplace transform of the system size distribution, when the input is in operative and non-operative. Assuming the steady state of the system, the steady state behaviour of the model is also analysed for both these states of the input source. Assuming the duration of the stay in the non-operative state of the input source as exponential, the explicit expressions for the system size distribution, mean queue length, emptiness of the system etc. for both states of input source are derived and analysed . This model includes the finite source M/M/interdependent queueing model when n_{21} tends to zero. This model also includes M/M/ interdependent heterogeneous queueing model with two states of input source, if the source size 'K' tends to infinite. This model includes M/M/queueing model when the dependence parameter 'ε' equals to zero, n_{12} tends to infinite and n_{21} tends to zero. Like this many more models can be generated for specific or limiting values of the parameters. It is also observed that as the dependence rate 'ε' increases the mean number of customers in both states of the input source are decreasing when the other parameters remain fixed. The probability of the system emptiness is increasing when covariance between arrival and service processes is increasing. These features are much useful in developing optimal operating strategies of the system.

In Chapter IV the finite source heterogeneous queueing models discussed in Chapter II are extended to multisever models. With all the assumptions made in earlier models given in Chapter II we further assumed that there are 'C' servers each serve independent of the other with equal efficiency. The number of servers influence the service rates of the system. When there are less than 'C' customers i.e. $n < C$, then, only *'n'* servers are busy. Here also we assume that the source size is finite and equals to the system capacity K. Using the supplementary variable technique the difference-differential equations of the model are developed and solved through Laplace-transformations. The Laplace-transformations of the system the size distribution, when the input is in operative and non-operative states, under transient conditions are derived. Assuming thc stcady state of the system, the system behaviour is also analysed. Assuming the duration of the input source is in non-operative state as exponential the explicit expressions of the system characteristics under steady state are obtained. The average number of customers in the system is a decreasing function of the dependence parameter when other parameters remains fixed in both states of the input source. The emptiness of the system is increasing function of 'ε' when other parameters are fixed. The mean queue length is a decreasing function of the number of servers 'C' when other parameters remain constant. This model also includes the finite source heterogeneous interdependent queueing model given in Chapter II when C is equal to 1. We also get the infinite capacity infinite source heterogeneous interdependent queuemg model when 'K' tends to infinite. This includes M/M/C heterogeneous queueing model when ε is equal to O. Since this model includes many of the earlier models as particular cases, this model can be viewed as generalised Poisson queueing model with two states of input source.

In this last Chapter V, the results derived in earlier chapters are summarised with conclusions. Some interesting topics for further research are also mentioned.

Future Areas of Research

The models developed in this thesis are much useful in analysing many practical situations much close to the reality. For example, consider a situation in analysing the recurrent communicable diseases. In diseases like Measels, Diphtheria, Diarrhoea etc., there may be a periodic outbreak of an epedemic nature. The infection is alive for some time and after some time the infection is controlled temporally medically. When the diseases appears to be controlled the medical control is terminated and the disease spreads once again. Such diseases are known as recurrent communicable diseases.

For efficient control of the disease the modeling of the recurrent communicable disease is needed which can be done by applying queueing models. Here the arrival process of the queueing system may be represented by the infection of the disease. Here also the calling population is finite, known as the population of the community under study. These diseases are also having two types of states like, infectious state in which there is significant infection rate, the non-infection state when the rate of infection is approximately zero. For the analysis of this type of communicable disease the finite source heterogeneous interdependent queueing model with two states of arrivals discussed in Chapter II is useful.

Scope for Further Research

In this thesis the descriptive analysis of the heterogeneous interdependent queueing models is carried out. It is also possible to develop perspective modeling of the heterogeneous interdependent queueing systems by considering various cost aspects and optimisation of the system parameters The inferential aspects of the queueing models developed in this thesis can be investigated by developing the estimators for the system parameters and their testing. All these problems require further investigations.

With the above discussions we can see that the heterogeneous interdependent queueing models have some realistic nature with their ready applicability. In situations where interdependence between arrival and service processes prevails and having different environments for the input source these models are more close in approximating the natural phenomenon. As these models include several earlier models as particular cases these models form a basic spectra of the Poisson queueing models. It is highly possible that many more queueing models with heterogeneous interdependent nature can be developed with various plausible assumptions in order to analyse the natural phenomenon more close to the reality and to utilise the natural resources more optimally.

Reference

1. C.S.R.L. Hanumantha Raw (1999) has to the Andhra university, Visakapatnam in partaial fulfilment of the requirements for the a ward of Doctor of philosophy in statistis and awarded ph. in the year 2002. So here (A) Vizianagaram

Chapter - 4

History

4.1 Impact of Tribal Policy

The studies so far conducted are incomplete and failed to explain the tribal phenomenon in its totality-in the context of present day socio-economicrealities. To fill the gap, the present study intends to probe the impact of state policies on the select tribes of Andhra Pradesh.

Objectives of the Study

The main objectives of the study are:

(1) To study the impact of the state policies (ITDPs) on the socioeconomic lives of the Chenchu, Koya and Gond tribes under study.

(2) To assess the developmental programmes for the tribal during plan periods with special emphasis on the Fifth Five Year Plan.

(3) To study the extent of success and effectiveness of the Andhra Pradesh State Land Transfer Regulations, the impact of Wild Life Protection Act on the tribals and to explore causes for the continuing tribal unrest.

(4) To study the reasons as to why the tribals still remain backward despite so many policies and programmes initiated by the state and central governments.

(5) To examine the extent of suitability of programmes for the different tribal areas vis-a-vis the social, economic and cultural values.

Method of Study

The data necessary for the study is collected from both the Primary and Secondary sources.

Primary data is also collected orally from the tribals living in the areas covered by three ITDAS, i.e., Srisailam, Utnoor and Eturnagaram. The researcher conducted formal interviews and informal discussions with several officials and representatives of the tribals and tribal youth. The researcher also attended the Governing Body Meeting of the ITDA, Eturnagaram, which was convened by the District Collector and Chairman, ITDA, Eturnagaram, and addressed by the ministers for Social Welfare, Tribal Welfare, Government of Andhra Pradesh and members of Parliament and Legislative Assembly.

The secondary data obtained directly from the records of ITDAS, Tribal Welfare Department, government of Andhra Pradesh and Tribal Cultural Research and Training Institute, Hyderabad.

The researcher also undertook extensive field-visits for the study by visiting many tribal villages of the three ITDAS. A formal interview schedule is prepared to collect the necessary information from ITDA project officers. Assistant Project Officers, Managers of GCC, DTWOs and the tribals of the area to collect the first hand information.

The literature also collected from documentary sources like Records, Reports, Action-Plans, Budgets, Office Files, and other documents of the tribal development institutions selected for the study. Besides these, the Census Reports, the publications of the Government of India and Government of Andhra Pradesh were also consulted for the study. Further, published literature in different journals and books on the subject of study were also used.

Need of the Study

The tribals have underwent the effects of *laissez faire* policy followed by the colonial rulers and the Nizam Government. After Independence, the tribals were approached by the policy of isolation, recommended by Verrier Elwin, the Panchasheel of Jawaharlal Nehru and ultimately by the integrational policy. A series of schemes came into operation. The studies relating to these developments so far were concentrated on their operational performance. They did not throw much light on examining whether the programmes were suitable for the different areas with reference to the prevailing socio-economic ground realities.

It is, therefore, felt necessary to study the impact on tribals in the light of the implementation of the state policies. It is in this context an attempt has been made to study the impact of Wild Life (Protection) Act 1972 on the primitive Chenchus of Nallamala. Besides, the study assumes significance in highlighting the grievances of the tribals in the light of the blind implementation of the policies by the administrative machinery. Such studies would be helpful not only in identifying and analysing the factors responsible for the grievances, unrest among the tribals, but also in formulating new policy initiatives necessary for defusing the tension in the tribal areas.

The present study instead of confining to a particular area or unit, covers the scheduled areas (Integrated Tribal Development Agency (ITDA) areas) of the three dominant tribes and it covers the Five Year Plan period from 1951 to 1985, with special emphasis on the Fifth and Sixth Five Year Plan periods. Because the major tribal developmental programmes wer e introduced during the Fifth Five Year Plan and its impact was observed during the Sixth Five Year Plan period.

For the purpose of present study, three important tribes viz., (1) The Chenchus, of Srisailam in Kurnool District, (2) The Gonds of Utnoor in Adilabad District, and (3) The Koyas of Eturnagaram in Warangal District, are taken up for the reasons given below:

(a) The Chenchus are considered the most primitive of all the tribes. It would be interesting to analyse how they are undergoing transition from food gathering stage to the settled life.

(b) The Gonds are the most conservative and superstitious tribe. The Gond area experienced two rebellions within a span of forty years, i.e., Babijheri uprising in 1940 during the Nizam's period and the Indravelli uprising in 1981 in a welfare state. It is interesting to probe into the various socio-economic and demographic developments of this naxalite prone area.

(c) The Koyas are the dominant tribe in Warangal District. They had numerous grievances from the forest authorities during Nizam's period. They had participated in the Telangana Armed struggle against the Nizam. Koyas were the only tribal groups which had taken in an appreciable degree to industrial employment in the Singareni Colleries.

Organisation of the Study

The present study is divided into six chapters. The First Chapter is of introductory nature, includes the review of the literature, objective, method of study along with chapterisation.

The Second Chapter deals with the Tribal setting of Andhra Pradesh with a special reference to the socio-economic, cultural description and historical background of the three tribes, (a) Chenchus, (b) Gonds, and (c) Koyas slected for the present study.

The Third Chapter reviews the Forest-Tribal policies, Legacy of the British, Impact of Nizam's Policy, Post-colonial Policy, A.P. Land Transfer Regulation 1959. Single Line Administration and Wild Life (Protection) Act.

The Fourth Chapter deals with the process and evaluation of Tribal Development and activities of the ITDA during the plan period. This chapter is divided into three section. Section A, deals with Chencus of Srisailam in Kurnool District, Section B deals with Gonds of Utnoor in Adilabad District, and Section C deals with Koyas of Etumagaram in Warangal District.

The Fifth Chapter presents a critical analysis and the impact of the tribal policies initiated by the Government and it also deals with an overall impact on tribes.

The Sixth Chapter is a concluding chapter which provides a brief summary of the findings, suggestions and remedial measures.

***

Each tribal area had a particular level of acculturation and the social structure is inhibitive of real development. This finding had been attested even by the report of the study team on tribal development programmes by the Planning Commission, which stated that the industrialisation of the tribal areas which was expected to improve the economic conditions of the tribal communities proved to be largely illusory. The task force on development of tribal areas constituted by planning commission in 1972, also observed that, special problems of the tribals such as, primitive methods of agriculture, land alemation, indebtedness, adverse effects of industrialisation, low levels of literacy, health and nutrition have not been solved.

The process of tribal development should not only generate the feeling of self-help in the minds of tribal people, it should also ensure their self-employment. If necessary alternative policy should be found for the elimination of various processes of domination and cultural hegemony of rising classes in tribal areas.

Since the advent of independence, emancipation of the tribal community has become the constitutional responsibility of Government of India. There has been a serious thinking over the tribal problem. The policy of "protected development" as suggested by Verrier Elwin and lauded by Pandit Jawaharlal Nehru has been the major approach towards the tribal problem. It has undergone several changes, additions and deletions from time to time, to suit to the changing needs and priorities.

The phase of planned development of tribal community has been marked with an honest and earnest zeal on the part of the national and state governments to effect a rapid but protected development of the tribal areas. Several commissions, expert committees and groups have been appointed from time to time to suggest measures for the rapid amelioration of the backward tribal areas.

The Government of India and Government of Andhra Pradesh have decided that atleast 6 percent of the total budget of each department should flow to Tribal sub-plan. But in practice the actual flow was only 3.72 percent and the actual expenditure was 3.07 percent. If we delete the expenditure on programmes like commercial forestry, medium irrigation, which do not benefit tribal economy, the actual relevant expenditure works to 2.36 percent. In view of the low level investments during V and VI five-year plans, the objective of bridging the gap in levels of development could not be achieved. On the other hand, the gap has widened due to progress in plain areas in corresponding plan periods.

The Sub-plan areas during the V and VI plan have been brought under the Integrated Tribal Development Project. The objective of the ITDA was to focus attention on the specific problems of the area and people in the region and formulate an integrated area development programme. Likewise, the long-term goals of sub-plan area, firstly, to narrow the gap between the levels of development of tribal and non-tribal areas and secondly to improve the quality of life of the tribal communities. The other related objective was the elimination of exploitation in all forms.

As a result of the introduction of developmental schemes, the Chenchus are presently cultivating their own lands. The percentage of families who leased out their lands decreased from 77.36 percent to 36.59 percent, while own cultivation increased from 22.64 percent to 63.40 percent. Another notable feature is the yield of food crops per acres has increased from 1.5 quintal to 3 quintal. But the Chenchu could not derive effective benefits from the supply of milch animals. As the Chenchus were not given any assistance to construct cattle sheds, the animals were left unprotected which resulted in the death of 50 percent of the milch animals due to wild animals attack. The milch cattle programme could not succeed, as there were no marketing facilities. Most of these animals were purchased from the delta areas of Krishna District and they are not accustomed to forest climate and uncared life and easily succumb to diseases.

Though the integrated tribal development project could not derive desired results in all sectors, it was able to create considerable awareness, confidence and hope among the Chenchus. They are exhibiting a remarkable zeal to adopt to modern way of life by shedding their traditional fears and inhibition to a greater extent and are participating in the activities aimed to improve their economic lot. The community which never knew thrift or saving habit has just began to save some amounts for the future in Nationalised Banks and Post Offices and has also began to demand specified programmes for the development, and participation in Panchayat Raj administration.

The programme implementation process has also brought changes in their outlook and way of life as was observed among the Chenchu inhabitants of Allipalem and Chilakacherla who were hitherto to living on highway robbery and cattle lifting by taking up cultivation. Some of the notorious gang-leaders of these villages were employed in the local ashram schools. These criminal Chenchus have completely given up their old habits and are sending their children to Ashram Schools. They are evincing keen interest to lead a settled life. Among food-gathering Chenchus the realisation that they have to depend upon some assured source of income by taking up agriculture has been noticed.

The entry of the Chenchus into the cash economy has come about mainly by the activities of the Girijan Co-operative Corporation. The sums obtained from the sale of minor forest produce are very considerable. In the year 1977 alone the G.C.C at Mananur purchased Minor Forest Produce worth Rs 5.50 lakhs. These purchase from Chenchus have made a decisive impact on their economy. Several Chenchu households at Srisailam and Mananur, who were exposed to urbanisation have acquired the habit of tea drinking.

The establishment of Rajiv Tiger Reserve in Nallamalai, i.e., the Primitive Tribal Group area has adversely affected the Chenchu villages as no development work could be taken up in the villages. Approximately 4350 Chenchu families are affected by the Tiger Reserve. 35 villages with a population of 2033 Chenchus are lying in the core area of the sanctuary. These Chenchus are facing many problems in eking out their livelihood. More than 2000 cattle were killed by tigers between 1981-86. The Chenchus are afraid to go to forest for collection of minor forest produce.

Studies conducted on tiger sanctuary areas of Chenchu habitat have revealed some disturbing trends. There is a strong belief in the Department of Environment that by saving the tiger, the entire eco-system will be saved. The primitive Chenchu tribals living there and part of eco-system are some how out of focus. Some times the tribals get a feeling that they are pitted against the wild life, the latter taking an advantageous position supported by legislation. Such a feeling has developed in the last decade, because some of the age-old tribal habitations had to be shifted from core areas to provide a habitat for tiger and tribal rehabilitation was not taken up in a satisfactory manner.

The milch animals, plough bullocks, goats etc., killed by tiger in core area will not get compensation. If tiger comes out of core area and kill animals, the owner is eligible for compensation. But, the compensation is low and the procedure to be followed is so cumber some that the delays frustrate the tribal who had already lost the economic opportunities due to the death of his animals. Even these payments are generally made at the end of the financial year. Tribals often complained that after the payment of mamuls (bribes), they get a compensation that is not even sufficient to buy a calf to replace their dead milch animal. Some of the Chenchus even questioned, "how do animals know about the core area and other area when we ourselves are not clear about this" ? the anger generated out of this frustration found expression when, recently, the ITDA staff visiting a Chenchu village were beaten up, their jeep and files were burnt by the Chenchus. This aggressive reaction from the mild Chenchus is first of its kind in the Chenchu belt and it is an indicative of a clear message to correct the officials.

The award of contract (1980) for the exploitation of bamboo on the upper Amrabad plateau to the Sirpur paper mills, has adverse effects on the Chenchus of Amrabad plateau. The depletion of the stocks of bamboo in the Amrabad forests has disrupted the Chenchu economy.

The improved transport facilities resulting in the progressive depletion of forests are depriving the Chenchus of their seasonal forest foods. While the Chenchus of roadside settlements registered remarkable progress, the Chenchus living in the remote villages, especially in the core area of the Tiger reserve are leading a precarious life, some times facing semi-starvation.

The Government has promised to distribute 41 acres of temple-land of Vempenta village to the Chenchus. Though many years have passed but the promise is not yet materialised. The proposed land distribution scheme is limited to the files alone. As a result frustration is creeping in to the Chenchus who have lost faith in the credibility of the officials and are turning to illicit manufacturing of liquor for their survival. The Chenchus opined that the inaction of the Government is forcing them to illegal activities for their survival.

The areas of Koya tribe registered all round development during the Fifth Five Year Plan Period. The land colonisation scheme executed by the Koya collective farming cooperative society was a success. The Eturnagaram tribal areas are blessed with rich ground water potential and this potential was utilised, the Eturnagaram tribal areas register highest percentage of irrigated area.

As a direct result of the "Dayyam vagu" irrigation project at Rangapur, in Etumagaram area, was developed into a successful growth centre with necessary infrastructure. The master plan irrigating an area of 56649 acres heralded a new era in the tribal areas of Warangal. In the Etumagaram Koya belt 10743 acres of land was assigned to the landless tribals, 11550 acres of waste land was brought under cultivation, net sown area increased to 125393 acres, and irrigated area increased by 162 percent during the V plan period. All these resulted in the surplus food grains production in Etumagaram, Gudurm and Mulug areas. In Mulug area 21 percent food grains and 100 percent cash crops produced were marketed. The road-side Koya villages reached the level to compete with plains cultivators.

The introduction of ginger cultivation in the tribal areas of Etumagaram has given highly encouraging results. Mulugu area of Etumagaram is in the forefront in use of modern inputs like fertilizers, pesticides etc. Per acre yield found doubled after the use of modern inputs in the tribal areas of Mulugu and Eturnagaram.

The improved agricultural position had increased the income of the Koyas and helped to acquire the assets like Radio, Tape Recorder, Gold, Silver. Considerable number of Koyas possess engines of irrigation. Whatever change that has taken place in asset structure was only due to the impact of the developmental programmes. The activities of Girijan Cooperative Corporation has brought down the indebtedness in the Koya belt. The value of G.C.C supplies to tribals has gone up to the extent of ₹ 9.44 lakhs by 1982-83. Because of their industrial and high agricultural base, the Koyas of Kothagudem area have incomes above the poverty line. They are directly approaching the government offices and asking for the assistance as their awareness regarding Government schemes has increased considerably. A.P Adivasi Prantheeya Sangam, representing Koyas, called for an agitation to achieve "self-governance" as in the case of "Darjeeling hill council" in West Bengal and Hill Council in Tripura. It may be concluded that the attitudes and awareness of the Koyas have changed over a period of time. Their participation in economic activities has also increased compared to the past.

As in the case of Gond area, the Koya belt is also not free from land alienation problem. Tribal areas of Mulug and Narsampet are under non-tribal attack. Settlers from coastal areas, by dubious means occupied roadside areas, such as Chelvai, Pasra, Buttaram, Rohir etc. Local officers are unable to enforce the Land Transfer Regulation as the settlers enjoy political support. Whereas in interior villages the Koyas retained all their lands and with well-built houses led prosperous life.

Gonds, unlike other tribal areas, the Gond tribal belt has been experiencing unrest right from Nizam's period. The granting of scheduled tribe status to the Lambadas has unleased the process of large scale population migration into Adilabad district from the neighbouring Maharashtra State. This population growth increased pressure on the for ests causing dwindling of minor forest produce and encroachment of Gond land.

4.2 Federalism in India in the Context of Administrative Relations Between Centre and States

Summary and Conclusions are presented in the following paragraphs.

The Constitution of India adopted in 1950 was drafted discussed and approved by men of outstanding expertise and eminence. It was thoroughly examined and freely commented upon by intellectuals all over the world. Most of whom feel that the document has by and large stood the test of time. Several provisions of the Government of India Act of 1935 with which the country was familiar found their way into the new Constitution. Besides, the experience gained in welcoming of federal democratic systems obtained in several western countries. was also made use of. Yet, the framers of the Constitution of India have created a unique federal system suited to the requirements of the country. They were caught in the dilemma of creating a federal system with the constituent units exercising considerable autonomy while ensuring the creation of a federal government powerful enough to hold the country together in any enventuality. India was merely described as a Union of States and the use of expressions like 'federation' were tactfully avoided. The Constitution was described as 'unique' in its spirit as it contained distinguishing federal features as well as strong unitary tendencies.

Interestingly enough, as long as the Congress Party was in power at the Union as well as the state levels. the federal system was neither questioned nor found to be defective. It was only after the fourth general elections which brougtt some non-Congress parties into power in some states and more recentlly with some regional parties emerging power that the efficacy of the federal system was seriously questioned. To begin with, a large part of the criticism was directed at the misuse labuse of the constitutional authority by the Union Government but later they started questioning the provisions of the Constitution that have conferred such powers on the Union Government. It is significant to note that a large number of those responsible for the controversy were politicians while the academics and the intellectuals did not question the basic structure of the Constitution. The main contention of those who challenged the federal set-up was that undue importance was given to the Union Government, rendering it almost impossible for the States to function as autonomous units in spheres exclusively allocated in them by the Constitution. On the other hand, the defenders of the Constitution maintain that the present set-up was deliberately created to contain the fissiparous and secessionist tendencies that may emerge at any time in future. In a way, it is parodoxical that at a time when some people in Punjab, Kashmir and even in Assam wish to secede from the Union, the position of preeminence envisaged for the Union Government to contain such elements only, is seriously questioned. An extreme and absurd view point was expressed by those who described the Union as a myth. Such expressions eminate from members of regional political parties who could never think of exercising the powers of the Union Government, except as junior partners in coalitions.

The concept of 'federalism' is not new to the comity of nations. Several countries at different times have established federal structures to suit their political requirements. Consequently, no two federal structures look alike today. With each having peculiarities of its own. For instance, the federating units of U.S.A. were anxious to avoid creating a powerful federal system that would overtook them. Hence one set of functions to be vested in the Union they listed out only others for themselves. But in India Union while retaining all government run from Delhi which enjoyed it was the preeminence while the provincial governments played only a secondary role. Consequently, the centralised tedencies in the federal system of India may also be viewed as a part of our British legacy.

The issue of Centre-State relations was examined by the Administrative Reforms Commission, appointed by Government of India and the Radmaannar Committee, appointed by Tamilnadu Government and more recently by the Sarkaria Commissions appointed by the Government of India. No doubt, the views expressed by such Commission have extensively been debated and commented upon but none of the proposals have been seriously implemented. The debate today involves a re-examination of the concept of 'federalism' in the Indian context and analyse the preculiar federal characteristics as designed by the framers of the Constitution and as evolved over the past four decades. Though the focus of the present study is the examination of federalism in India in the context of Centre-State administrative relations, it is found necessary to discuss some of the collatora factors that have an important bearing on such relations. Discussions involving ideal models or theoretical constructs have limited relevance in the present context. Even otherwise it is no longer the same theory as it was during the times of Wheare or Livingston. Domination of either levels of government over the other is out of context today. It is the age of co-operative and participative federalism in which levels of government function with mutual trust, understanding and coordination. The Sarkaria Commission has rightly observed that it is cooperative federalism which is the spirit of the Indian Constitution and that both the Union and the States should function in that spirit.

It is alleged by several critics that the division of functions between the Centre and the States lacked rationality. They feel that the State Governments do not enjoy any co-ordinate authority at present, eventhough the Constitution has contemplated the same. The Constitution- makers have adopted the Canadian or the Australian model than the American system in regard to the division of functions. Thus, the legislative powers are not only divided between the Centre and the states but some of the functions on which both the governments have concurrent jurisdiction are also separately mentioned. More importantly the residuary powers are vested in the Union. Further. the provisions of the Constitution relatinq to the temporary transfer of functions from the State to the Centre are also subjects of controversy. No surprise, non-Congress State governments have been consistently demanding that the Constitution should do away with the Concurrent List. They ignore the fact that division of powers between the two units into watertight compartments is not only undesirable but impracticable. if not impossible. Many of the items in the Concurrent List are important matters of concern both for the Union and the States. Normally they are carried on by the State governments except where the Union acts on them. Even then any State activity not inconsistent with the central 'will', will remain. In fact, the Concurrent List is in the nature of a shock absorber in the sense that it enables the Union and the States to go beyond their own exclusive legislative spheres when the necessity arises to meet the exigencies without transgressing the boundaries already drawn for each of them by the Constitution. It is unfortunate that they also ignore the need to secure uniformity throughout the country as well as the need for securing coordination berween States in respect of certain functions requiring Centre's intervention through concurrent jurisdiction.

Another important area of conflict between the Centre and the States is the place and invocation of certain Articles in the Constitution. Articles like 248, 249 and 252 have become the bone of contention and hence a number of non-Congress (I) State governments demanded the deletion of these Articles from the Constitution or suitable amendments to be made as the residuary powers of legislation should belong to the States and that no State could be deprived of any legislative power which belonged to it, without its prior concurrence. But, as pointed out by many scholars, the rationale of giving residuary powers to the Centre is a move in the right direction as it would be beyond the skill of any draftsman to guarantee that no potential subject of legislation, unknown and unsuspected at the time of framing, may not arise afterwards. Hence, it is evident that the makers of the Constitution were eager to avoid the long process of evolution of federal powers through other means as it happened in other federations. Again, if the struggle for political unity, integrity, stability and economic prosperity have been dependent on judicial interpretations for the enhancement of the federal powers, the very objectives of achieving these ends would not have been possible. Again, the Constitution also had to provide measures for any contingency that might arise in future. And a Central Legislature with residuary power of legislation is therefore a more powerful guarantee against such future exigencies than the enumerated powers which may not arm the Centre with sufficient strength when required by it. The utility of Article 249 is very much felt because it provides the necessary scope for making temporary adjustments in the scheme of division of powers. The absence of a provision of this nature has been very much felt in other federal constitutions like the United States and Australia when pressing socio-economic problems called for uniform legislation. Hence this provision is essential and should not be tampered with. Also Article 252 is highly beneficial in promoting uniform legislation for the benefit of the contiguous states, especially in matters of common and general interest. Hence, the demand of some States, that Articles 248, 249, 252 and 254 should either be deleted or suitably amended, is based on narrow and partisan outlook.

Some non-Congress (I) State governments also demand the deletion of Articles 200 and 201 from the Constitution in their present form. Also they stress that it should be a constitutional obligation on the part of the Governor to give his assent to the Bills passed by the State Legislatures. The benefit of Articles 200 and 201 is that they make available legal and constitutional guidance to the State governments which might be lacking in this regard and secure as far as possible uniformity in laws without jeopardising the legislative autonomy of the States. However, it can be suggested that a time limit of six months should be provided for the exercise of presidential veto. If the presidential assent is not received within the stipulated period of six months or if the Bill is not referred back to the concerned State legislature with suggestions and objections, if any, the concerned Bill should be considered as assented to A provision to this effect may be made in Articles 200 and 201 through amending the Constitution.

Many non-Congress (I) State governments have also expressed their views against the Articles 256 and 257 of the Constitution. According to them, these Articles which empower the Centre to issue directives to States and also Article 365 which empowers the Union to take remedial measures, are repugnant to the spirit of a federal entity in as much as the operation of these Articles reduces the States into administrative units of the Union

Government. The State governments have expressed their views against these Articles, mainly on the ground that these Articles, especially 365, have been misused by the Union Government. However, these provisions are essential because if the Parliament, in any particular case, thinks that in passing a law which relates to the concurrent field, the execution ought to be retained by the Central government, Parliament shall have the power to do so. If the Centre did not have power to issue directives to the States, it would become impossible for the Central government to secure execution of its laws. On the other hand, if the execution of laws made by the Union Legislature is not in compliance with the Centre's guidelines, by any State government, it would be open to a citizen to challenge the action of a State executive in an appropriate court and obtain redress. This would be apart from any action which the Union government may itself choose to take under its power to give directions. Here, one should not lose sight of the fact that there is no exclusive Union agency in the State for the adminstration and execution of the Central laws in India. Anyhow, keeping the fact in view that the remedies provided in the Constitution for disobedience of the directives of the Centre are rather stringent and harsh, it would be, better that the Centre should resort to the process of Presidential intervention, only after exhausting all available methods of persution and negotiations. In this context the Sarkaria Commission has rightly pointed out that Article 356 should be invoked for Central intervention in the States very sparingly and only as a last resort measure.

Again many non-Congress (I) State governments have often been pointing out that law and order is a State subject and hence the prerogative of the States in this matter should fully be respected. But due to the growth of fissiparous tendencies all over the country. along with the threat of regionalism and sccessionalisrn looming large in India, in times of crisis it is better that the Government of India is allowed to act on its own than to depend on the State administration. In fact, the post of the Governor was never as relevent as to-day when there are several secessional tendencies raising their heads. Article 356 helps the Union Government (which, includes the Parilament) to hold the country together in an extreme case of any part trying to secede from the Union. Also, the issue of deployment of armed forces has become an irritant in the Centre-State relations and some State governments are of the view that unless requisitioned by a State, the union armed forces should not interfere, as the law and order maintenance is purely a problem of the State government. However, the Sarkaria Commission, having explained the issues of 'public disorder' and 'internal disturbance' rightly pointed out that a State government may be unabale or unwilling to suppress an internal disturbance and may even refuse to seek the aid of the Union armed forces. In fact, there are extreme cases of the

State Government sponsored bandhs being organised in some parts of the country. And so the Union should always have the power to deploy its armed forces wherever and whenever it is convincingly regarded as essential. However, in such an event of deployment it is desirable that the concerned State government is consulted wherever feasible, and its co-operation sought, though prior consultation with the State government is not obligatory.

The All-India Services also have become an important irritant in Centre-State relations in India. Many non-Congress (I) State governments have expressed their strong resentment against the scheme of the All India services. Most prominently the States which have come under the rule of the regional political parties and the leftist parties always viewed the All India services as an instrument of the Union government to keep the State governments under their watch. Even at the time of independence Punjab, Bengal and Sind provinces openly opposed the scheme of All India services on the ground that such services were aqainst the federal spirit of the Constitution. On many an occasion the non-Congress (I) State Governments have demanded an amendment to be brought about to the Constitution in such a way as to enable those State governments which are not favourable to these services, to opt out of the scheme. The main reason for the continuation of the All India services was certainly the consideration of efficiency. Also, it ensured the uniformity of the administrative system throughout the country. Again, as the recruitment is done on All India basis, they have always been attracting the best talent that is available in the country. The nature of the services is such, that it contributed largely to the cause of national integration as well. The personnel of these services are prepared to walk into any State in the country and work for its prosperity as if it were his own State. Such an outlook is highly essential in a sharply divided society as ours in the sense that they function against petty parochial and local forces. Their loyalty, to both the State and the Union governments, makes them truly federal to a large extent. Accordinq to the Sarkaria Commission, the continuance of these services is highly essential as it would ensure a unified approach to the myriad problems of the country as a whole. The All India services in the process of their working bring to the national level policy-making, practical experience of implementing decisions at the State level. This quite often lends a touch of realism to the administrative process at the Centre. And when once they revert back to the States they take back with them a wider appreciation of the nation's needs and priorities. All India services also constiute a dependable means of c,reating public functionaries who in course of their employment gain a varied experience, a breadth of vision and outlook, a special capacity to co-ordinate and synthesise various conflicting interests and a deeper understanding of the social economic development of the country at large without losing sight of the needs of the constituent units at the sametime. The recommendation of the Sarkaria Commission that any move to disband the All India services or to permit any State government to opt out of the scheme must be regarded as a retrograde step deseries to be appreciated and taken note of.

There has also been a demand from various non-Congress (I) State governments that Article 263 should be put to more effective use by the creation of an Inter-State Council for better and smooth working relations between the Centre and the States. The presently prevailing situation in the country, wherein different political parties are ruling in many States and no single political party showsany prospects of securing majority to form a government on its own, it is essential that a suitable and stable machinery is evolved to provide for mutual discussions, consultations and necessary negotiations between the Centre and the States on various pressing problems. In fact the Administrative Reforms Commission, the Rajamannar Committee and also the Sarkaria Commission have recommended the formation of such a machinery, though they differed on the details relating to its structure and functioning. It is in the fitness of things that the Government of India had taken a very serious note of this recommendation and very recently created the Inter-State Council in order to provide for a fair 'and speedy resolution of various problems of national importance so that the same do not, through neglect, assume dangerous dimensions. However, it is too premature to make any assessment of the working of this Council.

Yet another federal arrangement which has been significanlty contributing to the confusion in the relations between the Centre and the States is that of the Finance Commission. Its working has been criticised on the ground that lack of any agreed formula and considerable confusion in the criterica adopted by various Finance Commissions in determing central assistance has contributed to a very unhealthy cornpetiton the States to indulge in bargaining and manipulation to obtain larger amounts of assistance from the Centre Surprisingly enough, there is no demand from the States for deletion of the provisions relating to the Finance Commission, inspite of the bitter criticism and various shortcomings with respect to its functioning. Various political parties, especially those in the opposition demand that all kinds of financial transactions between the Union and the States should be handled by the Finance Commission only and not by any other agency. The devolution of revenue resources by the Finance Commission for non-plan expenditure once in five years and leaving it to the Planning Commission to assess the financial requirements to sustain an extended plan each year is leading to serious difficulties in the management of the finances of the nation. So it is essential that only one agency should deal with all financial transfers, both plan and non-plan, which could best be handled by the Finance Commission. However, it is necessary that the Planning Commission is made a statutory organisation governed by a Parliamentary Act, clearly describing its role and position. Again, this Commission should consist of reputed economists, technocrats and management experts in order to bring about a coordinated effort for better economic development. It is also necessary that this body is kept away from all pressures from the Union government and is made available to represent various States in turns on a Zonal basis. At present the role of the Planning Commission as a 'super cabinet' influencing the economics' of the entire nation including the States is another Source of irritation for the States. Not only its role should be statutory defined but its functioning should be scientifically streamlined. The present practice of finalising the plan outlay for the State on the basis of 'oral' promises of Chief Ministers to raise more funds is most unscientific and political, leading to unrealistic boosting of plan outlays to attract more central assistance. The recommendation of the Sarkaria Commission that planning and implementation should be a difficult process between the Centre and the State to be given due recognition.

The National Development Council and its working is also the target criticism by various opposition political parties infact, the Council's meetings have been reduced to a ritual and little scope is provided at its meetings for any meaningful and useful discussions on important national issues. In order to bring about a better understanding and co-ordinated effort, the National Development Council should function more as a real deliberative, purposeful and compact body. The Council must meet at least thrice every year, and all the members of the Finance Commission as well as the Planning Commission may be invited to participate in its deliberations. The Five Year Plan may be approved only after constructive deliberations among all those concerned. Thus, the establishment of a permanent Finance Commission, a Planning Commission with the necessary statutory status, coupled with a truly co-coordinating, deliberative and business like National Development Council shall provide a now ground for the building up of an economically strong, politically viable and socially accommodating India.

The emergency provisions in the Constitution have also been the subject of serious discussions in the post-independent India and there is a strong demand from various opposition parties for suitable safeguards to be written into the Constitution for better and well considered use of emergency provisions. There are many who strongly demand the deletion of article 356. This Article, more often than not, has been interpreted and applied differently in similar situations to suit the political interests of the party in power at the Union level. In fact, the unwholesome use of this Article in

1977 and 1980 has been regarded as certainly against the Constitutional norms even by the Sarkaria Commission. As observed by this Commission, the emergency provisions of the Constitution form a fasciculous of nine Articles giving the President overriding authority to assume and exercise powers to deal with different types of extraordinary situations like external aggression, internal disturbance, armed rebellion and breakdown of constitutional machinery in any one or more States. In fact, these provisions are a result of well considered situation under which the republic came into existence and the threat of the sub national cultures made it necessary that a duty be cast on the Union to ensure that the governance of every State is carried on in accordance with the provisions of the Constitution. In a situation of grave emergency whereby the security of India or any part of its territory is threatened by war or external aggression or armed rebellion, the Union Government could resort to action under Articles 352, 353, 250, 354, 358 and 359. In the same way, a situation involving breakdown of the Constitutional machinery in a State i.e. where the government of the State cannot be carried on in accordance with the provisions of the Constitution can be tackled by resorting to action under Articles 356 and 357. Articles 355 and 360 are also provided for tackling situations of emergency. With respect to the doubt relating to whether 'external aggression' or 'internal disturbance' is to be read as an indispensable element of the situation of failure of the constitutional machinery in a State, the existence of which is a pre-requisite for the exercise of the power under Article 356, the Sarkaria Commission rightly pointed out that it need to be so. The Commission very rightly felt that 'external aggression' or 'internal disturbance' may not necessarily create a situation where government of a State can not be carried on in accordance with the provisions of the Constitution. However, a failure of the constitutional machinery in a State may occur, without there being a situation of 'external aggression' or 'internal disturbance' Hence the Commiossion rightly opined that a fialure of the consititutional machinery may occur in a number of ways as factors which contribute to such a fialure are diverse and imponderable. while strongly recommending the retention of Article 356, the Commission categorically stated that it need only to be used as a last- resort power and that it is difficult to give an exhaustive catalogue of all situations which would fall within the sweep of the phrase the government of the State can not be carried on in accordance with the provisions of this Constitution. However it is also in the interest of good centre-state relations that a warning should be issued to the errant. State in specific terms before resorting to action under Article 356 wherever feasible. Again, the Commission's recommendations that the material facts and grounds on which Article 356(1) is invoked should be made an integral part of the proclamation, would further brighten the prospects of good

Centre-State relations. This is a truism as this would make the control of the Parliament over the exercise of this power by the Union more rational. Anyhow, the recommendation that normally President's rule in any State should be imposed on the basis of the Governor's report under Article 356 (1) doesnot prohibit the Union from imposing President's Rule even without such a Report as sometimes the Governor may be reluctant to submit a Report even when such situation really existed. Except for the above mentioned, the emergency provisions need no changes and the growth of regionalism, parochial attitudes, linguistic chauvanism, large scale violence in the political field and the threat of secessionism demand such power to be with the Union. To protect the unity and integrity of the country and to action against any State which acts against such interests, the emergency powers need to be retained, but with a degree of restraint to be exercised by the Union government.

The institution of Governor in the Indian federal scheme infact, occupies a position unrivalled by any other office in any other federal system in the world. However, this institution has come under severe criticism in the recent past, especially after the fourth, general elections. The manner in which the office has been thoroughly politicised by different political parties ruling at the Centre, resulted in doubts being expressed regarding the very desirability and place of this office in the federal set-up of India. There is a strong demand, of course from the opposition parties for the abolition of this office. The partisan role played by many Governors, especially at the instance of the Centre in toppling the duly elected State legislatures, in withholding assent to the duly passed Bills of the State governments, withholding or causing undue delay in clearing a number of key appointments on political grounds, not providing an opportunity to the opposition parties even where they are eligible for forming government in many States, recommending President's rule on filmsy and purely political grounds have infact strengthened the demand for the abolition of this office. However, keeping the vital role assigned to the Governor by the Constitution, and also the recommendations of the Administrative Reforms Commission and the Sarkaria Commission in view. Efforts should be made to redeem the office to its original glory. The most important steps, for improving the efficiency of this office, to be taken are that:

(i) Only persons who are eminent in some walk of life should be appointed as Governors;

(ii) Persons only from outside the State should be appointed to this office;

(iii) Persons detached and not so intimately connected with local politics of the State should only be appointed to this office; and

(iv) Persons who have not taken too great a part in politics in general should alone be appointed as Governors.

However, a politician of the ruling party at the Centre shall not be appointed as Governor of any State, in particular any State ruled by the opposition party or a combination of other parties.

The process of consultation on the appointment of the Government of State with the concerned State Chief Minister should be prescribed in the Constitution itself, if necessary by amending Article 155 of the Constitution. However, consultation should not be considered as concurrence of the concerned State Chief Minister. The Governor's term of office of five years shall not be disturbed except very rarely and that too for only compelling reasons as this would provide individuality and security to the Governor's office. As a matter of convention the Governor, on demitting his office should be eligible for any other office of profit except for a second term as Governor or election as Vice-President or President of India. This keeps them away from the active politics and makes the office a real source of strength for both the Union and the States. While appointing a Chief Minister – under conditions when no single party secures majority, the Governor should honestly, without being influenced by any force, keeping the welfare of the state and the country at large in view, select the one who in his judgment would most likely command a majority, in the Assembly. Any issue relating to the question of majority of the Chief Minister has to be decided, only on the floor of the concerned State Legislature and never outside by the Governor himself. Again the Governor should refer any Bill for the consideration of the President only when it is really required to be reserved and not by applying political standards. The President also on his part should return the Bill within a reasonable time, as recommended by the Sarkaria Commission, of course without incorporating those changes in the Constitution and the same applies to issue of ordinances also. As rightly left by the Sankaria Commission, the discretionary powers of the Governor as provided in Article 163 should be left untouched. And it is necessary to recognise that it is neither feasible nor advisable to regulate its exercise. Its scope by any amendment to the Constitution.

In India there are many rivers which flow through more than one State and hence there is ample scope for inter-State disputes with regard to the sharing of the waters among the concerned States. The Constitution makers very rightly anticipated that with the accent on development of irrigation and power resources, the number of inter-State disputes might be on the increase regarding the sharing of the river waters and therefore the Constitution has a special provision for resolving such disputes under Article 262. Eventhough Entry 17 of List II empowers the State Legislatures to legislate on the regulation and development within the territory of the conceded State, even in case where in the source of the water is an inter-state river or river valley, the Parliament may by making the requisite declaration in public interest in terms of Entry 56 of List I, enact a law for the regulation and development of such inter-State river and river valleys under the control of the Union. Thus, the Parliamentary law would, to the extent of its operation, have the effect of ousting the power of the State Legislature under Entry 17 of List II. Against all this, some State governments have been demanding that (i) 'water' should be made a Union Subjects and/or (ii) Entry 56 of List I should be deleted and the expression, "Subject to the provisions of Entry 56 of List I" in Entry 17 List II also should correspondingly be deleted. Other issues involved of are (i) relating to the appointment of a Tribunal under the Inter-State River Water Disputes Act, 1956 and (ii) that there is no machinery for the implementation of thc award of a Tribunal.

Since the jurisdiction of a State by virtue of Article 245 is territorially limited, only Parliament can effectively regulate by law the beneficial use and distribution of such inter-State river waters among the States. As the power given to the Union is exercisable only when it is found necessary and not otherwise, the existing arrangement of power distribution between the Centre and the States should continue and there is no need to make water a Union subject. As recommended by the Sarkaria Commission and Administrative Reforms Commission a Tribunal should be appointed once an application under Section 3 of the Inter-State River Water Disputes Act, 1956 is made by any of the concerned States within one year from the date of the receipt of such an application. For this purpose the Act may suitably be amended. Thirdly, in order to see to it that an award made by the Tribunal is implemented without fail, an amendment should be made to the Inter-State River Water Disputes Act, 1956 in such a way as to make the concerned State treat the tribunals award as almost an order or degree of the Supreme Court, as then only it becomes binding on the concerned party.

A dispassionate view of the Indian Federal System reveals that the makers of the Constitution have by and large created a structure suitable for a country with varied cultural, linguistic and religious complexities. Their wisdom and foresight in developing a unique federal system can best be approbated today when forces of disintegration are threatening the very existence of the Republic. It is most unfortunate that a good system is badly used by those in power. If the politicians running the Union Government abuse their power and misuse authority for political and partisan ends and if those in power at the state blame the Union Government for their failures and demand autonomy in areas where strong Union action is justified it is wrong to blame the Constitution.

4.3 Implementation of Jawaharlal Nehru National Urban Renewal Mission: In the Mission City of Hyderabad

I. Urbanisation and the Challenges

Unbalanced and unregulated growth, the typical characteristic feature of Indian urbanisation is contributing to severe strain on the urban infrastructure and services apart from other developmental concerns like increasing urban poverty, polarisation of social groups and deteriorating public health. Though the severity of the problems has been worsening fast, the governmental response has been largely abysmally slow and ineffective.

It is only in the post 1990s that certain reforms were initiated in the backdrop of liberalization policies and the quantum of financial assistance for the urban sector is being increased though it is grossly inadequate to meet the existing as well as the emerging needs. Focus on infrastructure and efforts to streamline the urban service delivery systems are gradually increased through various urban development initiatives which culminated in the launching of the Jawaharlal Nehru National Urban Renewal Mission in the country in 2005 promising a new era in the Indian urban sector development.

Migration from rural areas to urban areas in search of employment, establishment of business in search of livelihood, for social connectedness, education and for professional development, etc, increases the burden on cities / urban areas regarding civic services, employment, housing etc. Poverty has been the centre point for the influx of rural people to urban areas who generally prefer to move towards cities for livelihood. Keeping all these aspects in view, the Government of India has introduced several urban poverty alleviation programmes with an objective to uplift the urban poor in their socio-economic conditions. The poor people migrated from rural areas in search of employment normally find accommodation in old part of cities or outskirts of the cities either increasing the existing slum population or creating new slums. Thus, the ercation of new slums has become an additional problem to civic administration. Apart from Urban Poverty Alleviation and housing schemes, several other programmes have been introduced in urban areas to provide infrastructural facilities like roads. drains, streetlights, sanitation and water supply in thc mega cities, million plus cities and other cities by the Government of India as introduced.

Dr. V Gangaiah has his Ph. D in Public Administration under the supervision of Prof. S. Bhoopati Row (R), Professor of Public Administration, os mania University, Hyderabad (2017).

2. Urbanisation in Telangana State

The urban population of the Telangana state was 98.53 lakhs in 2001 which increased to 136.09 lakhs by 2011 registering 36 percent urban growth. Of the ten districts. the district of Hyderabad is 100 percent urbanised while the adjoining Ranga Reddy District has 70.225 urbanised as per 2011 Census. In other districts, it various from 14.99 percent in Mahaboobna gar to 28.5 percent in Warangal. It means, if Hyderabad district is 100 percent totally urbanised the Mahboobnagar district is the least urbanized in the state. From the growth trend point of view. the Ranga Raddy district registered highest growth of 91.92 percent during 2001-2011. The Medak district with 89.78 percent and Mahaboobnagar district with 63.64 percent. Warangal district with 59.23 percent and Nalgonda district with 53 percent followed in descending order. Interestingly. the Hyderabad district which is 100 percent urbanised experienced a meagre 2.97 percent growth rate which explains that the growth is now shifting from the core city of Hyderabad to the hinterland and the adjoining districts. The Waranagal being the next major urban centre, the future growth appears to be in that corridor. The interesting feature of urbanization in the Telangana state is that the urban growth center around the Hyderabad Metro Region. In fact, the Hyderabad Metropolitan Region spreads into the adjoining district of Medak. Ranga Reddy, Mahaboobnagar and Nalgonda districts.

3. Launching of the Jawaharlal Nehru National Urban Renewal Mission

Jawaharlal Nehru National Urban Renewal Mission (JNNURM) is a massive city modernisation scheme launched by the Government of India under Ministry of Urban Development. It envisages a total investment of over 1,00,000-00 crores over seven years for selected 63 Mission Cities in India. Named after Jawaharlal Nehru, the first Prime Minister of India, the scheme was officially inaugurated by Prime Minister Manmohan Singh on 3nd December 2005 as a programme meant to improve the quality of life and infrastructure in thc cities. It was launched in 2005 for a seven-year period (up to March 2012) to encourage cities to initiate steps for bringing phased improvements in their civic service levels. The government has extended the tenure of the mission for two years, i.e., from April 2012 to March 3. 1. 2014.

4. Scope of The Mission

The Mission comprises two Sub-Missions as described below:

(1) Sub-Mission for Urban Infrastructure and Governance (UIG): The UIG Sub-Mission is administered by the Ministry of Urban

Development through the Sub-Mission Directorate for Urban Infrastructure and Governance. The main thrust of the Sub-Mission is on infrastructure projects relating to water supply and sanitation, sewerage, social waste management, road network, urban transport and redevelopment of old city areas with a view to upgrading infrastructure therein, shifting industrial and commercial establishments to conforming areas, etc.

(2) **Sub-Mission for Basic Services to the Urban Poor (RSUP):** This is administered by the Ministry of Urban Employment and Poverty Alleviation through the Sub-Mission Directorate for Basic Services to the Urban Poor. The main thrust of the Sub-Mission has been on integrated development of slums through projects for providing shelter, basic services and other related civic amenities with a view to providing utilities to the urban poor.

(i) Implementation Status of UIG Projects

(1) The urban development initiatives in GHMC area have picked up with thc launching of the JNNURM. Firstly, a comprehensive development frame work emerged for taking up different projects. Though master plans are being prepared, the approach of City Developm ent Plan under the JNNURM Mission commendable.

(2) Under UIG, 22 projects in total were undertaken in Hyderabad, The storm water works were executed by the GHMC while the water supply projects were executed by the Hyderabad Metropolitan Water Supply & Sewerage Board (HMWS&SB). The overall progress indicates that out of the total approved cost of Rs. 2406 crores, a sum of Rs. 822 ACA was approved by the Central Government and to remaining to be borne by the state government and implementing agencies. Out of this 79 percent of amount was utilized on projects till June 2014. As far as ACA utilisation is concerned, about 80 percent utilization is equal to Visakhapatnam and better than other two cities. In terms of number of projects, 10 projects were completed totally, over 80 percent work was done in respec t of 6 six works and 50 to 80 percent work is done in respect of remaining works.

(3) The various projects taken up more the water supply, sewerage, roads and public transport areas are part of the overall CDP. In fact, JNNURM provided major financial assistance to initiate different projects in the above areas and more such projects are needed to realise the CDP goals and objectives.

(4) As far as execution of projects is concerneds the tender issues and land acquisition problems appear to be the main hurdles. The sewerage sector has more operational issues due to congestion and traffic problems in the older Parts of the city.

(5) Under JNNURM, the Road Transport Corporation, Hyderabad has received funding in segregated manner for construction of commuter amenity centres in Hyderabad with sanctioned fund of ₹ 22.69 Cr which has been released. The work of commuter amenity centres is completed. The RTC has also received an amount of ₹ 71.91 Crores for 973 buses during 2009 and ₹ 29.34 Crores for 210 buses during 2013 under JNNURM from the Central Government. The RTC has also received an amount of ₹ 12.97 Crores as the State Government share for bus funding project of 210 buses under JNNURM. As of now the RTC has completed the earlier of project of acquiring 937 buses under JNNURM and the second project of 210 buses is in progress[1].

(ii) Implementation Status of BSUP Projects in GHMC

(6) The BSUP gives more housing and habitat focus to the slum development programme in India. Housing for all is reflected the RAY programme too. In simple terms, the BSUP Sub-Mission aims to provide housing and basic services in the slum areas so that the physical environment improves. The other UPA projects like Urban Livelihoods focus on providing employment opportunities to the urban poor through self and wage employment initiatives. These two and other poverty related projects have to dovetailed and implemented in an integrated manner so that the development of slums and urban poor objectives could be more effectively achieved. In India, most of the urban development projects are run parallel with least inter-link ages.

(7) As far as the BSUP projects in GHMC are concerned, out of the total 17 projects taken-up for implementation, 5 projects were reported as completed as on 16th September 2015. The Central Government has funded around ₹ 734.03 crores out of ₹ 1631.81 crores while the approved sanctioned amount was about ₹ 680.39 crores. The physical progress achieved so far under these 17 schemes reveal that 64,300 Dwelling Units (DUs) were constructed out of proposed 72390 DUs were constructed while remaining 8090 DUs are still in progress. Out of completed 64300 DUs. 45945 DUs have been occupied constituting 71.45

percent by the beneficiaries while remaining DUs are still in the process of identification of beneficiaries and allocation of DU to the beneficiary.

(iii) Implementation of the Reforms

(8) Urban government system in India is inherited from the British regime. Efforts to Indianise the system has been slow. Further. with the increasing urbanisation and the emerging problems, the urban institutional needed strengthening. And reforms assume vital importance in strengthening the urban institutions both, from administrative and financial perspectives. Though thc urban reforms were being implemented since about three decades in India, the slow pace and ad hoc approach could not make thc much needed impact.

(9) The JNNURM scheme gave big push for serious implementation of urban reforms toward achieving concrete results. Reform implementation, no doubt, is a continuous process and the momentum has to be sustained as the results and total impact of administrative reforms takes longer time.

(10) The implementation status of these reforms reveals that about 67 percent of progress is achieved compared to the 70 percent target as per the reports of the State Government. The planning function is shared with thc Directorate of Town and Country Planning Department and urban development authorities along with the ULBs. The Urban Land Ceiling Act is abolished and efforts are being made to bring down stamp duty to 5 percent from existing 9.5-7.5 percent. The community participation law is brought-out to implement the ward committees as per the 74th Constitution Amendment. Public Disclosure law is also implemented. The implementation of provisions of the Constitution is being made especially the mandatory provisions like reservation, ward committees Election Commission, State Finance Commissions and District Planning Committees, etc. are implemented. The implementation of the Metropolitan Planning Committees is not implemented in the state similar to other states as this function is being performed by the Urban/Metropolitan Development Authorities. The Rent Control Act has been amended by Act no. 17 of 2005 with effect from 28-05-2005.

(11) With regard to the implementation of the ULB level reforms, Hyderabad achieved 59.5 percent overall progress as per the state

government reports. Apart from this overall performance, the individual ULB level reforms discussed in more detail in the following. Most of the mandatory reforms are implemented in GHMC under the JNNURM except full cost recovery in services like solid waste management and implementation of services in the slum areas. In fact, the slum development is being done on a continuous basis because the slums are not de-notified after development. In regard to solid waste management, surcharge is not levied to generate continuous income. This appears to be a common problem in all the ULBs in India. Though some ULBs make efforts to recycle some waste and produce manure, it is not sufficient to make this service self-sufficient.

(12) As per the Government reports, 90 percent overall progress is achieved in implementing the optional reforms in Andhra Pradesh. Except the property title certification, all other reforms are being implemented by the ULBs. The legal changes in the building permission process is simplified in 2012 by the state government. The re-use of waste water and water harvesting are being implemented slowly at ULB level. The ULB level discussion reveals certain improvements in the public private partnerships like door to door collection in solid waste management and developing infrastructure facilities through PPP mechanism.

5. Study Purpose and Design

The available literature on urban issues is quite wide covering aspects like urbanisation, urban development, environment and pollution, urban economy, urban politics, urban services, urban poverty, etc. Not many studies are available in India focusing on urban infrastructure and governance in a comprehensive manner. The researcher found a fertile research space in this area.

JNNURM is the new programme introduced on a mission mode in selected cities in the country. In Andhra Pradesh, Hyderabad, Visakhapatnam, Vijayawada and Tirupati cities have been selected under JNNURM for the implementation of different projects based on the requirement of individual cities. The present study intends to evaluate the projects undertaken under JNNURM in the Mission City of Hyderabad. In the recently carved-out Telangana State, Hyderabad is the only Mission City under JNNURM.

6. Objectives of the Study

Within the broader framework of the study outlined above, certain specific objectives are formulated for studying the various issues, problems and deficiencies in a focused manner. The objectives formulated are:

(1) To assess the progress achieved in the implementation of the projects taken-up under JNNURM in the City of Hyderabad;

(2) To critically evaluate the implementation of the reforms taken-up as part of the urban governance improvement programme under JNNURM;

(3) To record the perceptions of the institutions involved in the implementation of JNNURM; and

(4) To offer suggestions for policy and administrative corrections to guide the similar urban development programmes focusing on the urban infrastructure and governance front in India.

7. Hypotheses

i. The Mission of JNNURM launched in India in major cities for improving infrastructural services and urban governance has opened wide opportunities for innovations in the urban sector development in India.

ii. Mere increased funding without proper administrative delivery mechanisms does not automatically ensure improved infrastructural services.

iii. The institutionalisation of urban reforms under the JNNURM has been poor which raise the questions of sustainability of reforms for improved urban governance.

8. Area and Scope of the Study

Present study of "Implementation of Jawaharlal Nehru National Urban Renewal Mission: A Study of Hyderabad City" is confined to the Mission city of Hyderabad but the findings of the study will have wider relevance especially to the policy-makers and administrators to rework-out the implementation strategies for effective implementation in other Mission cities across the country. The new schemes namely. Smart City Programme and the Atal Mission for Rejuvenation and Urban Transformation (AMRUT) are also launched to provide continuity and future directions. The present study covers most of the projects proposed under these schemes hence, is useful as a feedback and learning. The implement ation of the JNNURM projects is done by multiple organizations in Hyderabad, through the Hyderabad civic body. GHMC is the core agency. The study, therefore, covers all the projects taken-up by these executing agencies to assess the total perspective of the JNNURM.

9. Methodology

Primary and secondary sources are used to collect relevant data for the completion of the study. Primary data is collected through discussions and interactions with the officials associated with the preparation, implementation and monitoring of JNNURM programme at different levels. An interview schedule was administered to the officials to record their perceptions on the implementation and impact of JNNURM. Simultaneously, a structured questionnaire was administered to 300 identified slum dwellers of Mission City of Hyderabad to record their perceptions on the implementation and impact of BSUP projects under JNNURM. Random sampling technique was followed to identify the samples. Secondary data is collected through books, government reports, brochures, records, unpublished material, from the office of nodal agency and concerned ULB. The study primarily applies the case study method to arrive at concrete conclusions and lessons.

10. Chapterisation

The present study is entitled as **"Implementation of Jawaharlal Nehru National Urban Renewal Mission : In the Mission City of Hyderabad City".** The study is comprehensive covering several aspects relating to the policy and reform framework, sub-missions, projects, institutional set-up, implementation and the emerging perspectives. It is divided into seven chapters for detailed assessment and analysis.

The introductory chapter provides the study framework . It discusses the conceptual and policy background, previous attempts of urban development programmes in thc country, emerging urban reforms and genesis of the mission mode approach and the JNNURM. This chapter provides the framework for the present study including the aspects like purpose, aims, objectives, scope, methodology, etc.

The Second Chapter is on the .JNNURM Programme and Institutional Framework. It discusses at length the details of the JNNURM. The programme components, projects, funding, etc., pertaining to the two sub-missions namely, Urban Infrastructure and Governance (U IG) and the Basic Services for the Urban Poor (BSUP) are described. The institutional set-up for implementing and monitoring at the central, state and ULB level is discussed clearly. The JNNURM is a reform oriented urban development programme. The urban reforms initiated are backbone for the sustenance of the Mission objectives. Hence, the aspect of urban reforms is discussed at length.

The Third Chapter provides the state level picture of the .JNNURM in Andhra Pradesh. The aspects like the state urban growth scenario, cities selected under the JNNURM, the state level institutional set-up and the profiles of each selected city are discussed. The state of Andhra Pradesh is recently divided while forming the new Telangana State. The Hyderabad is the only city selected under JNNURM in Telangana state. All these issues are discussed in this chapter.

The Fourth Chapter is devoted to the study of JNNURM programme in the Hyderabad city. The Hyderabad is the fifth largest city in India in terms of population and growth. The urban development programmes like JNNURM are needed to strengthen its infrastructure in tune with the growth. The projects taken-up, the progress achieved in implementation, the success rate, the organisations involved, coordination issues. etc.. are discussed at length in this important chapter. The case study provides some useful insights into the JNNURM.

The Fifth Chapter discusses the implementation of the JNNURM programme on the city infrastructural services in slum areas in the GHMC. The implementation of BSUP projects including peoples' perceptions is discussed at length in this chapter.

The sixth chapter is devoted to the implementation of urban reforms under JNNURM in GHMC. The reforms taken-up and their implementation status are discussed critically in this chapter.

The Seventh Concluding chapter provides broad conclusions of the study. Some useful suggestions also given to improve the programme further. This chapter also provides the emerging perspectives on urban development programmes in the country in the light of the recently launched new Missions namely, SMART City and AMRUT programmes.

11. Findings of the Study

The study brought-out certain important aspects relating to the implementations of the JNNURM Programme in Hyderabad. The insight brought-out in UIG projects. BSUP projects and the reforms is briefly outlined in the following.

(i) Findings on U1G Projects

1. The various projects taken up under the JNNURM like water supply, sewerage, roads and public transport areas are part of the overall CDP framework. In fact, JNNURM provided major financial assistance to initiate different projects in the above areas

and more such projects are needed to realise the CDIP goals and objectives.

2. As far as execution of projects in concerned, the tender issues and land acquisition problems appear to be the main hurdles. The sewerage sector has more operational issues due to congestion and traffic problems in the older parts of the city.
3. The development of cities is complex and continuing process. The cities could withstand the demands only when they implement the plan objectives through various development projects. The JNNURM has given the required push and it should be continued. Still several areas are left like solid waste management, roads. etc. which should be given push in the next phase. The city especially needs a comprehensive drainage and sewerage system which should also get attention in future in the infrastructure front.
4. It is hoped the current SMART City Programme will continue the development momentum with much more speed and IT interventions. JNNURM is thus could be considered a beginning for future urban moment of the city of Hyderabad.

(ii) Findings on BSVP Projects

The analysis of above projects under BSUP shows that GHMC has undertaken various projects for construction of dwelling units and provision of infrastructural facilities in its area, wherein the occupation rate is dismal. Though DUs have been constructed in most of the projects, the number of DUs occupied shows that government has been unsuccessful in mobilising beneficiaries and allocate the DUs to the beneficiaries.

It has been observed by the officials that GHMC is facing financial problems because of non-payment of 30 percent of the beneficiary contribution. Houses were built with GHMC funds. The beneficiaries are expecting free housing by the Government.

Another problem relates to delays and the contractor issues. For instance, in Unni Kota Housing Colony, the beneficiaries of Unni Kota colony have come forward lor the payment of beneficiary contribution but the contractors are reluctant to complete the construction process, saying that rates have been increased drastically.

It is interesting to note that though the Central Government released Rs. 734.03 cores as against the approved Central share of Rs. 680.39 crores, an excess of Rs. 53.64 crores, the Commissioner mentions that the GHMC is facing financial problems due to non-contribution of beneficiaries' share which is 30 percent. This is the main cause for dismal occupancy relate of mere 70 percent. Unless the beneficiaries come forward with their share, the goal of the Mission remains unfulfilled. The Government has to take initiative to sort-out of this problem with bankers. This appears to be the core of the problem pertaining to housing schemes under the JNNURM.

At the other spectrum, perceptions of the slum dwellers and the beneficiaries' brings out other set of problems and issues. Though there has been some perceptible change and improvement in the slum areas, there is a long way to go. The demands and needs increase with the increase in population and new slums emerge and the old slums need constant improvements. The dissatisfaction of the slum dwellers remains in some form or other.

The study brought-out that though the basic civic infrastructure like water supply, waste disposal, drains, street light and roads is provided, the maintenance is not proper. Thereby, the slum dwellers do not get the intended benefits. In a way. this problem is common in almost all the other areas in cities and towns in India. However, the facilities like schools, health centres and accessibility through public transport are missing in some slums. In certain slum areas drainage is reported to be a problem and the people wanted the authorities bestow attention on these missing things. The study in general brought-out that the civic services need to be maintained regularly and properly.

Regarding housing projects under BSUP. JNNURM, certain interesting findings were noted. At the outset, the beneficiaries are expecting free dwelling units. Though they are reluctantly accepting for beneficiary contribution as it is integral part of the scheme, they are finding difficulties in mobilising bank loans or loans from family sources. Their poor asset base and income levels may be the main reason especially, in getting bank loans.

Funding has been thus a critical aspect in the entire slum housing projects in India. The delays in project implementation accentuate the problem of mobilising the beneficiary contributions on time. Some respondents even suggested for instalment based payment. The authorities have to consider this suggestion positively and search for completing the projects on time with alternate arrangements temporarily. In fact, the GHMC has done some projects, it is putting more burdens on its meager revenues. The policy-makers have to come out with some alternate models of funding by easy methods while retaining the beneficiary contribution component.

Apart from funding issues, quality of construction has been observed as another major problem. The respondents in general are not satisfied with the quality of construction. The quality has been bad especially, in respect of poor construction material used. The result was frequent water leakages, drainage problem, etc. demanding annual repair works.

The funding, facilities and quality related problems had an impact on the occupancy ratio too. The overall occupancy ratio was about 70 percent and it needs to be increased to 100 percent for deriving the benefits of the scheme totally and to make the projects sustainable. All these factors led to the dissatis-faction of the beneficiaries.

Better maintenance of civic facilities and services, finding viable methods to improve compliance of beneficiary contributions and improving the quality of construction of dwelling units by better control and monitor ing mechanisms are the main deficiencies observed in the study.

(iii) Findings on Implementation of Reforms

In Andhra Pradesh, the status of implementation is slow but steady. Though the legal changes are made, their actual implementation is very slow on the ground. Broadly, concrete results are achieved in the property tax, accounting and community participation areas. The other areas are lagging behind in progress. Though the state level reporting shows very good progress compared to other states in India, lot is to be done at the ULB level. The administrative systems are established but there is a long way to go in this respect.

The state government should take active role in monitoring the progress at the ULB level and the monitoring mechanisms also should be strengthened going beyond the mandatory reporting. For instance, though the system of property tax assessment has been streamlined but the coverage is not improved. The GIS based surveys are being initiated similar to Karnataka state, but it is only in the beginning state far from reaping the benefits in the form increased incomes. Periodic revisions are not made which affects incomes adversely over a period. Similarly, water charges in the user charges category are yet to be made self-sufficient which requires realistic pricing. Though water harvesting is mandatory as per the planning rules, their actual implementation is lagging due to lack of people's cooperation. Citizen charters are provided but people are ignorant of them and they are hardly followed by the authorities.

The governance and service level improvements could be achieved only when reforms are actually implemented in true spirit at the ground level. A system of citizen report card is therefore, essential to assess the impact in true sense.

In GHMC, while most of the mandatory reforms are implemented, the optional reforms are being implemented slowly. The reform implementation status in GHMC reveals some positive points like property tax improvement, accounting reform and e-governance initiatives. The accounting reform and e-governance initiatives in GHMC are noteworthy and could be considered innovative worth emulating by other ULBs. The service sector is, however, lagging behind especially in implementation of the citizen charters, redressa of citizen grievances, cost recovery in services like water supply and solid waste management, etc. It is hoped, the GHMC bestow attention on these aspects in the future programmes.

12. Testing of Hypotheses

Hypothesis-I: The Mission of JNURM launched in India in major cities for improving infrastructural services and urban governance has opened wide opportunities for innovations in the urban sector development in India.

According to the High Powered Expert Committee (HPEC) Report 2011, urban investment in India is estimated at around Rs. 39.2 lakh crores. Through JNNURM, states have been given the power to identify infrastructural gaps and challenges to improved urbanised services. Under JNNURM, opportunities have opened up for states to implement infrastructural projects by allocating funds for road development with an estimated budget of ₹ 17.3 lakh crores, sanctioned budget of transportation is ₹ 4.50 lakh crores, water supply, sanitation, sewerage, solid waste management, storm water drainage - ₹ 8 lakh crores, renewal and redevelopment is allocated a budget of ₹ 4 lakh crores. Schemes under JNNURM have led to increased infrastructural development around Indian cities/ towns with an aim to provide adequate housing and infrastructural facilities which are divided UIG and BSUP. The details presented in Table 5.1 show that GHMC alone has constructed 64300 dwelling units out of 72390 sanctioned units, out of which 45945 units have been occupied by the beneficiaries. Under UIG, GHMC has also taken steps to improve the basic services amount to ₹ 2,40,632 lakhs. This shows that JNNURM has provided opportunities to state governments to take measures for implementation of welfare schemes for the poor, provide improved basic services to the poor by developing roads, providing electricity, improving transportation facilities and improving the sewerage and storm water drainage. With sanctioned budget under JNNURM and guaranteed central assistance to the states and ensuring beneficiary participation has opened up wide opportunities for the governments towards innovation and infrastructural development. Hence. Hypothesis-1 is tested and proved to be true as per the details presented in Table 5.1.

Hypothesis-II: The Mere increased funding without proper administrative delivery mechanisms does not automatically ensure improved infrastrue-tural services.

Under JNNURM, there is an allocated budget of Rs. 19.90 lakh crores towards Operation and Maintenance for better allocation of resources and timely completion of projects. Under BSUP, GHMC had constructed 64300 DUs out of which 45945 DUs were occupied. It is important to note that the remaining DUs were not occupied and the reasons cited by the respondents reveal that the delivery mechanism is not accurate as beneficiaries reveal that they faced challenges in mobilising funds (Table 5.21) and could not get loans through banks (Table 5.22). More importantly, the beneficiaries revealed that the quality of construction was not good (Table 5.24) as there were water leakages in building (Table 5.25) and other infrastructural facilities like water supply, drainage, roads, sanitation, street lights, and storm water drainage were not present (Table 5.26). Since, the dwelling units were constructed away from the cities, the beneficiaries did not find the houses useful as many reported that the location was far from schools, hospitals, etc (Table 5.27). Almost all the beneficiaries who participated in the study, reported that the construction quality and layout was not good and it was located away from the core and peripheral city. Moreover, the status of projects as mentioned under Table 5.1 wherein still 8000 DUs were left to be construction, around 20000 houses were unoccupied and under UIG, out of 22 sanctioned projects to GHMC, only 10 projects were completed as shown in Table 4.2 Considering the status of projects and opinion of beneficiaries, it is assumed that no matter how huge the budget is sanctioned for improving infrastruetural services, proper delivery mechanism is essential and the lack of it has resulted in incomplete projects and unoccupied dwelling units. Basing on this, the Hypotheses-It is found to be true as per the primary data, project status of UIG and BSUP in GHMC.

Hypothesis-III: The institutionalisation of urban reforms under the JNNURM has been poor which raise the questions of sustainability of reforms for improved urban governance.

The institutionalisation of urban reforms under JNNURM has been good considering that public participation was the core of the project. Under BSUP, the beneficiary share is around beneficiary share is around 30 percent and this has resulted in reduced participation from the people as they could not mobilise funds, either through banks or from private sources, While institutional development at central and state level was robust and enabled sanctioning of projects, the progress of the sanctioned projects reveals that the City level monitoring committee did not ensure the timely completion of projects, either in UIG or in BSUP, as many DUs and projects were still to be completed. Hence, it is understood that institutional setup under JNNURM at the city/ULB level does not ensure timely completion of the projects despite the steering committee making efforts to allocate funds to the state for improving the basic services and providing dwelling units to the identified beneficiaries. Hence, the Hypotheses-III is found to be true as institutionalisation of JNNURM at city/ULB level is poor due to which sustainability of programmes could not be achieved.

13. Recommendations and Suggestions

The development of cities is complex and continuing process. The cities can withstand the demands only when they implement the plan objectives through various development projects. The JNNURM has given the required push and it should be continued. The present study brought-out certain important findings which are discussed in the above paragraphs. In this section, certain broad suggestions and recommendations are given in the following to make urban development sustainable contributing to the national development on a wider scale.

(i) Infrustructure Development

Urban infrastructure development in the metropolitan cities like Hyderabad are really challenging to the governments and the urban institutions. Various projects are being implemented but their implementation has been suffering due various administrative factors like institutional backwardness, lack of inter-institutional linkages, inability to involve the private sector in a workable and effective manner, funding constraints, lack of citizen awareness and lack of political commitment to long term goals in a sustainable manner.

Some useful suggestions are given in the following towards improving the situation:

(1) Several projects are taken-up and some implemented and some in part. Still several areas are left like solid waste management, roads, etc. which should be given push in the next phase. The city especially needs a comprehensive drainage and sewerage system which should also get attention in future in the infrastructure front.

(2) The transportation projects are take-up in isolation by the GHMC and the RTC. Though strategies are discussed so many times, a comprehensive transportation programme has not been taken-up. Therefore, instead of preparing plans and strategies and reformulating again and again, concrete steps must be take-up on a

sustainable manner over longer period say 20 years without changing the broader vision strategy. This is essential because traffic and transportation plans and strategies have been discussed since long time: no concrete initiatives emerged till now.

(3) In India, most of the urban development projects are run parallel with least interlinkages. This has been the bane of urban development programme in India since Independence. Therefore, effective functional linkages across the stakeholder institutions must be established and maintained.

(4) Most of the projects suffer due to inability of the institutions to mobilise funds for implementation. The plans remain visions only if no concrete steps are taken to fund them. Innovative methods of mobilisation of funds should be taken-up as the traditional sources have dried-up. The concrete financial plans are to be devised and implemented in this respect.

(5) Political commitment to the programme and projects have been adhoc and change as the governments change. This has been the perennial issue in urban governance and development in India.

(6) The PPP approach must be implemented more effectively. Though certain administrative issues are being faced, they should be implemented with more commitment, innovative and partnership focus.

(ii) BSUP and Urban Housing

Urban poverty area has received much attention in India since Independence. But, in tune with the increasing urban poor, the problems continue to challenge the administrators. New slums are emerging every day and the demands are increasing ever. In this situation, increased efforts are needed to overcome the problems. The main areas are infrastructure development, civic service maintenance, employment and shelter and housing areas. The problems mainly concerns with lack of people's involvement and participation, poor quality housing delays in implementation, rehabilitation issues, developing employment opportunities and poor maintenance of services. The solutions regarding thc BSUP projects are lie in the problems themselves. The following suggestions are offered in this study.

(1) Though the poor maintenance of civic services common across urban areas in India, better maintenance of civic facilities and services in slum development projects becomes cssential to realise their goals not mere targets. Community level initiatives and participative methods will deliver better results rather than mere administrative interventions.

(2) Funding is a common problem in housing projects in India. Hence, finding viable methods to improve compliance of beneficiary contributions, providing alternate methods for funding, etc. may yield better results in slum areas.

(3) Poor quality of public housing in slum puts more financial burden on the urban poor. Therefore, improving the quality of construction of dwelling units by better control and monitoring mechanisms is essential.

(4) The study brought-out that local level participation of the slum dwellers has been poor. Earlier community development approach is to be reinforced to improve peoples' participation. In fact, the scope for community level participation is more in slum areas than in the better of areas in cities and towns. This is because the urban poor has become more aware in recent years and they only proper support system to bank-on.

(5) Identification of the beneficiaries has been reported as a big problem by the civic authorities. The reasons lie mostly in the background of the slum dweller. The slum dwellers may be seasonal migrants to cities and they maintain their identity in their native places. In slums also they try to maintain identity by obtaining cards like ration cards and voter identity cards. These people are highly mobile people in search of employment. Due to the family and employment problems and mobile nature, they identity is riddled with several administrative issues. Now, this problem could easily solved with the Aadhar Cards which are being linked various other cards including the bank accounts. The identity issue could be sorted-out with this. The other problem relating to identification is their poor economic conditions. This creates credibility problems for getting loans and other purposes. The government should come out with some solutions like relaxing the guarantee rules and making their different card systems integrated through digital processes. These actions could solve the identity problems and credibility issues.

(iii) Urban Reforms

Urban reforms are of recent origin in India which gained importance with the international funding and other borrowings. The loan based funding necessitated institutional reforms to their efficiencies and financial systems so that they become strong enough to obtain and manage loans. All the financial reforms like user cost recover, accounting, taxation, etc. started with this objective. The other set of reforms relate to governance aspects, The accountability, transparency and participation which are basic to the good governance concept, necessitated certain governance reforms like citizen charters, citizen grievance reddressal system, digitalisation of municipal operations, PPPs, etc. All these have become the reform agenda of the central government which are new linked to the urban development projects through the JNNURM.

Governance reforms in general in India are implemented very slowly due to adaptability and acceptability issues in the public organisation. The dangers of misuse also make the authorities to go slow. Urban reforms are no exception to these problems. The hesitation is visible in the way they are implemented and slow pace of progress. Some sections still believe that the reforms are unnecessary burden than instruments for changes and development. The institutional reluctance and adaptability issues appear to be the main causes for slow progress. There is therefore, need for changing this perspective of the governments and implementing institutions. Following suggestions are made to improve the implementation process of the urban reforms.

(1) At the outset the state authorities and institutions implementing the reforms must commit in spirit not mere formal commitment. In a federal system, each level government has autonomy but that should not make reform process casual making it ineffective. The committed action will make the implementation smoother.

(2) The adaptation problems are natural and they should be tackled with tact and patience.The easy going and old ways will not work. There should be concerted efforts by the authorities by mobilising the peoples' acceptability and timely corrective measures in identifying the problems and resolving them.

(3) As reform is a learning process, proper capacity building and training should be imparted to all the concerned officers periodically to up-date their skills and understanding.

(4) Sustainable efforts are needed to implement the reforms as the process of reform implementation is a long term initiative.

(5) Reform is innovative in approach and method. There is need for devising innovative methods to implement the reform objectives.

(6) Reforms under the new schemes namely, SMART City Programme and thc AMRUT programme. Efforts are made to make the reform process more focused for better and effective implementation. These reforms should be implemented with more focus and commitment.

To sum-up the discussion, the study clearly brought-out certain issues, problems and loopholes in the implementation of the JNNURM projects. JNNURM has longer and broad vision of developing the urban areas in a comprehensive and integrated manner. Now. the programme is remodeled under different nomenclature like SMART City and AMRUT. Though they have similar objectives and goals, etficient administration and effective response to the issues and urban problems appear to be the main focus. The main challenge here is mobilising the mindboggling investments needed to fund the mega projects in the mega cities like Hyderabad, The funding available under the centrally sponsored programmes though enhanced in recent years is to be supplemented by other funding mechanisms like accessing capital market, involving the private sector and increased allocations by the central and state governments for urban development. It is a positive trend to note that the GHMC is looking for alternate funding sources like capital market/borrowing and private sector involvement. It is hoped that the new programmes like the SMART City will continue the urban development momentum picked-up with JNNURM but with more focus, detcrmination and funding.

Notes

1. Corporate Office OPD (M&C) Wing Mushirabad. Hyderabad-500 624. Telangana State Road Transport Corporation. Lr. No. C2/10/(RTI)/2015-O PD(M&C), dated 09-10-2015.

Chapter - 5

Digital Library

1. Introduction

Philip Bell says that "The Internet is like an amazing library-except all the books have been thrown in the middle of the room".[1] Subject guides can be described as maps to library resources that fulfill the role of "an information locator for the library user whose search for recorded materials on a subject of interest is just beginning". Standard resources like online subject guides can be helpful for students, as these guides target the specific information need of the student by providing references to quality resources.

Through the use of subject guides, it is possible to link directly to online information. There is a vital necessity for identifying the sources to access the scholarly information and its logical organisation on Web. The present study involves identifying and organising the Web-based information resources on the subject Library and Information Science.

1.0 Background

Internet and its most used component World Wide Web (WWW) has turned into a biggest source of information with widest coverage and the fastest access. It is the most powerful rool for global communication and exchange of information. The amount of publicly available information on the web is increasing consistently at an unbelievable rate.

As per the World Internet statistics, http://www.internetworld stats.com/ Internet Usage and World Population Statistics as on June 30, 2010 shows the penetration percentage of population to be 28.7 percent. Internet usage in Asia as on 2010 is 21.5 percent with a growth of 621.8 percent between 2000 -2010. Out of which, in India itself the penetration of population is 6.9 percent and users growth is 1520.0 percent in between 2000 and 2010. These statistics reveal the impact and usage of internet.

The World Wide Web provides a seamless in formation space in the Internet. The Internet facilitates access to a large amount of electronic information. Index and search subsystems appeared hand in hand with the rapid growth in the amount of information and in the number of users having specific needs.

It has revolutionised the way that people access information, and has opened up new possibilities in areas such as digital libraries, information dissemination and retrieval, education, commerce, entertainment, government and health care.

The World Wide Web can be a great place to accomplish research on many topics but finding quality web materials and using them to our requirement can be challenging.

It is because putting documents or pages on the web is easy, cheap or free, unregulated, and unmonitored. It is a self-publishing medium, that is, anyone can publish anything. This means that not everything one finds on the Web is equally valuable or reliable.

Data (lowest abstract or a raw input) is processed to information (arranged to make meaningful output or observations of data"are done) which can be text, numeric, audio, video, image or a mixture (multimedia) and stored in a File (A piece of information stored) on a computer disk to transfer from one location to any other electronic means via telecommunications (both analog and digital communications occurring via modem over a telephone line).

The Original information (Primary source such as Statistics; Research articles, Blogs, Websites) its interpretation or analysis (Secondary sources such as Textbooks, Review articles) and a tool in understanding and locating in formation (Tertiary sources such as Databases. Subject Gateways, Dictionaries, Bibliographies) is allowed for intense long-distance exchanges between larger numbers of people through internet on Web with modern communication medium.

Information sources are primary sources of information, usually in the form of publications, such as journals, reports, and newsletters, meetings, conference proceedings, and trade publications which present and report information.

In the Web environment along with the text form of medium for the transfer and storage of information, the other media like audio, video and image are also used.

In the Internet era, the Primary sources or Information sources also include Blogs, You_tube, facebook, posters, podcasts, discussion forums, e-newsletters, listservs, e-joumals, Proceedings of conferences, records of organizations and associations.

Information resources generally organize information and facilitate retrieval or retrospective access to information, data and documents. Informations resources may include: abstracting and indexing services; bibliographic, factual and numeric-type databases; directories; catalogs; dictionaries; libraries and information centers. Information resources on the Web are Web OPAC, e-books, online dictionaries and Webliographies, websites and search engines also form the secondary sources of information.

One can always use more and better information sources. If there is too much information available, for anyone to effectively acquire and assimilate, information resources are important.

Secondary sources, notably abstracting and indexing publications and bibliographic databases, are information resources routinely organizing and summarizing information about information sources and their contents.

Information Sources are 'Where one gets things from while Information resources are "the things one can get from the sources."

Information sources form indispensable resources for any study and research activity. Therefore, every student, scholar, teacher and researcher depends on information sources such as books, journals, newspapers, conference proceedings etc. As the subject develops the literature and its access posed several issues in the pre-internet era. With the advent of Internet there is a wide range of resources available through the World Wide Web, the service of Internet, in every field of study. Library and Information science is not an exception for this.

As the growing field of study, Web-based information resources are abundantly available in the field of Library and Information science. A crude search of webbased resources with the help of search engine Google.com (http:// www.google.com) gives rise to about 48,000,000 results.

Another search category Yahoo.com (http://www.yahoo.com) gave rise to 120,000,000 results.

Another search category Alltheweb.com (http://www.alltheweb.com) gave rise to 122,000,000 results.

A search was also carried out using Meta-search engines, which allow submitting a search query to several search engines at once and then returning the results in a single listing, to know the web resources available in the field of Library and Information science. The results for few different Meta-search engines are as follows:

Search.com (http ://www.search.com./) gave 8,610,010 results.

ixQuick.com (http://www.ixQuick.com./) gave 137,999,824 matching results.

Dogpile.com (http ://www.dofpile.com) gave 2,310,000 results.

Whereas the search engine, Bing.com (http ://www.bing.com/) retrieved 73,700,000 results when tried to retrieve the web resources on 'Library and Information Science'.

And the Google Scholar (http:// www. scholar.google.com), a way to search for scholarly literature, also retrieved 28,90,000 results.

The above indicates that in the wilderness of web resources using powerful searching also denoted that there are enumerable web resources in Library and Information science. Then arise a question, whether all these are relevant and precise web resources to shoot the needs of the users?

The search from specific subject gateway, the Oxford Libraries Internet gateway, (http://www.bodleien.ox.ac.uk). an integrated library service of the Universiry of Oxford, for the Library, and Information science web resources retrieved about 1130 matching results; however access to these libraries is restricted. This site offers collections and services tailored to the needs of members of their respective colleges.

Many of the universities are having in their homepages are linking to their library websites and providing on line services through web OPAC's and giving links to the collections of various online resources useful to their clientele, but the access is restricted.

Most information consumers are not aware of, nor do they use, most electronic information resources. The results confirm, too, that the majority of information seekers are not making much use of the array of electronic resources (online magazines, databases and reference assistance, for example) that are available to their communities. Very few respondents use such resources regularly and the majority of respondents are not aware that they have these electronic resources.

King et al.(2003) in their study "Patterns of Journal Use by Faculty at *Three Diverse Utiersities"* observed that the faculty use the electronic collections much more than print, partly because of convenience and time savings. They have surveyed the readership at three universities with different levels of electronic journal implementation demonstrate how transition to electronic journal collections affects use patterns of faculty and staff. The survey was carried on three diverse universities, The University of Tennessee, The University of Pittsburgh and the Drexel University. The study revealed that the Drexel University had migrated to nearly all electronic journals (2002) and the University of Pittsburgh had acquired a large electronic journal collection, but with some duplication with print journals (2003).

OCLC, 2005, survey on *"Perceptions of Libraries and Information Resources"* revealed that 'the main purpose of a Library' according to a 23-year-old from the United States as a place "To gather as much literature and information as possible in one place, and to share that wealth of resources with that community. It is important to have a place where anyone can go to learn (be it news, research, films and music, fiction, or non-fiction". Whereas a 56-year-old from England feels the main purpose of a library as "To provide information on global issues from born past and present and offer usable in formation/ observations as to the possible future of all things". While a 71-year-old from the United States felt that "The internet has now put all the libraries of the world [at] your fingertips".

The OCLC Library & Information Center compiled data comparing current output, or current activity, with projections for 2007. The data was drawn from a wide range of sources principally from the developed world: traditional paperbased resources, full-text journal articles, respected Web sites, and personal correspondence with industry experts. The goal was to analyze worldwide trends and review the overarching information trends. The analysis looked at recent research into Web use. Recent research indicates that information seekers begin with the Web.[2]

Choice- According to the Pew Internet and American Life Project, most Internet users and some non-users expect to find reliable information online; most find the information they seek; and many now turn to the Internet first.[3]

Seven of Ten U.S. College students say they are successful at finding what they seek most of the time. Their first-choice web resources are search engines, web portals and course-specific websites.[4]

People from all walks of life use the Internet. E-mail is the first most popular Internet based application while searching for information on the Web is the second most popular activities in all the Web-based applications.

On the Briggs Library Research Guide the following statement appears: "Information is Power". Laribee considers information as an asset that should be managed rigorouslys. Information, defined as knowledge in communicable form, is recognized today as one of the main requirements for development. Indeed the ability to record and use data, information and knowledge is one of the most important human characteristics." - Unesco / PGl. Therefore, Information is some meaningful message must be transmitted from source to users. In this process information may be stored in information products and systems organised for providing a memory in numerical, sound and image forms. Information may also be communicated through interpersonal channels. The source may be documentary material, institutions or people.[6]

Bhat and Sampath Kumar (2008) in their study on 'Web citation behaviour in scholars electronic journals in the field of library and irformation science" analysed the extent to which scholars are using web-based sources in scholarly electronic journals. Results of the study shows that 81.49 percent of articles in the area of Library and Information science published in selected 9 electronic journals during 2000-2006 have web references. Out of 25,730 references 43.52 percent of references are web references.

Chowdhury, G.G. and Chowdhury, Sudatta (2007) stressed that the rapid development of the Internet, Web, and digital libraries necessitate the teaching of fundamental concepts, tools, and techniques of information organisation. In their book, Organizing Information from the Shelf to the Web, they attempt to cover the broad spectrum of information organisation in different environments—from print libraries to the internet, intranet, and web".[7]

The Web has enabled users to electronically publish information accessible relatively easy, but as the quantity of information grows, the ability of users to find relevant information becomes difficult. If a user is looking for a particular piece of information, there is a good chance that this informacion is stored somewhere in the Web. However, it is difficult to discover the location and the way in which the information is provided.

A Web page has a similar format to a page from a book or magazine, with text and graphics displayed in a layout, and is displayed in a normal computer application window. A Web page is a collection of information, consisting of one or more Web resources intended to be rendered as a single unit. Web pages are written in the HTML language and sent to Web browsers by a Web server using the HTTP protocol. There are billions of Web pages in existence on the Internet. Web pages have been published on almost every subject imaginable by almost every type of person and organisation.

In a Web-based environment, a user can navigate from a source page to the destination page through the hyperlink. If the destination page also has a hyperlink in it, the user can then navigate to another destination page, and so on. In usual, there are many hyperlinks in a source page.

Web search engines utilize robot-created databases of the Web. They are computer generated, therefore, not subjected to evaluation and quality control. They cover a far greater number of sites. Search engines enable to search across the Web using specific keywords. They provide the users with a large body of results by a 'click'.

Web searches reflect a diverse set of underlying user goals. Search methodology is often based on " trial and error" and is usually undertaken with no particular strategy. Liao[8] (2008) argues that we are facing information deluge on the Web and spend much time and effort examining the results provided by a search engine because search engines function with limited knowledge about users' preferences and search histories. Search engines help to retrieve digital information represented in a wide range of formats such as text, audio, video, data, and simulations. In this new information environment, users are no longer simply reading or printing information but instead are engaged in more complex processes such as reviewing, selecting, linking, downloading, installing, annotating, interpreting, and saving in a citation database.

Search engines are the only tool that attempt to index the whole Internet. A search engine sends out an automated program (called a robot, a spider, or a crawler) that goes around on the Internet and brings back information. The Internet is gigantic. There is simply no single search tool that searches through all of it. And search engines are updated at different rates.

In order to exploit the flood of information, sophisticated search facilities are needed which convert the outpouring of electronic data coming from numerous sources into real knowledge. From this knowledge a whole range of users will benefit. If a user is looking for a particular piece of information, there is a good chance that this information is stored somewhere in the Worldwide Web. However, it is difficult to discover the location and the way in which the information is provided. Since search forms or other discovery tools are developed independently, interoperability is difficult to achieve. In many cases, a user must contact more than one source to reach the final destination where the answer to his/her question can be found.

Web-based resources are rapidly becoming the user-preferred method of access to scholarly information. This being the state of preferredness, there is a need to identify and organize subject specific web-based information resources which are scattered over the Internet at one place. The formats of information resources are also more. Web provides information resources in text, audio, video and image forms and many a times a mixture of all the above. This is facilitating and creating more interest to the patrons.

Professionals and researchers all over the world have embraced the scholarly publication revolution from various disciplines, to which library and information science is no exception.

Library and information science began with the first effort to organize a collection of information and provide access to that information. In more recent years, with the growth of digital technology, the field has been greatly influenced by information science concepts.

Therefore, this research is taken up to identify Web-based information resources in Library and Information Science in all the possible forms in variety of formats and to organize them.

1.1 Significance of the Study

The Web is the most influential and important technologies of this century. Publishing huge amounts of information on the World Wide Web and proliferation of electronic information resources in a number of formats has posed several challenges in retrieving the right information. The Web is a bank of information. The Web exists for users. The very powerful added value of the Web is that users can access resources online electronically. The Web provides information and makes it online accessible, so that it can be used for all sorts of reasons: education, creative recreation, improvement of the economy, support for literacy, life long learning, cultural enrichment etc. The outcome of this use is the betterment of the individual and the community in which he lives. So, the Web resources are for use.

Previous user studies on 'how to obtain information from online information systems such as electronic journals' have indicated that people are well favored to the general concept of electronic resources. Characteristics such as speed of searching and printing, benefits of simultaneous access, and the fact that users can work from home having 24-hour access to resources are some of the main reasons why users enjoy using electronic resources. However, users adopt relatively unsophisticated, simplistic approach to searching, where browse facilities are used more occasionally than search. They tend to use single keywords and rarely use Boolean operators. Users want fast and easy access to information without being required to memorize usernames and password,s in order to use an online information system.

If a Web resource is not readily discovered and retrieved by the user, a frustrated user may miss the knowledge of the needed Web resource's existence. The Web resource may remain invisible indefinitely.

Need of the Present Study

Internet search engines tried to solve the information retrieval focusing on machine-oriented approach. Accessing the required information from all the available sources was not possible through the search engines. This statement has been supported by findings of several research studies.

Search procedure on the Web is a complex course of action particularly for those who are gathering information about a specific topic in a comprehensive approach.

Even though the required information exists on the Web, the user may not find it because of

The following reasons:

- The abilities of current search facilities are not sufficient to locate the information needed.
- The users' search experience is limited and she does not utilize the existing search facilities probably.
- The users' knowledge domain is limited and she does not use the correct *search term* to search.

Users expect to find everything full-text on the Web immediately. Information is abundant; attention is scarce: As resources, tools, and environments proliferate so does the attention available for any single one of them decline.

Therefore, if an experienced or trained person had searched for his given information she could found out.

To help users to find resources that are topically related, a well-organized and more categorized arrangement of various Web resources at one place with a correct link to Web resource, will match every Web resource its user. Therefore, the concern is towards human-oriented approach as another way to improve the access of desired information.

A number of studies have been conducted on the growth of library and information science literature. A study conducted by Bottle and Efthimiadis (1984) investigated the sampling issues of LISA (Library and Information Science Abstract, ISA (Information Science Abstracts, RZI (Referativnyi Zburnal Informatics Abstracts, BS (Bulletin Signaletique) and CCA (Computer & Control Abstracts) for the year 1983. The study clearly indicated that literature coveragc in the field of library and information science has increased dramatically.

One more study by He and Wang (2006) quantitatively analyzes the research activity in the area of Chinese Library and Information Science (LIS) from 1975 to 2004, based on Social Sciences Citation Index (SSCI). Results show that there are increases in the quality of publishing channels.

Ali (1985) provides an overall picture of growth of librarianship and information science literature (academic research and practitioner's literature) and various outlets available for reporting research findings, with special emphasis on United States and Great Britain. Another study by

Sharma (1999) reveals that Asian countries have been very active in publishing books and journals in the field of library and information science. The study deals with the development of Asian library journals with an emphasis on South Asia.[10]

Zahid Ashraf Wani (2008) study established that the growth of publication channels in the field of library and information science is increasing. The growth of library and information science literature is at a good pace. Developed countries are contributing a largc chunk of literature through various types of publications. Developing countries like India have also made laudable contributions to library and information science literature. The chronological study indicates that library and information science literature has been expanding its subject boundaries. Most noticeably is its extensive coverage of IT-related services since 1980. The maturity of the scientific aspect of the library science discipline has helped in increasing the literary output in the field o f library and information science. Further more, the countries with a well established tradition in the field of LIS are showing an explosive growth in the LIS literature. Literature is making itself available in different forms[11].

Taler, Izabella (2008) examined the landscape of online LIS published during 2000-2007 in his study *"LIS Open Access. E-Jounal-where are you?"*. The starting publications dates of each of the thirty-one e -journals that were established in the 21st century are analyzed. His studied showed an increase in the number of LIS e-journals significantly.

Dwived and Verma (2007) in their study on *'Web Information Retrieval: Exploring new dimensions with word sense disambiguation [WSD] for naive users"* felt the necessity of alternate methods to search engines to improve the performance of the information retrieval on the web. The study identified that the web is a massive collection of static and dynamic pages and the practical situations of web information retrieval do not portray a positive image. The naive users did not get what they actually desire. The information that is stored on the web is unstructured and finding the absolute information is a difficult job for the naive users.

Safari (2004) in his study *"Metadata and the Web"* has emphasized the inappropriateness of traditional schemes of resource description for web resources. The rapid increase in the number and variety of resources on the World Wide Web has made the problem of resource description and discovery. He felt the necessity to structure the contents of the web and consequently to enhance its effectiveness.

The subject gateways emerged in response to the challenge of 'resource discovery' in a rapidly developing Internet environment in the early and midnineties. The subject gateways began operations in 1995.

The present information era has also brought about a radical alteration in the output of library and in formation science literature. There has been a marked increase in the growth and output of literature in LIS. The growth of published literature plays a vital role in the development of any discipline or subject field.

There is a conviction that the effective use of information resources in learning and research depended on its access and discovery.

Dempsey, Lorcan (2000) feels that there is a need to provide managed collections of resources, supported by effective resource description and subject access, available for browse and search access. This is expected to give shape and definition to an information space in a particular subject area . The aim is to save the time of their users, to connect them to resources which support their learning, teaching and research interests, and to make sure that information abour useful resources was effectively disclosed[12].

In view of this a study on "Web-based information resources in Library and Information Science: a study" will be a significant one, that may explore the various information resources available in various forms in Library and Information Science on web.

Further, the literature review presented in Chapter 2 reveals that so far there is no study carried in this area. Therefore, the study is carried out with the following Statement of the Problem.

1.2 Statement of the Problem

"Web-based information resources in Library and In formation Science; a study".

1.3 Operational Definitions of the Terms Used in the Statement

Web: The web is an abstract (imaginary) space of information. On the web the connections are hypertext links. Hypertext is the ability to have web pages containing links, which are areas in a page or buttons or graphics on which one can click a mouse button to retrieve another document into the computer. The web contains information beyond plain text, including sounds, images and video. For its resemblance to a spider's construction, this world is called the 'web'.

The web exists because of programs which communicate between computers on the internet.

Web-based: In a Web-based environment on Internet, a user can navigate from a source page to the destination page through the hyperlink. If the destination page also has a hyperlink in it, the user can then navigate to another destination page, and soon. Generally, there are many hyperlinks in a source page.

Information: Dictionary definitions on Information range in scope. Merriam Webster defines it as "facts or detail" and Xrefer as "data, common knowledge, general knowledge, know-how, skill and aptitude". X refer online defines data as collections of more or less isolated facts, whereas Information is "data with a shape and a potential use, or conclusions drawn from data".

According to Belkin, 'Information is a process of social communication among human beings'. According to Daniel Bell, 'Information is the accumulation or collection of processed data'. Therefore, Information is a synergetic resource and shareable. The nature of information is that it is an element of a knowledge spectrum. Information is an important input or basic resource and link between a variety of activities, intellectual and material in the society. The information could be in any form, audio, textual, video and may be obtained from a variety of sources.

Resource: A resource is a means or supply of ability. According to the Concise Oxford dictionary, 'Resource means supplying what is needed, the stock that can be drawn, available assets which a person or country can use'. A resource is an asset. It can be a material, finance, real estate, forest wealth, water wealth, power or any machinery.

Information resource: Kaniki (1995) defines an information resource as 'a space or building in which human and other information resources in a variety of media are arranged or made accessible in an appropriate manner'. The information resource is a source may be library / book / person / e-book / web page, with specific information for a certain target group. Information resources are generally designed to provide support for a specific group of users in a given content area (Milheim & Harvey, 1998). Khosrowpur & Yaverbaum consider an information resource to be a resource consisting of various forms of data (text, image and voice) that can be disseminated through different systems, i.e., communication systems like the Internet.

Information resource is an electronic resource in which Information (usually a file) is stored in the form of electrical signals, usually on a computer. This Information is made available on the Internet. An information resource is identified by a Uniform Resource Identifier (URI) or a Universal Resource Locator (URL) and may be a Web page, an image, a video or other piece of content. Hyperlinks present in resources enable users to easily navigate their browsers to related resources.

Library and Information Science: Wikipedia defines Library Science or Library and Information Science (LIS) as an interdisciplinary field that applies the practices, perspectives, and tools of management, information technology, education, and other areas to libraries; the collection, organisation, preservation, and dissemination of information resources.

Library Science includes how information resources are organised to serve the needs of select user groups, how people interact with classification systems and technology, how information is acquired, evaluated and applied by people in and outside of libraries as well as cross-culturally, how people are trained and educated for careers in libraries. There is no generally agreed distinction between the terms library science, librarianship, library and information science. LIS can also be seen as an integration of the two fields library science and information science.

5.1 Library and Information Science Digital Library

FINDINGS

1. The Worldwide Web is a HYPERMEDIA. Hypermedia is used as a logical extension of the term hypertext in which graphics, audio, video, plain text and hyperlinks interlink to create a generally non-linear medium of information.
2. The 21st Century Library is a HYPERMEDIA DIGITAL LIBRARY. Hypermedia Digital library is a database, storing data of different type (text, static and moving (video) images, animation, audio or other media), which is structured in a way to allow easy manipulation and use.
3. Web technologies help organizing hypermedia digital libraries by providing a means to structure and present them in a hypermedia manner. Users are allowed to quickly move across subject-related topics in a non-linear way. These topics may include sets of objects, such as text, images, audio and other media, which relate to one another via hyperlinks.
4. Skills are required to find and retrieve information effectively from WWW The skills required to achieve the maximum potential of electronic resources are much greater than those required for searching printed sources.

   These skills include knowledge of the structure of the database, the instructions that the searcher must enter into the computer, and an understanding of the ways these instructions are linked to one another.

5. In the global information communications technology (ICT)-dominated world, "The impact of moving from text-based to resource-based learning has involved heavier use of library materials and a demand for more and varied media sources".
6. Electronic resources greatly increase access to information. E-resources provide access to a wide range of information in various formats and types modern libraries provide a strong link between the highly technological information environment and the users, advising on search strategies that help the user to focus the topic better and evaluate the information even as the user is able to access library catalogs and databases from home, office, or anywhere.
7. Philip Bell says that "The Internet is like an amazing library-except all the books have been thrown in the middle of the roorn".[1] Subject guides can be described as maps to library resources that fulfill the role of "an information locator for the library user whose search for recorded materials on a subject of interest is just beginning". Standard resources like online subject guides can be helpful for students, as these guides target the specific information need of the student by providing references to quality resources.

   Through the use of subject guides, it is possible to link directly to online information that has been picked by subject specialists at the library.
8. WWW as Information Resource. Web has all the information related to Library and Information Science but is scattered in various types of sources in various formats. Web provides access to Web-based information resources such as e-books, e-jourals, reference sources, e-newsletters, e-mail discussion groups, forums related to Library and Information Science which are distributed graphical.

   Web gives information about various LIS associations around the world and updates about the information regarding the Conference and Seminars. One who is interested in pursuing the LIS education can get the details about the universities all over the world along with the courses they are offering. Distance education and continuation of education is also possible through web-based material available through audio, video, podcasting and webinar options. This proves the Hypothesis No.1 of the study to be true, which states that Web is global information resource that hosts information resources on all subjects including Library and Information Science.

9. The internet is the largest global collection of information, but "this collection of information is not as well organised as it should or will be". There is no one system that classifies and organises all the information on the internet. The Web is a complex construct for both information transfer and as a repository of information content. The Web represents an information source but it is not a library of those information resources. Information on the Web has no evaluation criteria. Anyone can publish anything on the Web. The Web as a whole may not be organised to the degree to meet the standard of a library.

José-Marie Griffiths (1998) offers a four-point argument against the Web as library:

- despite appearances to the contrary, the Web does not offer access to all information;
- the Web lacks authority and quality control;
- the Web is inadequately catalogued;
- Web search interfaces and other tools are ineffective and simplistic.

In a library, which is a collection of sources, resources and services are organised for use. The information in libraries is organized and categorized so as to enable the patrons to locate the desired information under the Library of Congress or Dewey Decimal System or any scheme of Classification. The Web has no system for organisation and consistency. The refore, the Web is not a library but Web pages and Websites can be collected and categorised selected from the Web. This finding disapproves the Hypothesis 2 of the study.

10. Questia is the first online library that provides 24/ 7 access to the world's largest online collection of books and journal articles in the humanities and social sciences, plus magazine and newspaper articles. One can search each and every word of all of the books and journal articles in the collection. One can read every title cover to cover. This rich, scholarly content — selected by professional collection development librarians.

To complement the library, Questria offers a range of search, note-taking, and writing tools. These tools help students locate the most relevant information on their topics quickly, quote and cite correctly, and create properly formatted footnotes and bibliographies automatically. Questia provides a comprehensive research environment to meet students' academic needs.

11. My Library offers libraries a single source for content hosting, archiving, discovery, access and purchasing. With access to nearly 250,000 e-book titles and adding 5,000 new titles per month, My Library is the fastest-growing and most comprehensive online e-content platform on the market today.

No proprietary e-book reader is required. The MyiLibrary platform integrates easily into OPAC systems for easy searching alongside other information resources.

12. WorldCat (the OCLC Online Union Catalog) is the World's largest bibliographic utility, representing content held by libraries all over the world.

WorldCat is dedicated to offering access to the widest possible range of resources. One can search for any collection and the collections of many other libraries worldwide using WorldCat, the world's largest network of library-based content and services.

WorldCat has a global reach; it is possible to see information about our collections and links to our services up front. Everything one needs is displayed right within the WorldCat record, including location and availability information for the item, and prominent button links to reserve or request an item or directly view electronic content such as the full text of an article.

13.Web not only facilitates electronic information resources but also provides information resources necessary for procuring the Printed material in the libraries. **Google Books** (previously known as Google Book Search and Google Print) is an excellent service from Google that searches the full text of books that Google has scanned, converted to text using optical character recognition, and stored in its digital database. FetchBook. Info is a free service aimed to provide the best shopping tools for librarians. Every book price comparison is done in real time and scans 145 book stores. High Beam Research is your one-stop resource for book reviews.

14. Libdex is a searchable Worldwide Online directory of libraries homepages across the World. Its Web-based OPAC's, Friends of the Library homepages maintained by Peter Scott of the University of Saskatchewan Library is an Library Index. **Information and Library Network (INFLIBNET)** Centre is an Autonomous Inter-University Centre (IUC) of University Grants Commission (UGC) involved in creating infrastructure for sharing of library and information resources and services among Academic and Research Institutions in India.

15. Web 2.0 is increasingly entering the field of Library and Information Science. It is a new way for searching the Web in a collaborative and interactive way. **Web 2.0** encourages users to become more involved in the creation and manipulation of the data. With the advent of these new "2.0" technologies in the library world, the mechanisms for social interaction and the dissemination of information has changed.

16. Library 2.0 constantly makes changes to encourage user participation and reaching out to users in ever changing and innovative ways. Innovation include incorporating Web 2.0 tools as online reference, IM chat, bookmarking, tagging, and rating systems into a library website. In Library 2.0, users can tag the library's collection and thereby participate in the cataloging process. A full-featured Library 2.0 OPAC makes the users to involve in the process of interacting with the catalog and sharing content. This shows the change of flow of information from the user back to the library.

17. RSS gives the users the updates of the 'subscribed' interested information as soon as it is available on the Web. Therefore, there is no need of searching and checking the web for the updates in the users' interest area. **LibWorm** is a professional development tool and a current awareness tool for library and information professionals and to those who care about libraries.

18. Podcasting is a communication enabler, reaching out to a wider community. Podcast is an Information tool. Podcasting usage provides lifelong education opportunity. Podcasting is a new and exciting format: Integration into classroom assignments Publish it online. Every group member can take part in projects. It creates a culture of knowledge-sharing and interdisciplinary collaboration.[3] A webinar is a collaborative web conference and provides question and answer sessions to allow full participation between the audience and the presenter.

19. YouTube videos are very useful to students of Library and Information Science as well as to those who are interested in the subject. The visual medium being the powerful medium of Communication. The lessons are recorded and produced by reputed institutions so, they are reliable and authentic in source. These videos can be played as many times as they want till they get the subject digested.

20. Blogdigger is a search engine for RSS and blogs. LISZEN is a library and information science blog search engine. There are many blogs on web which update the current information that it useful to LIS community such as providing information about Indian Library and Information Science Book Reviews, 'the future of library cataloging and metadata creation'. There are many LIS blogs which are offer information to the students of LIS regarding Admission Notification and lessons for Courses in Library and Information Science (LIS) and also inform them regarding Upcoming

Seminars, Conferences, Workshops and Refresher Courses in Library and Information Science (LIS) in India. OEDb, the Online Education Database has a blog.

21. A library wiki as a service can enable social interaction among librarians and patrons, essentially moving the study group room online. Wikiversity is a community effort to learn and facilitate others' learning.

22.Twitter is a rich source of instantly updated information. Twitter is useful in talking and hearing from the users and helps as Announcement channel. While MySpace and FaceBook enable users to share themselves with one another. Delicio.us enables users to share Web resources.

Library Thing enables users to catalog their books and view what other users are reading. LibraryThing enables users to recommend books to one another simply by viewing one another's collections. It also enables them to communicate through blog, and "tag" their books. This proves the Hypothesis 3 of the study that the change in information environment from print to electronic has impact on collection tools, techniques and approaches in Libraries.

23. Library 2.0 is a mashup. It is a hybrid of blogs, wikis, streaming media, content aggregators, instant messaging, and social networks. Library 2.0 remembers a user when they log in. It allows the user to edit OPAC data and metadata, saves the user's tags, IM conversations with librarians, wiki entries with other users (and catalogs all of these for others to use), and the user is able to make all or part of their profile public; users can see what other users have similar items checked-out, borrow and lend tags, and a giant user-driven catalog is created and mashed with the traditional catalog.

24. In the past the information flow was mostly one way, from library to user. With new Web 2.0 tools in formation can be released to flow in every direction (library to user, user to library, library to library, and user to user). The heart of Library 2.0 is user-centered change. It is a model for library service that encourages constant and purposeful change, inviting user participation in the creation of both the physical and the virtual services they want, supported by consistently evaluating services. It also attempts to reach new users and better serve current ones through improved user-driven offerings. Each component by itself is a step toward better serving our users. Stephens believes that "Library 2.0 will be a meeting place, online or in the physical world, where [library users'] needs will be fulfilled through entertainment, information, and the ability to create [their] own stuff to contribute to the ocean of content out there". This finding proves the Hypothesis 4 of the study that Web has changed the flow of information in Libraries.

25. The openness of Library 2.0 extends to the software and hardware that libraries use, including integrated library systems (ILS). Modifiable automation systems and catalogs are preferable to proprietary, closed systems.

Some examples of this are Aigaion, ERAMS (e-resource access and management services), refbase, RefAware, and Library World.

Conclusions

In this era of information technology, the digital library is the need of the hour and can play a vital role to enhance research and development in the country.

Digital libraries, including Web-based collections, are redefining both the role of electronic in formation storage and retrieval as well as the role of traditional libraries. Digital libraries include collections of books, journal articles, graphics, audio and video podcasts, and other material in digital format; collections of electronic content. To be a library, that collection should be organised according to some standard, and then the Web can be seen as an extension of and as a tool for libraries. Web-based information resources have great role to play in Libraries as research tools.

In fact, no library can ever fully meet the "access to all information" test. The Web can be organised, collected, and managed. Libraries, necessarily digital libraries, can be and are constructed from Web resources.

As information multiplies and becomes readily available in a range of formats, users are becoming more confused over which types of resources are acceptable. In order to meet this changing demand, the services of librarians are required to help to navigate the information. The duties of librarians are changing; librarians are, indeed, needed more than ever to assist in these new endeavors. No longer are librarians just keepers of the books. Librarians must be professionals who are knowledgeable and proactive in reaching out to their patrons in a responsible way. Library and information professionals need to be well-versed with the online information world and its new technologies.

The infrastructure of the libraries also must change with change in information environment. Modern libraries must have multimedia computers and high speed internet connection in order to facilitate the hybrid information available in web resources such as e-text, audio, video and graphics.

There have been a number of approaches and proposals to categorize, index, and catalogue the Web. One of the more important is Dublin Core, a major and comprehensive effort to describe Web resources. The Dublin

Core elements list and semantic headers represent a loosely constructed thesaurus in which index terms are author supplied.

Very recently, from the beginning of July 2010, OCLC has transitioned its OAlster database to being included in WorldCat and they are transitioning metadata harvesting to the WorldCat Digital Collection Gateway.These changes offer several advantages for repository managers.

Future Study

Web-based information resources in libraries are very recent incorporated. E-journals are being used froms last 5 years but the other forms of resources are new to libraries and its users. So, the utility and evaluation of these are not involved in this study.

The collection and organisation of web resources in libraries in the subject area of Library and Information Science are only covered in the present study. Web preservation is not covered. This is the upcoming problem involved with web resources. Exhaustive study is necessary in this direction.

Future study after a period of time can be done in this direction.

5.2 Housing Policy and Programmes in Urban Bhopal : A study in Social and Environmental change.

The State of Madhya Pradesh lies in the very heart of India, The State is located mainly on the table-land of India. Initially the manpower in the state is not well educated and not so skilled when compared with other states in India. Moreover the increase of people to the existing unskilled and uneducated manpower really pulls back the rate of economic growth and overall development.

After independence, India has seen four decades of planned economic development with the basic aim of growth with social justice. It was envisaged that an egalitarian society would be established and hunger, want and oppression will be totally eliminated from our society. A considerable section of our society who particularly shifted from villages to cities in pursuit of employment still remains homeless.

In India there are social, political and economic injustices galore. The glaring inequalities, the shocking ill-treatment and denial of fundamental rights and even elementary justice to millions leave them without hope or any certainty of getting two square meals daily, not to talk of assured shelter of some kind and minimum clothing or of reasonable opportunities for earning their livelihood and living with dignity and privacy. Previously the National Front Government has declared 1990-91 as the year of Social justice. It is no matter how much progress has been achieved in this line.

About half a century ago, Bhopal was an unpromising town. Its prosperity shot up when it became the capital of Madhya Pradesh in 1956. With the addition of a Railway Coach Factory, the establishment of the Forest Management Institute and other such big organisations and institutions the population of Bhopal is likely to go upto 15 lakhs by 2000 A.D. According to 1991 census Bhopal has become the Second big city in Madhya Pradesh with a population of 10,63,662 persons.

In 1959-60 Arera colony was partly barren and mostly agricultural land. The first bungalow was constructed in Arera Colony by Late Mr. R.C. Murah an retired I.A.S. Officer. At that time it was a lone house in the entire area. Formerly, it was known is Pensioners Paradise, but now several big business magnets have constructed palacial bungalows in ultra-modern designs with advanced facilities.

There are many reasons for the fabulous progress of Bhopal city once famous for Shikar and Hockey play. As the capital city of the city of the state, it has attracted traders from the neighbouring states and Delhi specially. There are at least more than 50,000 Maharashtrians, 20,000 Malayalees, and Tamilians permanently settled in Bhopal providing skilled, unskilled labour besides government and private employment. The salubrious climate of the city, which is next to Pachmarhi, indiced the majority of retired persons to settle down in Bhopal, not only helping their offspring's to get higher eduction but also suitable employment.

The basic concept of the constitution of India is to provide a good set up under which social justice is assured, exploitation of poorer sections of society eliminated and the economic condition of the masses improved so as to promote equality and prevent imbalances. Article 36 of the Constitution says that the State shall strive to promote the welfare of the people by securing and protecting as effectively as it may, a social order in which justice, social, economic and political shall inform all the institutions of national life. Clause 2 of the Articles 38 further requires the states to strive in particular for minimizing the inequalities in income and eneavour to eliminate inequalities in status, facilities and opportunities, not only among individuals but also among groups of people residing in different areas or engaged in different vocations.

Shelter is a basic human need. Most human settlements in urban areas reflect poverty and squalor. Population and the aspirations of families are ever increasing, to ensure the dignity of the individual and preserve the living standard of the essential. In terms of the quality and quantity the gap between supply and demand in the housing sector in urban areas has ever been widening. If there are 100 million houseless families in the world,

India has about 23 million families without any shelter. This will grow to an alarming tune by the turn of the century.

The housing scene is rather alarming with a backlog of 7 million houses in urban areas. By the year 2001 the figure is expected to shoot up to 16 million houses in cities and towns. This is mainly due to the rapid industrialisation and heavy influx of population from rural areas to cities. It is also due to population growth, break-up of joint family system and above all a general lack of housing standards.

The present housing scenario of India shows that 23 lakh people are not having any house and 572 lakh people live in slums and more than 50 per cent of the housed wellers live in congested and one room accommodations. This is really a sorrowful picture that even after a lapse of 41 years of plans in the country, the housing sector is not getting its due priority and significance. On the contrary investment in housing sector as a proportion of total budget under the Five Year Plans has been gradually declining. In the First Five Year Plan (1951-56) investment in housing was 1,150 crore rupees formed 34 per cent of the total outlay. No doubt over the successive plans the investment in housing in absolute terms has been increasing but as a proportion of the total plan outlays it has been shrinking from plan to plan. In the Seventh Five Year Plan (1985-90) the investment in housing was Rs. 31,458 crore which was only 9 percent of the total budget outlay.

The national housing scenario appears even bleaker in the light of the haphazard and unplanned growth in the urban population. The percentage of urban population living in Class I cities including metros, to the total urban population increased from 50 per cent in 1961 to 60 *per* cent in 1981. The government of India has made a firm committment with its new housing policies and programmes to provide a housing unit to each family by 2000 A.D. This would mean that between 1991 and to the beginning of the 21st century 105 million housing units are to be provided.

Housing stock of Bhopal

The M.P. Housing Board during its life period of 20 years has constructed number of multistoried buildings, residential flats, commercial complexes etc. in Bhopal. However, the progress of construction of houses to the needy is somewhat not at the par with the required level. Several hire purchase schemes are in vogue. In different hire purchase schemes the M.P. Housing Board has provides nearly 6000 houses of different categories to the Bhopal population. Out of this large number of Janata quarters to the poor people were given numbering to 2,377 houses. Upto the year 1978 the benefitted persons were nearly 32000 persons if a family consists of 5 members. Large number of houses numbering 5,200 were constructed in Kotra Sultanabad which are of different types - Jr.MIG, MIG, LIG and 3,556 Janata quarters. A large number of LIG houses were constructed under Hire-purchase schemes upto 1963-84 in Machna Colony, Ravishankarnagar Market, and in large mamber in Subhash Nagar colony. At Koh-i-Fiza, the Housing Board has constructed large number of houses and now the colony is looking very bright and prosperous. However, from the present study the housing policy, which aims at providing houses to the poor and needy, has definitely undergone the threats of sources, forces and vested interests. It is true that the house-building agencies have been successful in adding to the housing stock in Bhopal, but the policy adopted in the recent years has, by and large, excluded the poor and houseless persons specially of lower middle income group persons.

It is noticed that whenever a new scheme is floated in the market and the houses get constructed, the first priority is being given to rich and resourceful persons who make cash down payments. The pity is that the formalities and procedures to these people will also be made simpler and easier. Persons with meagre incomes, and straight forward and sincere have thus to wait for years for their turn in the main gate and afterwards they become frustrated by knowing that the houses were already given by backdoor policies or on cash payment. Besides these, there are special quotas at the discretion of the Board top officials and other political personalities. Private houses have been built in the vacant places in government colonies mostly by influential officials bypassing all the rules and regulations of environmental protection. The situation is so grave that houses were built and shops were opened on the big nalas also.

Another pitiable condition in Housing sector in Bhopal is that houses so built by M.P. Housing Board or by B.D.A are not occupied by the owners. All these houses are given on rents of exorbitant rates specially to such organizations or to the high officers working in those like General Insurance Companies or Banks etc. Rules framed by the government, in regard to the charging of rent from allotters who own houses, is not being implemented strictly. Specially the lacunas in framing the rules or in implementation of these rules need through revision. To be vary frank the resourceful persons and the influential cases those who are getting preferences in getting allotment of houses on priority basis should be discouraged and stopped forthwith.

In Madhya Pradesh more than 10 percent of the combined cost of plot and house is charged for registration itself. As Madhya Pradesh is economically poor and on the path of development, this hard rule is both ill-conceived and illogical for the upliftment of poor and weaker section people.

The Housing Board was busy in carrying on the twin operations of building houses on the vacant land already buy it and developing more and more land for farther construction of houses. Several colonies were developed in Bhopal. The Bhopal Development Authority was established in 1978 initially with the appointment of only six members. The creditable feature of B.D.A. is that it has not constructed even a single house for the high income group in the first phase. The Bhopal Development Authority is responsible for the planned development of Bhopal city in accordance with the specifications of the approved plan, keeping its activities within the budgetary provisions. Keeping in view the increasing demand of house building for the economically weaker sections, the B.D.A. has made provisions for poor people. Upto 1991 the Bhopal Development Authority has constructed 1595 houses and 4729 flats. Besides construction of houses it has developed plots of 10,674 in number in different localities. It has also developed a housing scheme for gas victims on a 400 acre plot in Karondkala.

The Bhopal Development Authority had developed 1404 plots on 0.26 acre land in Panchsheel Nagar and constructed houses also before 1980 itself. The B.D.A. has also constructed several commercial-cum-residential building in Maharana Pratap Nagar in 1978. In the years 1989 the B.D.A. has constructed 48 flats in Meera Complex, and in Aamer complex 80 flats, 60 in Chittod Complex and 120 in Shabri complex, thus providing lot of houses to middle-income group.

During the present study in a personal investigation houses provided by two organisations viz. The United India Insurance and the New India Insurnce Companies has been collected. These two organisations have purchased flats for allotment to their officers in different localities and different type of flats.

The United India Insurance Company Ltd., in Bhopal has purchased 1 HIG flat constructed by B.D.A. in the year 1986 and allotted to their Asst. Manager. In the year 1982 it has purchased 4 flats in Baghira Apartments from M.P. Housing Board costing each 80,000 rupees and allotted to their A.O. and A.A.O.

The New India Insurance Company Ltd., in Bhopal has purchased seven MIG flats, with 90,000 rupees each in year 1964. Afterwards it has purchased four H.I.G. flats each costing about 2,15,000 rupees and ten NIG flats each costing 1,35,000 rupees for the allottment to their officers. In the year 1984 the company has purchased with ₹ 2.15 lakh each, three 'C' Type bungalows and one Kothi for ₹ 6.25 lakh which is having the area of about 1600 sq.ft. for their Regional Manager. Afterwards also the Company is purchasing flats in small numbers every year for providing suitable accommodation to their officers and other staff.

The information regarding providing of houses to their officers has also been collected from the Food Corporation of India office situated in Bhopal. In Bhopal the Food Corporation of India is having nearly 87 officers and 515 Class III and IV staff posted in different branches. The Food Corporation of India has purchased two HIG houses were purchased in Gitanjali Compolex and five MIG flats in Shivani Complex with a total cost of ₹ 4,17,348. Twelve senior MIG flate in Anjali Complex with a cost of ₹ 7,06,770 and ₹ 21,42,179 respectively. The problem of searching suitable accommodation by the officers working in this organisation has been solved by the Food Corporation of India through purchase process and allotting to their employees. Actually this procedure is very good and it increases the workmanship of the employees. Different Co-operative societies were formed with the members living in some areas and also by some persons working in alike organisations. They have purchased land from the B.D.A. and constructed houses through the help of private contractors. In this way also some shortage of houses have been covered. However, now the people of Bhopal, are not so worried about getting a suitable accommodation because in the decade of 1980-1990 several houses were constructed through different agencies in Bhopal.

During the year 1990-91 the Bhopal Development Authority is having the following programmes in hand.

1. Construction of a Multistoryed Building in Maharanapratap Nagar, Bhopal.
2. In Kotrasultanabad a plan has been chalked out for construction of a commercial use building and a residential accommodation complex in 4.62 acre land.
3. A plan is in progress in Karanakala, Berasia road construction of buildings for E.W.S. on 419.83 Acre land. The survey of land has been completed.
4. The plan was agreed for construction of 64 houses in Tila Jamalpura for E.W.S. people.
5. Near Indrapari hire purchase scheme has been submitted for construction of 70^0 LIG, MIC houses with the assistance of Central Government.
6. In Shahpura Manisha Market was almost completed.
7. In the plan of clearing slums near Board office a plan was there for construction of Multistoried building.

The M.P. Housing Board, since its inception has constructed 1,39,912 housing units through the state. The M.P. Housing Board has built 10,489 houses in 1987-88, 17,868 houses in 1988-89 and 20,543 houses in the year 1989-90. It has achieved gradual progress and attained the goal of providing many houses to the people of state.

The housing scene is rather alarming, in spite of the progress achieved by different organisations because of abundant influx of population to the urban areas. The present backlog of 7 million houses may shoot up to 15.5 million houses in cities by 2001 A.D. It is due to the social change in urban agglomeration. In cities both wife and husband are nowadays working people, and they are facing lot of difficulties in rearing their children, specially infants during the office hours. Several people are forced to keep one or two of their elderly members bringing from rural areas for proper care of their children. This has also created the problem of big accommodation to each such family.

The migration of rural population to cities in the national level was recorded as 22 persons in every one thousand per years in cities. Whereas the influx of rural population in Bhopal has been taken as 80 persons in each thousand per year. This increased influx of population from rural areas to Bhopal has increased encroachments and erection of new slums. However, formation of slums in Bhopal certainly increased the environmental problems in different areas of pollution. Industrial development in the area has also added more and more problem of pollution in water, air etc.

Environment protection

Man is becoming a Robot. Money has become God. Everything except life and arms is costly. Peace is elusive. Manners, morals, values, virtues, sacrifice and sentiments are becoming the articles of archaeological importance now-a-days. This is the legacy one new entrant in this society one inherits. Even in the childhood of a new born will have to witness on earth the devoid of soil cover, polluted water and cursing greenery, full of filth and dust. Adulterated food to eat, polluted air to breath, chemical waters to drink, wearing earplugs to keep the deadly noise out. It is rather crime on the part of a parent to bring a new born to this world of dreadful atmosphere. It is rather difficult to say that a newborn will ever smile hopefully for a happy survival on this earth.

Attaining the goals by foul means, achieving the targets by manipulated figures, wrong implementation of plans, have resulted in inequality, corruption, and imbalances of different types in this society.

The Housing shortage in Bhopal has given way for several encroachments and forming of slum colonies in different localities. The living of people in slums is very sub-standard because of their poverty. They are much worried about their square meals than about their accommodation and privacy. The root cause of pollution in Bhopal is more and more slum colonies that too in between posh localities.

In the pursuit of protecting environment the Madhya Pradesh government has established The Environmental Planning and Coordination Organisation (EPCO). The Environmental Planning and Coordination Organisation was registered under the Department of Housing and Environment as a society and acts as the Principal Advisory body to the Govt. of Madhya Pradesh in protection of the Environment in the State. EPCO was established on the World Environment Day, i.e. 5th June 1981 in Bhopal with the main object of creating public awareness with regard to environment and for promoting environmental studies and coordinating with field agencies on specific environmental problems. The area of EPCO is spread in 54 acres of land in Bhopal and called as 'Paryavaran Parisar'. The aims and objects of this body are as follows:

1. To assist and advise the Government of Madhya Pradesh in the formulation and implementation of an environmental policy for the State in the determination of priorities for environmental action.
2. To create public awareness with regard to environment generally and in relation to Madhya Pradesh in particular and to keep the public informed in this field.
3. To assist and advise the Govt. of M.P. and other agencies in the management of the human environment including inter-ali reviewing environmental action, improving human living conditions through better regional, urban and architectural planning protecting and conserving ancient monuments and other places of social, cultural, religious and aesthetic significance.
4. To improve the environment of these social and cultural and historically important places, monitoring prevention and control of pollution and other environmental hazards, formulation, monitoring and enforcement of environmental quality standards and environmental safeguards.
5. To safeguard environment, inculcation of environmentally appropriate forestry, wild life, agricultural and animal husbandry practices conservation of energy and development of alternative energy sources, recycling of resources and utilisation of wastes, inculcation of proper standards of environmental health and hygiene, sound management of natural resources, conservation of biotic communities, ecosystem and watersheds and inculcation of appropriate land use practices.

6. To assist in environmental impact studies and collect monitor and assess data on important environmental issues, particularly of Madhya Pradesh.
7. To organise and encourage conferences, lectures, seminars and public debates in matters relating to environment.
8. To organise educational and training programmes for manpower development in the field of environmental sciences, technologies and management.
9. To establish libraries and information collection documentation and retrieval services and undertake or assist in the publication of journals, research papers and books relating to environment.
10. To offer consultancy services in regard to all matters concerning to environment,
11. To develop a cadre of professionals and experts in the field of environment and maintain information on the availability of diverse expertise in this field.
12. To constitute or cause to be constituted regional centres at convenient places to promote the objects of the society.
13. To provide facilities to the Institute of Environment of Barkatullah University and similar institutions of other Universities for research and study on all aspects of environment and to enter into collaborative arrangements with universities and research centres for conducting research in relation to specific environmental problems.
14. To institute academic positions, fellowships, scholarships, awards etc. for furtherance of the objectives of the society.
15. To encourage education on environmental matters and interest in the significance of environmental factors in schools, colleges and other academic institutions by initiating various other participative activities.

The EPCO has already succeeded in achieving their objectives such as:

(a) A traffic and transportation study of Bhopal city, incorporated a set of recommendations for improving the Road Transportation network.

(b) A study on urban slums has already been done.

(c) A study on the present status of Rural Housing activities in Madhya Pradesh has also been completed.

With enormous growth of population in cities the environmental deterioration increasing day by day. This has obstructed in the overall development aimed at environmental protection. The health of the city agglomeration depends on the fertility of soil and natural resources. Maintenance of the purity and safety of the environment in the face of increasing urbanisation and industrialisation is emerging as the most challenging problem for mankind.

The huge quantities of pollutants like solids, liquid and gaseous which are being let out into air, water and land systems are investing the relationship between man and nature. Some of the statistics pertaining to the environmental scenario are quite revealing. At present nearly 70 per cent of the available water in India is polluted. Over 73 million work days are lost annually due to water related diseases in India. In the last two decades in Bhopal, there is a tenfold increase in number of vehicles pumping pollutants into air. No wonder, a breath of fresh air is becoming a rare commodity in the city.

For the protection of environment and controlling pollution some standards must be laid down. In this direction, standards of operation, maintenance, house keeping and systems control are the major factors for improvement environment management. the following aspects will certainly help in protecting the environment:

1. To strike proper balance between the requirements of economy and environmental protection measures.
2. To suggest means for reducing pollution loads.
3. To monitor the extent of pollution in the outgoing effluents.
4. To prescribe limits for various characteristics of the outgoing effluents.
5. To lend assistance in minimising the toxicity of wastes generated.

The moat important way of standardising is to correlate the interests of economy with ecology. There is a continuous conflict between the needs of improving the standard of living through rapid industrialisation and the need of preventing degradation of the environment. In the exercise of waste management, vital significance attaches to the means which can help modify and reduce the toxic character of the outgoing effluents.

The Bureau of Indian Standards (BIS) has visualised the dimensions of the problems well in advance i.e. before early sixties end supplied nearly 250 standards covering codes of practice, methods of testing etc. To maintain the purity of natural water, the BIS has suggested nearly 80 standards including the methods of treatment of effluents to reduce, modify or eliminate their pollution loads.

Control of sir pollution and proper disposal of solid wastes represent other challenging areas. Noxious emissions and callous dumping pose a grave threat to human health, soil fertility, ground water quality, damage to civil structures and corrosion of metal installations and equipment, and the BIS has given 50 standards to provide guidelines in this regard.

The Central Pollution Control Board (CPCB) was constituted in September 1974 under the Water (Prevention and Control of Pollution) Act, 1974 which became effective from March 23, 1974. Also in all the 25 states of India, State Pollution Control Boards have been constituted. Since May 1981, the Central and State Pollution Control Boards have been entrusted with the additional responsibility of Air pollution control under the provision of the Air (Prevention and Control of Pollution) Act, 1981. The scope of activities of the boards is further widened with the enactment of the Environment (Protection) Act, 1986, for enforcement of measures for the protection of the environment.

The main functions of the Central Pollution Control Board are:

1. To advise the Central government on all matters concerning prevention and control of water and air pollution.
2. To provide technical assistance to State Polution Control Boards and coordinate these activities for effective implementation of the pollution control programmes.
3. To lay down standard for the quality of air and water.
4. To impart training to personnel for enforcement of pollution measures.

The status of environment is regularly assessed by conducting surveys and by monitoring the air and water quality. Seventeen problem areas where pollution was found to be severe and alarming were identified by the Central Pollution Control Board, out of which 13 areas of problem have been surveyed to assess pollution load and quality of ambient and receiving water bodies.

With the introduction of the Motor Vehicles Act, 1988 there is now a greater emphasis on pollution control from the exhaust of vehicles. It prescribes safe exhaust pollution standards for both newly manufactured and vehicles already in use. In case of petrol-driven vehicles, the permissible limit for four-wheelers has been prescribed as 3 per cent carbon monoxide at idling, whereas for two and three wheelers the limit of 4.5 per cent carbon monoxide has been fixed. For dieasel-driven vehicles, the safe emission limit is 65 Hartridge smoke units measured by Free Acceleration method. The violation of these provisions has been made a punitive offence with fines of Rs. 1000 and more.

Mass emission standards for newly Manufactured Motor Vehicles prescribed by the Motor Vehicles Act, 1988 have come into force from April 1, 1991, which will ensure that new vehicles will have low pollution levels because of improved engine technology.

To enable the vehicle owners to frequently check their vehicles, the State Government has to authorise some private petrol pumps and workshops to provide tuning and rectification facilities in addition to pollution checking as was done by Delhi authorities. The Vehicle owners should go frequently to these checking points and ensure that their vehicles do not contribute to air pollution. However, the success of these preventive measures depends on the vehicle owners.

The worlds biggest conference to protect the planet from pollution and to protect the environment was organised in Rio-de-Jenaro and 119 countries have attended the summit which started on 3rd June 1992. In his first lecture the Indian Prime Minister has briefed the measures taken by India to protect the Environment. The summit has declared the principles on general rights and obligations on environment protection initiated by the participants. The text of Rio declaration on environment contains 27 points of Human rights, general principles for protection of environment and strict measures to be taken to control the pollution activities. In this summit the world countries have amply recognised the fruitful measures taken by India and its contribution in protecting the environment.

A good environment means not only conditions that are favourable to the maintenance of physical health, but also certain emotional and aesthetic qualities of the surroundings. The unfettered use of technology, which is the hallmark of our era, has led to profoundly ambiguous results. On the one hand, technology has given those, who have mastered it, unprecedented economic growth and on the other, that same mastery has brought us the threat of disaster, in the short term from nuclear war, and in the longer term from irrevocable damage to the global environment.

Man is eating away the earth resources without thinking what that earth needs in return of its contribution to humanity. Poverty related environmental problem is the main issue. The resources of earth are limited. One cannot go on extracting the natural wealth for human use for an unlimited time.

As mentioned earlier, slums are the result of increasing population and in Bhopal the main contribution towards degradation of the environment and polluting the atmosphere is of slum population. Needless to say that the main contribution to pollution of water and air in Bhopal is of industries. There is a general absence of social services and welfare agencies to deal with the major social problems of families living in sub-standard conditions victimizing themselves with serious biological, paychological and social consequences.

Actually, this housing sector problem is indirectly has inter-relation with other sectors of social life like education, medical facilities, employment and poverty alleviation programmes. Employment generation and poverty alleviation are closely connected to growth. But this growth has many facets like adequate food supply, control on inflation, and provision of shelter. This has a great impact on social service sector include reduction of birth rate to 26 per thousand, reduction in infant mortality rate to 70 per thousand live births, improvement in nutritional status of pre-school children, etc. Also this will reflect the eradication of adult illiteracy, diversification of vocational programmes, provision of drinking water to all villages and towns with a population below 20,000 provision of 10 million households in rural areas with at least one electric light connection each and all these are the highlights of the Eighteen Five Year Plan.

In the housing sector the backlog to be cleared upto 2001 is estimated to be around 23.3 million units and the new demand will be to the tune of 63.8 million units in the country. However, the long term goal is to provide 'Shelter for All'.

In the direction of environmental protection the most successful attempt in Bhopal is the First National seminoar on "Ecological Socialism" which was held from November 14 for two days. The seminar has been organised by the Society of "Ecobalance", the local voluntary organisation for promoting environmental awareness among local residents. well-reputed scientists, environmentalists and sociologists in large number have attended the seminar and contributed their knowledge in protecting the environment. This is the first seminar of its kind which included environmental ethics, environmental problems in regional planning, energy saving means and energy alternatives, held at Bhopal in the year 1992.

The Ministry of Environment and Forest has started a scheme of "ECOMARK" for products considered as environmentally friendly to enhance the public awareness towards the protection of environment. The ECOMARK is started from January 1992, initially started printing on Soaps and detergents and on all other products which are related to environment in which the regulations and laws of environment are strictly followed and by manufacturing and using these products there is no environmental problem and all the principles of protection of environment are followed.

It is evident that in 2000 A.D. the house construction activity in Bhopal will absorb a large number of workers than it does at present. The shortage of skilled labour masons, plumbers and carpenters which is felt more now will not be there in 2000 A.D. The pace of construction can be accelerated if special attention is given to the requirements, the availability and the mobilisation of resources of money, material and skilled labour, the environmental constraints etc.

On the basis of the discussion mentioned earlier, the following suggestions are drawn for the result-oriented programmes of housing in Bhopal and also to protect environment and control of pollution.

1. The rules relating to the sale of plots both by Public and Private sectors should be made simple and easy.
2. The rates of plots should be at subsidised rates both for low paid government employees and to the members of weaker sections of the society.
3. The material needed for house construction should be made easily available to the needy persons.
4. The State government adopt such a policy for its government employees to grant owning rights of the quarters alloted to them while in government service, after retirement by taking nominal cost keeping in view the rent already recovered from them.
5. In case of deceased government servants, the state government should provide a house on easy installments and for subsidised rates.
6. The government should also restrict the government employees or private parties to own more than one house in one city.
7. Slums should be cleared as early as possible and till then the population living in slum colonies should be provided with minimum facilities like drinking water, sanitation, health facilities, electricity etc.
8. The Bhopal Municipal authorities should be watchful about the needs of slums, hutments etc.
9. The influx of population to cities, from rural areas should be discouraged.
10. The rural people may be given employment opportunities sufficiently in villages by establishing new units of industries.
11. Poverty alleviation programmes should intensified.
12. Adult literacy programmes should be given more significance and widely propagated.
13. Social institutions be given more economic aid to eradicate illiteracy specially in rural folk.

14. In cities environmental awareness programmes be given wide publicity.
15. The cooperative movement in housing is to be strengthened while luxury housing is to be discouraged by relevant disincentives.
16. People should be educated in proper form so as to enable them to utilise the finances provided by National Housing Bank and Housing & vrban Development Corporation (NHB AND HUDCO) etc.
17. The environmental problems should be solved from the home level i.e.
    (i) Put the brakes of global warming and acid rain by saving energy at home, at work and on the road.
    (ii) Preserve forests by planting trees, using recycled paper and avoiding tropical hard woods which have not been sustainably harvested.
    (iii) Reduce waste by recycling glass, paper, cans and kitchen wastes and avoiding chemicals.
    (iv) Cultivate the habit of growing kitchen gardens.
    (v) Be conversant and informed about local regional issues by joining conservation programmes and organisations.
18. Control pollution in water, air and noise in local and regional levels as much as one can do.
19. Avoid noise pollution on roads and in houses by keeping their vehicles fit to run on roads and by use of controlled audio-video equipment.
20. Awareness of environment and controlling pollution is must.

Notes

1. http:/ /www.ibiblio.org/ libraricsfaq/ faqidx.htm
2. http.// www5.oclc.org./downloads/community/ information trends.pdf
3. hltp:/ / www. pewinternet.org/reports/toc.asp?Report=80
4. OCLC White Poper on the Information Habits of College Students, June 2002.
5. Laribee, J.F: Information resources Management : Topics, Concepts, and Resources for teaching IRM to Business students, 1992.
6. Mont viloff, V: National Information policies, Unesco, 1991.
7. Chowdhury, G.G. and Chowdhury, Sudatta (2007).Organizing Information from the Shelf to the Web. London: Facet, 2007.
8. Liao,Y.C.(2008). A weight-based approach to information retrieval and relevance feedback. Expert Systems with Applications, 35 (1-2) 254-261.
9. He, Tianwei, & Wang, Wei. (2006), Library and information science research in China: An international perspective. *The International Information & Library*

Review, 38(4), 185-191. URL.: http://www.sciencedirect.com/science?-ob=ArticleURL&udi=B6WGP-4MOBHS11& user=2248543&-coverDate= 12%2F31%2F2006&rdoc=1&-fmt=&-orig=search&-sort=d&view=c&-acct=C000056730&-version=1&-urlVersion=0&-userid = 224854 &md 5=8f7d177e32fbac4fc80b703aed9af9fb.

10. Ali,S.Nazim. (1985). Library and Information Science Literature: Research Results.

    International Library Review. 17(2), 117-28.

    URL.:http://www.eric.ed.gov/ERICWebPortal/custom/portles/recordDetails/detailmini.jsp?-nfpb=true&-&ERICExt Search-Search Value-O= EJ318722 & ERICE xtSearch SearchType-oeric-accno&accno=EJ318722.

11. Zahid Ashraf Wani, Ishrat Majeed Bakshi, & Sumeer Gul. (2008). Growth and Development of Library and Information Science Literature. *Chinese Librarianship: an International Electronic Journal,* 26, URL.: http: // www.iclc.us/cliej/c126WBJ.htm.
12. Dempsey, Lorcan (2000).T he subject gateway: experiences and issues based on the emergence of the Resource Discovery Network. Online Information Review, 24(1), 8-23.
13. http://'w.w.w. ibiblio.org/librariefaq/faqidx.htm.
14. Haughey, M & Anderson, T: Networked Learning. The Pedagogy of the Internet, Montreal, 1998.
15. Harris, H & Park, S (200R) Educational usages of podcasting. British Journal of *Educational Technology* 39 (3): 045-551.
16. Michael E. Casey and Laura C. Savasrinuk ; Library 2.0; Service for the next-generation library; Library Journal, 2006; http: //www. library journal.com/article/ C-\6365200.html.

Chapter - 6

Analysis (Core Chapters)

In this chapter an attempt has been made to present the overall analysis of the presented material in the Chapters from 2 to 5 chapters both are inclusive. In the second chapter, 3 Ph.D. theses and 1 M.Phil. dissertation have been presented in order to identify and recognize the set patterns in the spheres of structural research leading to final component. The major themes are related to Regional agricultural Geography of Andhra Pradesh has been selected by Dr. Y.V. Ramanayya, S.V. University, Tirupati (1984).

2.2 deals the material content related to planning for integrated Area Development. A case study of Tanuku Taluk west Godavary District, Andhra Pradesh, India by Dr. K.L. Narasimha Murthy, Department of Geography, Andhra University, Waltair (1984);

2.3 deals with Location, structure, problems and prospects of Small Scale Industries in Telangana has been presented by S. Ramakrishna, Department of Geography, Osmania University, Hyderabad under the supervision of Dr. K. Vithal Reddy, Professor & Head, Department of Geography, Osmania University, Hyderabad (1988) and

2.4 deals with "Impact of cyclone on Development: A case study of Yanam" presented by Kamesvari, Varanasi submitted to Andhra Pradesh Open University, Hyderabad (2000) for the award of Master in Philosophy in Development Economics.

In Chapter 3, 3.2 deals with human resource accounting and it is directed and related to the organised sector, mainly deals in the issue of employer - employee relationship. Human resources as capital which arises from the fact that while other assets are owned by an organisation, human resources and not so owned. Further, identified that organisation pays only wages or salaries to its employees, which are of a revenue types, and as such are treated as cement costs and it was never thought that investment in human resources could be treated as capital.

In 3.3, Prof. V. Madhava Rao has presented the thesis, "Planning & Management of Rural Electrification: A case study of Medak Region of Andhra Pradesh and it is an exemplary study which help the administer and Manage electrification system. No. 3.3 CSSRL CSSRL Hanumantha Rao has presented and submitted thesis "Heterogeneous queues and Queues with independent arrival and service processes" Department of Statistics, Andhra University, Visakhapatnam, A.P. India (2002).

4.1 Abdul Khader, S. has submitted the thesis, "Impact of Tribal Policy on the select tribes of Andhra Pradesh" to Sri Krishna Devaraya University, Anantapur for the award of Doctor of Philosophy in History (2000).

4.2 R. Gangadhara Sastry has submitted the thesis, "Federalism in India in the context of Administrative Relations between centre and states" to Osmania University, Hyderabad for the award of Doctor of Philosophy in Political Science & Public Administration (1987).

4.3 "Implementation of Jawaharlal Nehru National Urban Renewal Mission: in the Mission City of Hyderabad" was the entitled thesis by v. Gangaiah under the supervision of Prof. S. Bhoopathi Raw, Professor of Public Administration" to Osmania University, for the award of the Degree of Doctor of Philosophy in Public Administration (2017).

In Chapter 5, 5.1 deals with the library and information Sciences Dr. Kandimalla Bharathi has submitted thesis, for the award of Doctor of Philosophy in Library Science, to Osmania University, Hyderabad entitled, "Digital library" (1988).

5.2 deals with, "Housing Policy & Programmes in Urban Bhopal: A study in Social and Environmental Change" thesis has been submitted by B.M.K. Mohan, Sociology faculty for the award of Doctor of Philosophy to Baraktullah University, Bhopal (1992).

An attempt has bean made by the editor to present the changing scenerio of traditional pattern to additional tools of technology adoption in theses.

The above 12 theses were studied in depth to identify and recognize the changing patterns of traditional research methodology to modern types of technological methods for analysis. In this process all the 12 theses are described from 2nd to 5th chapter (both are inclusive) and in this chapter methodologies are specially examined in depth as well in detail for discussion and finally suggest model methodology for a thesis building and layout.

2.1 Agricultural Geography

"Regional Agricultural Geography of Andhra Pradesh" entitled thesis has been submitted by Dr. Y.V. Ramanayya, Department of Geography,

S.V. University, Tirupati (1984) under the supervition of Prof. N.B.K. Reddy, Professor & Head, Department of Geography, S.V. University, Tirupati, perhaps, it was the first thesis on agricultural geography under his supervision at Tirupati

2.2 Planning for integrated Area Development

Planning for integrated area development - A case study from Andhra Pradesh, "is an attempt in the field of rural studies relating to micro-level planning and its problems. Taluka is perhaps a viable unit for the separation of a development plan. It seeks a spatial framework of development particularly for land use, human settlement. Social services and amenities for people. Tanuka taluk is homogeneous in its physical structure but heterogeneous characteristics are noticed in respect of social facilities. Micro-level planning is a prerequisite for reaching balanced and integrated area development.

An attempt has been made by the author in this thesis to make a few proposals for its spatial, functional and developmental activities of the study region. The author have presented the following aspects such as economic development, Tanuku Taluk, Andhra Pradesh, Economic Planning Regional Planning Tanuku, Andhra Pradesh, Economic Geography Tanuku, Andhra Pradesh and Rural Development, Tanuku, A.P.

This study focuses on its physical structure and social development. On the grounds of a multifaceted survey, the author pats forth his suggestions for the spatial, functional and developmental activities in the study region. These suggestions would be of use to geographers, regional economists and planners of rural space in visualising development in a broader spectrum".

The major tool used in this analysis are (1) Gravity Model (2) Christaller's Central place theory and (3) Cost-Benefit Analysis for social facilities.

Suggestions

It is assessed that factor analysis method may be quite apt to regional planning and spatial planning exercises. This statistical tool give precise calculation of variations and it decides the levels of development quantitatively.

Christaller's Central place theory may be primarily used to identify the growth centres service centres and central villages based upon weight age and scoring techniques. Geographical cartographic techniques helps to visualise spatial variations and levels of development.

2.3 Location, structure, problems and prospectus of small scale industries in Telangana.

The author of the entitled thesis "Studies in industrial geography by Indian Geographers since 1940 has been systematically analysed the spatial distribution of industries and geographical factors operating in their location and features of industrial landscape and further presented that this study considers small scale industries as a solution to enhanced comprehensive development to overcome the shortcomings of regional disparities, unbalanced growth and development".

Dr. Rao's study also highlights the nature of the small scale industrial development in Telangana region of Andhra Pradesh further identified that, the abundant resources available for development, the study region continues to be lagging behind economically. This study attempts a geographical assessment of the possibilities of multiple issues of available resources at minimum cost for economic development with a view to uplift the region from the economic backwardness and methodology dopted was location quotient (L.Q.) for analysis.

Index numbers are employed to identify the magnitude of number of units, employment and investment in small scale industries and also used the method, to determine the level of small scale industrialisation, the equation of manufacturing industries has been used.

Finally, Spearman's Rank correlation method (Location factor) has been applied to calculate the relationship between size of small scale industrial units in the region and size of the workforce employed by the units. The unity localisation of small scale industries for each district over the time period has been analysed though the compilation of location quotient for every district in Telangana region and for each region of Andhra Pradesh".

Cartographic technique such as super imposed technique has been used in order to identify the development and deviation of small scale industrial units, workers and capital investment in small scale industries in Telangana Region.

Suggestion for future researchers

1. Industrial Geography of Telangana State: A Geographic study (1980-2018).
2. Industrial profile of small, medium and major industries spatial variation.
3. Spatial variations in industrial growth - North & South Telangana State, India (1970, 1980, 1990, 2000, 2010 and 2018).

2.4 Kameswari, Varanasi, "Impact of cyclone on Development"-A case study Yanam: has been submitted for the award of M. Phil degree.

The author has dealt the aspects, such as 1. Ragionalisation in India 2. deals with regionalisation Meso and Micro regions and opined that the macro planning regions and larger areas of diversified natural conditions and resources. The Meso naming regions have been divided on the basis of potentialities of the region. Micro regions should satisfy some of the basic needs and desires of people. Structural, functional and organisational aspects, should be viable for direct interaction which determine the main issues of area development. In this study, the author has identified the need to study the resource base and included these aspects such as:

1. The geographical location of the case.
2. The climatic conditions of the areas.
3. The quality of human resources.
4. The area under irrigation, cropping pattern and agricultural productivity.
5. Number of industries and their composition - Agro based, heavy, and cottage industries etc.
6. The service sector.
7. Mines.
8. Fishing.
9. Financial institutions
10. Educational institutions and
11. The institutions that promote trade and commerce.

The resource base of the region has been discussed terms of land resources water resources, livestock and the role of co-operatives for agricultural development of the region.

She opined that a comprehensive plan to be evolved and implemented by taking into considerations such as agricultural, biotic, industrial resources in order to achieve integrated development of the region.

Suggestions for future resources:

1. Factor analysis method may be more useful for identifying the growth processes and development. Functional integration and spatical integration are quite helpful for achieving integrated development of the region, taking "population" as norm and "Area" as norm.
2. Rank correction method may also be useful and gives utility while analysing the data on scientific lines.

3.2 Commerce and management studies:

From the Commerce and Management studies, Dr. Anjaneyulu has taken Ph.D. in 1996 from Kakatiya University, Warangal, Andhra Pradesh on, "Human Resource Accounting". This thesis is an outstanding work of the candidate as well under the capacity, calibere and capability of the supervisor on human capital. Human resources are considered as human capital as well as an asset It is such in economic literature, that land, labour, capital and organisation are subjected to process which in the process, the derivatives are rent wages, interest and profit. It is to say that the above four elements are basic sources and considered mainly as resources besides derivatives for further processing to form capital. To form human capital, human resources including human skills in are considered as property of a District / State / nation fits in an hierarchic system. It is a system within the total system for growth promoting or growth retarding in an economy leading to human capital accounting and also assessing assets.

Dr. K. Anjaneyulu has reviewed the literature as back drop of the prospect and the works of Renarde, Adam Smith, Alfred and Marshall, later has reviewed that the American Accounting Associations views as basis for accounting system related to human resource accounting some people opined that it is a process of developing financial assessments of people and groups of people within organisation and has further identified that the importance of human resource development and its accounting has been receiving increased importance for the last two decades.

He has presented the resource for using HCD and also distinguished the factors and special factor of human resources with other resources as a first step in the process of HR Accounting and methods which are suitably be made. The following aspects are vitally considered such as (1) Trading practice in Accounting, (2) Shortcomings in Traditional accounting or conventional accounting regarding hum an resources. History of Human Resource Accounting for (A) Companies and (B) Corporations were presented to understand the concept of human resource accounting in a case study.

3. Ideal meaning of HRA, 4. Objects of Human resource accounting, 5. Merits of HRA, 6. Limitations of HRA, 7. Valuation of HR Accounting, 8. Cost Models, 9. Historical Cost Method of valuation, 9. Critical appraisal of this methods, 10. Replacement of cost-method merits and demerits of this methods, 11. Standard cost method, 12. Opportunity cost method, 13. Competitive Bidding method - its merits and demerits besides Branch Lev and Aba Schwarts Model present value of Future earning birth a formula. The formula is given here as.

Vr = T = X

Vr = human capital value or a person with year old

E (t) = persons expected annual earnings upto retirement

r = a discount rate

t = retirement age.

with an example of Bharat Heavy Electricals Limited for critical appraisal and adjudication.

The following models are critically examined. They are 1. Eric Flamhottis model 2. Jaggicured lalis model 3. Hermanson's model 4. S.K. Chakrabathis Model and 5. Dr. S.M. Shukla's Model.

At least he has identified that Human Resources as an Asset.

He concludes that, "Government should also give recognition to HR as an asset and part 1 of Schedule VI of the Companies Act, 1996 should be amended so as to include Human resource as an independent asset rather than including it any of the existing groups of assets". The editor congratulates both the researcher and supervisor as Human Resources and which is to be accounted for academic assessment and this achievement is not to oneself but for both. It is an excellent piece of work as a modest work of a modest person.

3.3 Economics

Role of rural electrification corporation, State Electricity Board and rural electric co-operatives operating in Telangana region, assessing problems and associated factors in the promotion of rural electrification are important aspects which may uplift rural society through rural electrification. It is nothing but promoting quality of life of people living in rural areas. There is every need to suggest technological alternatives in the light of the problems that are being faced in any region should have to be identified and find solutions by the Engineers/Governance.

Power supply to rural areas has a telling effect especially to the farmers for growing food crops (essential). At the time of peak time in agricultural season, if the power is not supplied, there is stand still to the crop as well to its sustenance.

3.4 Statistics

CSRL Manumantha Rao has presented queuing models in operational research under the faculty of statistics, Andhra University, Waltair. It is observed that "a queuing system in which the total service capacity utilized at any given time was a variable under the control of a decision maker.

Steady state probabilities expected queue lengths and frequencies of change in capacity were to be evaluated for a vide class of possible control schemes and the optimisation procedures have to be out timed".

Further, it has been identified that, "the heterogeneous system is compared with a homogeneous system and a condition showing the efficiency of the heterogeneous system was obtained, this condition involves only the traffic intensity and the service rates.

Finally opined that, "it is highly possible that many more queuing models with heterogeneous interdependent nature can be developed with various plausible assumptions in order to analyse the natural phenomenon more close to the reality and to utilise the natural resources more optimally".

4.1 S. Abdul Khader has submitted the thesis, "Impact of Tribal Policy, on the select tribes of Andhra Pradesh," under the guidance of Dr. K. Krishna Naik, Associate Professor & Head, Department of History, Srikrishna Devaraya University, Ananapur (2000). Keeping in view of the gap in literature and to fill up the gap, the present study has been taken up, identify the impact of state policies on the select tribes of Andhra Pradesh.

The author has studied the impact of state policies (ITDP) in the socio-economic lives of the Chenchus, Koya and Gond tribes under study and also to assess the developmental programmes for the tribal during plan periods with special emphasis on the fifth five year plan.

Further studied the extent of success and effectiveness of the A.P. State and transfer regulations, the impact of wild life protection Act on the tribals and to explore causes for the continuing tribal unrest and has identified the reasons as to why the tribals still remain backward despite so many policies and programmes initiated by the state and Government of India. Beside the above, the author has examined the extent of suitability of programmes for the different tribal areas vis-a-vis the social, economic and cultural values.

Data has been collected for this study was from primary and secondary sources. Primary survey has been conducted from tribals orally in the areas covered by three ITDA (e) Srisailam, Utnoor and Eturnagaram. Dr. Khader also undertook extensive field surveys from tribal villages of three ITDAS. A formal interview schedule has been prepared to collect the necessary information from ITDA project officers, Assistant Project officers, Managers of GCC, DTWOS and the tribals of the area to collect the first hand information and further published literature in different journals and books on the subject of study.

This study would be helpful not only in identifying and analysing the factors responsible for the grievances, unrest among the tribals, but also informating new policy initiatives necessary for defusing the tension in the tribal areas and has covered the five year plan period from 1951 to 1985, with special emphasis on the fifth and sixth five year plan periods.

Geographically, the Chenchus of Srisailam in Kurnool District, Gonds of Utnoor in Adilabad District, the reasons being rein in Wararngal District were taken up, the reasons beings:

1. The Chenchus are considered the most preventive of all the tribes, and has analysed how they are undergoing transition from food gathering stage to the present settled life and Gonds and are the most conservative and superstitutions tribe. The Gond area experienced two rebellions within a span of 40 years, i.e. Babijheri uprising in 1940 during the Nizam's period and the Noravelli uprising in 1961 in a welfare state. It is interesting to proble into the various socio-ecnomic and demographic developments of this naxalite prone area.

Koyas are asunderant in Warangal district and they have many grievances from the first authorities during Nizam's period. They had participated in the Telangana armed struggle against the Nizam - Koyas, the only group which had taken in an appreciable degree to industrial employment in the Singareni Collieries.

4.2 Political Science (interpretation of Constitution of India) R. Gangadhara Sastry has submitted his thesis to Osmania University, Hyderabad, "Federalism in India in the context of Administrative Relations between centre and states". He opined that the constitution was described as 'unique' in its spirit as it contained distinguishing federal features as well as strong universal tendencies. It has been noted that after the 4th general elections, which brought some non-Congress parties into power in some states in India and of the relevent are with some regional parties emerging more peaceful that the efficacy of the federal system was generously questioned.

The main essence to challenge the federal setup was that undue importance was assigned to the union government, rendering it almost impossible for the states to function as autonomous units in spheres exclusively allocated to them by the constitution. Further opines that the context of "Federalism" is not new to the country of nations. Several countries of different times, have established federal structures to suit the political requirements and consequently, the centralised tendencies in the federal system of India may also be viewed as a part of our British legacy.

The focus of the present study is the examination of federalisation in India in the context of centre - state administrative relations, it is found necessary to discuss several of the collateral factors that have an important bearing on such relations and it is the age of co-operative and participative federalism in which levels of government function with material trust, understanding and co-ordination. Dr. Sastry has identified the aptness of the Sarkaria Commission, which has rightly observed that it is co-operative federalism which is the spirit of the Indian constitution and that both the union and the states should function in that spirit. The provisions of the constitution relating to the temporary transfer of functions from the state to the centre are also subjects of controversy. Rightly said that vacancy of the items in the concurrent list are important matters of concern both for the union and the states. The most important area of conflict between the centre and the states is the place and invocation of certain articles in the Constitution. Articles like 248, 249 and 252 have become the bone of contention and hence a number of non-Congress (I) state governments demanded to dilation of these Articles, from the constitution or suitable amendments to be made as the residuary powers of legislation should belong to the states and that no state could be deprived of any legislative power which belonged to it without its prior concurrence.

Finally, Dr. Sastry concludes that, "A dispassionate view of the Indian federal system reveals that the matters of the constitution have by and large created a structure suitable for a country with varied cultural, linguistic and religious complexities, their wisdom and foresight in developing a unique federal system can best be appreciated for today when forces of disintegration are threatening the very existence of the republic. It is most unfortunate that a good system is badly used by those in power. If the politicians running the Union government abuse their power and misuse authority for political and partisan ends and if those in power at the state blame the Union Government for their failures and demand autonomy in areas where strong union action is justified it is wrong to blame the constitution".

Editors Comments

This politico-administrative and constitutional amendments may help really the administrators as well as practitioner of the Indian Constitution. The Constitution of India, by and large, has been widely taken from so many constitutions to formulate vulnerable, viable and sustainable enough to cater to the needs of the people and area keeping in view of the unified structural mindset of heterogenerous people and finally brought into unified structure presents the 'federalism which will not harmful and strain the centre-state relation vis-a-vis Indian land and Indian population and their structural composition. Though it has been imposed structurally in the color of democratic, norms but its strature has its own identity among the constitutions of the globe and governments (Dr. K. L. Narasimha Murty,

Editor). It is imperative to Government of India through parliament, the amendments to the Indian constitution may be made as and when circumstances and environment warrants to do so to the extent of not loosing the spirit and purpose for which it has been evolved but many processes were involved to make constitutional amendment such as the recent 73 constitutional Amendment was an important one which devolve power to municipalities to exercise functional structures and progress to redress woes of the people of the lower administrative hierarchy and administrative machinery should be vulnerable enough to people to redress their problems as and when it warrants.

4.3 Public Administration

Implementation of Jawaharlal Nehru National Urban Renewal Mission in the mission city of Hyderabad." This entitled thesis has been submitted for the award of degree of Doctor of Philosophy in Public Administration in 2017 by Dr. V. Gangaiah under the supervision of Prof. S. Bhoopathi Row (Retd.), Professor of public administration, Osmania University, Hyderabad, Telangana State, India. He has analysed the following aspects in this study. They are: 1 . Urbanisation - challenges - Government of India has introduced several urban poverty alleviation programmes with an objective to uplift the urban poor to step up the socio-economic condition of poverty.

Dr. Gangaiah opined that, "apart from Urban poverty alleviation programmes and housing schemes, several other programmes have been introduced in the urban areas to provide infrastructural facilities like roads, drains, street-lights, sanitation and water supply in the mega cities, million plus cities and other cities by G.O.I. as introduced. He has presented the aspects such as, l) Urbanisation in Telangana (2) Leveling of Jawaharlal Nehru National Urban Renewal Mission, (3) Scope of the Mission and submissions such as urban infrastructure and Governance (BIG) (2) Basic services to the urban Poor (BSUP), and implementation status of GI projects, JNNURM, Implementation status of BSUP projects in GHMCs and implementation of the reforms.

Further upined that the JNNURM Scheme gave big push for serious implementation of Urban reforms toward achieving concrete results. Reforms implementation, no doubt is a continuous process and the momentum has to be sustained as the results and total impact of administrative reforms takes no longer time.

The present study intends to evaluate the projects undertaken JNNURM in the Mission city of Hyderabad in the recently carved-out Telangana State, Hyderabad is the only Mission city under JNNURM.

V. Gangaiah has assessed the progress achieved in the implementation of the projects taken-up under JNNURM in the city of Hyderabad, evaluated critically the implementation of the reforms taken-up as part of the Urban governance improvement programme under JNNURM and recorded the perceptions of the institutions involved in the implementation of JNNURM and offered suggestions for policy and administrative connectnees to quite the similar urban development programmes and it has its impact on the Urban infrastructure and governance front in India.

Methodologically, this study is very much innovative and evaluation of the project in its true spirit accrue urban development through this mission. The sample study relates to 300 identified slum dwellers of the Mission city of Hyderabad-Random sempling technique has been adopted to identify the samples and the study primarily adopts the case study method in order to arrive at concrete conclusion and lessons and so on.

The author has identified that, "the current SMART City programme will continue the development momentam with much more speed and IT interventions JNNURM is thus could be considered a beginning for future urban momentum of the city of Hyderabad".

Finally arrived at this novel point is that, "the funding available under the centrally sponsored programmes through enhanced in recent years is to be supplemented by other funding mechanisms like accessing capital market, involving the private sector and increased allocations lay the Central and State Governments for Urban development".

This study truly help both the academicians and administrators, plan execution really with the governments decision and governments mechinery when fund, are squared, nothing could be done. As programme progresses, the funds should be accrual to complete the programme as plannet financial flow should be in permanent form so as to get largest results.

5.1 Library Informatics and Urban Information

Dr. Kandimalla Bharathi has concentrated upon web technology and received the Ph.D. from Osmania University, Hyderabad, in library and information science. She has identified some important and interesting findings from her study.

1. The worldwide web as a hypermedia, Hypermedia is used as a logical extension of the term by pestext in which graphics audio, video, plain text and hyperlinks interlink to create a generally non-linear medium of information.
2. She has further identified that skills are required to find and retrieve information effectively from WWW. The skills require to

achieve the maximum potential of electronic resources are much greater than those required for searching printed sources. These skills include knowledge of the structure of the database, the instructions that the searcher must enter into the computer, and understanding of the way, these instructions are linked to one another.

3. Electronic resources greatly increase access to information E-resources provide access to a wide range of information in various formats and types, modern libraries provide a study link between the highly technological information environment and the orders, advising on search strategies that help the user to focus the topic better and evaluate the information even as the user is able to access library catalogues and databases from mouse, office or anywhere".

Comment

1. The author finally opines that traditional way of conducting research has been done away with and the digitalization has given new path, new way for conducting research intensively in order to have good links with latest technologies to adopt them at various levels of study.
2. An intensive study and research that has been presents that how technological revolution may help the librarians and associated staff in the development of library information i.e. storing, creation of database and retrieval of information and so on. If we examine the technological revolution in library and information science that one compared to the traditional approaches, many aspects of change may appear in the following paragraphs.

1. Varma, Manoj Kumar and and Brahma Krishna	:	"ETD contribution to Shodhaganga by Indian universities with status of potential for excellence (UPE).
2. Mahapatsa, Ralindra K	:	"Information needs and seeking behaviour of the scientists of Krishna Vigan Kendras in Odisha: A study.
3. Lal, Jawaharlal	:	"Research Trends in Library and Information Science in India : During 2000 to 2010 - A study".
4. Narasimha Murty, K.L.	:	"Current Trends in Geographical Research - Applied Bibliomatric Methodology".

5. Pareek, A.K. and Hada, K.S. : Mapping of the publication patterns in European Journal of Education : A Bibliogremetric study".
6. Singh, Rajesh Kumar : Qualitative analysis of Collaboration and authorship trends in papers published in annuals of Library and information studies (ALIS).
7. Savatagi, Vinayak or Patil, S.B. : Bibliometive analysis of Indian Journal of Agricultural Economics: 2008 - 2015.
8. Singh, Suchita : Specialized course in Agricultural librarianship in Central University of India : A study.
9. Singh, Kunwar and Vcrma, Neha: Global visibility of Asian country Open Access Insti-tutional Repositories.
10. Shukla, B.B. : Sampling Techniques for Research Scholars.

Observations of important points

1. It is observed that from the above data base that out of 10 articles, five articles belongs to 'E' system electronic media based research papers which accounts for 50 percent and the remaining papers belongs to traditional type of research in library and information science.
2. It is strongly believed that electronic media has been playing an important and pivotal role in the study and research in all the branches of sciences and has no exception to library and information science.
3. Web studies related to web design and format of information creation and retrieval of information as an important item in the current and modern research. The role of librarian has been ever changing from keeping books (storing) and disbursing them to the students and so on (the precions function of a librarian) where as the current work of a librarian is to identity, recognize and make cataloging and ordering the books through online then physical processes modern trends and role of the librarian may help if he undergoes proper skill development training and keeps himself abreast of the latest technologies that are introduced in many branches of sciences and engineering".

5.2 B.M. Krishna Mohan has identified that there are social, political and economic injustice galore. The glaring inequalities, the shocking ill-treatment and denial of fundamental rights and even elementary justice to millions leave them without hope or any certainty of getting two square meals daily, not to total of assured shelter of save kind and minimum clothing or of reasonable opportunities for earning their livelihood and living with dignity and privacy. Article 38 of the Constitution and stated that the state shall strive to promote the welfare of the people by securing and protecting as effectively as it may, a social order in which justice, social, economic and political shall inform all the institutions of National life, clause 2 of the Article 38 further requires the state to strive in particular for minimizing the inequalities in income and endeavour to eliminate inequalities in status, facilities and opportunities not only among individuals but also among groups of people residing in different vacations engaged in different occupations.

'Shelter' is a basic human need most human settlements in urban areas reflect poverty and equator. In terms of quality and quantity, the gap between supply and demand in the housing sector in urban areas has ever been widening.

From the present study, the housing policy, which aims of providing houses to the poor and needy, has definitely undergone the threats of souls, forces and vested interests the author opined that, the pace of construction can be accelerated if special attention is given to the requirements, the availability and the mobilisation of resources of money, material and skilled labour the environmental constraints etc. B.M.K. Mohan has submitted the Thesis, "Housing Policy and programmes in Urban Bhopal: A study in Social and Environmental Change" for Ph.D. in Sociology, Barkatullah University, Bhopal (1992).

Suggestions are as follows:

1. Housing plots should be provided at the subsidised rates both for low paid govt. employees and to the members of weaker sections of the society.
2. The material needed for house construction should be made easily available to the needy persons.
3. The State Government adopt such a policy for its employee to grant owning rights of the quarters allotted to allow while in government service, after retirement, by taking nominal cost keeping in view of the rent already recovered from them.

4. In case of deceased govt. employee, the respective state government should provide a house on easy installments and for subsidized rates.
5. She influx of population to cities from rural areas should be discouraged.
6. The rural people may be given employment opportunities sufficiently in villages by establishing new units of industries.
7. Poverty alleviation programmes should be intensified.
8. In cities environmental awareness programmes be given wide publicity.
9. People should be educated in proper form so as to enable them to utilize the financial assistance which it to be provided by National Housing Bank and Housing & Urban Development Co-operation (NHB and HBDCO) etc.

B.M.K. Mohan's work on "Housing Policy and programmes in Urban Bhopal : A study in social and environmental change" is an important document and has presented important suggestions for M.P. Government, Bhopal, while taking steps for the environmental protection and also a Critical appraisal has been designed to follow it totally. The author has presented an in-depth study relating to Housing policy and programmes in Urban Bhopal. Directly, this study has its utility to Madhya Pradesh State Government to carry-out important business in this sphere. Sociological aspects have been presented, this type of work may encourage many social scientists such as Economists, Demographers, Geographers, politicians Scientists and Public Administrators. This study should, be multidimensional and multi-disciplinary nature keeping in view of the current scenario.

Dr. B.M.K. Mohan's work in the area of urban Sociology is quite praise-worthy and this document indeed serve the purpose to the needy people and administrators at the top level. It is an excellent document that has been prepared by the researcher, Dr. B.M.K. Mohan and this may find good place in Government department, as an instrument.

Chapter - 7

Role of Remote Sensing and GIS in Social Science Research

(Geoinformatics Applications in Development studies")

Introduction

The application of Geospatial technology in India in various sectors namely in wasteland and watershed management, water resources, irrigation, drinking water, health, infrastructure, road network, agriculture and other sectors of development, has brought in visibility, knowledge and scientific decision-making at all levels, in a time and cost saving manner. We are presently positioned at the outset of twentyfirst century with the fast growing trends in computer technology, information systems and virtual world to obtain data about the physical and cultural worlds, and to use these data to do research or to solve practical problems. The current digital and analog electronic devices facilitates the inventory of resources and the rapid execution of arithmetic or logical operations. These Information Systems are undergoing much improvement and they are able to create, manipulate, store and use spatial data much faster and at rapid rate as compared to conventional methods.

GIS Technology is proving decision supporting tool at local level for judicious and rational decisions, by integrating all knowledge base at village level and has the capabilities of modelling, scenario generation and strong visualisation for making the communities and people participate in the process of development, more vigorously and with scientific inputs. Spatial technologies facilitate generation of knowledge base up to cadastral level (land parcel level), where household socio-economic data is embedded on this layer on a GIS platform, with all graphic features of house type and house, hold linked, to enable all stakeholders to take decisions in a dynamic mode.

A GIS application in rural development Is thought to comprise of all Information of rural areas in a comprehensive manner, present, past and probable future scenarios, for empowering people at local level. Development of GIS will require preparation of base map showing revenue village boundaries along with boundaries of all tiers of governance starting from the Gram Panchayat, with various socio-economic and administrative features, and integration of all demographic, legacy and cultural features, for planning, implementation, monitoring and evaluation of rural development projects.

The land parcel map of village digitized and geo-coded with the help of GPS points and Google reference points, is spatially adjusted for mosaic and matching the boundaries. The settlement map is prepared village map and further spatially adjusted to fit properly in the spatially corrected map of cadastmas. After preparation of the Settlement Map, the settlement boundaries are prepared with due consultation of Patwari, Sarpanch and the house owners and proper boundary adjustments of houses are made, with depiction of ownership with photo of owner, bank loan,: land use, land category, cropping pattern details. etc as per Record of Rights (RoR). The settlement maps will consist of all the details of the houses like ownership/family details with photos and all the house wise details including livelihood. The location of schools along with attribute details, health center, plot wise soil details, gives very useful planning and decision support capabilities at local level.

For MGNREGS Employment Guarantee Programme, Geoinformatics is used to minitor structures and assets constructed at local level under MGNREGS, Watershed or other RD programmes, along with their location and other details, to facilitate updation of the data (locational and attribute). Satellite imageries for Rabi and Kharif seasons help assessing changes in the vegetation status and changes in water bodies and vegetative cover, and assess the impact of land, soil and water at local level. Many other available location based like Geomorphology, Lithology, Soil series, Soil capability, Water bodies, Drainage line, Ground water, cultural features and the value addition and comprehensiveness.

The Participatory Rural Appraisal (PRA) prioritizing the needs of local people on the basis of spatial spread, resources, infrastructure, available governmental programmes, along with attribute database on education, skill development, health, water resources, employment opportunities, Immunization, rural energy, agriculture and related aspects, demography viz. age, sex, education, occupation etc, asset structure, income particulars, land use and land 'cover particulars from satellite imageries and cadastre, and other useful information like social status, ration card, marital status and related data, along with photographs of each household family member comprise of a powerful decision support system' empowering local communities in rural areas.

GIS in rural development sector has inherent significance from the point of decentralized governance and Constitutional Mandate of empowering people at local level. There can't be a better tool than GIS for providing a powerful decision support system to the people to take their own decisions, analyze situations, assess potentials, plan for future, model and simulate and generate scenarios. Technology is enshaping mankind and with rapid strides of development in GIS Software and in the Information and Communication Technologies, and with price slashing in cascades, not only GIS will be an affordable tool in the hands of local people but would usher an integrated end to end solution based system for local bodies, NGOs, Government Departments, and people at large. GIS with GPS, Internet connectivity, high resolution satellite imageries and attribute data can revolutionize the entire thinking process of mankind in coming years. Rather than e-governance, it would be possible to implement G-Governance (GIS Governance) at all levels, anytime, any place, making information flow and decision making a real time dynamic process ensuring total participation and involvement of local people. Mobile GIS facilitate capturing photographs along with exact location of development work taken up under any programme, making monitoring realtime and enabling social audit with sharing of information on schemes, expenditure, physical achievement etc.

Geospatial Technology Applications

Geoinformatics Technology based planning, monitoring, modelling, decision support systems on Watershed, MGNREGA, Agriculture Development, Environmental Assessment, Conservation practices, Resources Planning, Infrastructure Development, Village Planning, Disaster Management, Micro Level/District Planning, Customised Applications, Catchment / Command Area Development, are proving beneficial for implementing development programmes at local level.

Agro-climatic Planning and Information Bank (APIB)

APIB (Agro Climatic Planning and Information Bank) is a single window Knowledge base for Agricultural and allied Sector. It will help the Government and farmers to make decisions for improving agricultural productivity. APIB has designed a database structure to contain information on both spatial and non-spatial elements namely mapping, GPS survey, soil survey, GIS and Image Processing analysis, fertilizers use, plant protection, seeds/ seedlings, package of practices, agricultural implements, climatological data, credit/ insurance schemes available, infrastructure for processing and marketing, demographic details, etc. The strength of APIB is a powerful state-of-the-art image analysis and GIS facilities to assess the natural resources endowments to any agro-climatic regions and would present them in the spatial and temporal domain. The Natural Resources databank are generated for the 18 themes at 1:10,000 scale. All the database are generated at 1:10,000 scale level, except in case of very steep and steep hilly areas under forest where the level of mapping will be reduced to 1:50,000 scale.

Generation of Action Plans/ Detailed Project Report for Watershed Development

By a process of extraction of contours and drainage layers from toposheets and integrating with Satellite Imageries, TIN, DEM, aspcct, flow accumulation and sink are generated in ArcGIS Hydrology Model. This forms the basis for suggesting appropriate treatment structures for watershed development with decision rules on a very reliable and scientific basis. Hydro-geomorphology, Soil, Land Use/Land Cover etc are also generated from satellite imageries which give significant inputs for scientific and cost effective watershed development Plans.

Geo-Informatics based Monitoring and 'Evaluation of Watersheds

Monitoring and evaluation are vital components of watershed development planning. Advanced technology of Remote Sensing and Geographic Information System provide a sound scientific platform in this endeavour. For the study Field survey was conducted at 300 watershed locations falling under Bhilwara, Barmer and Jaisalmer Districts of Rajasthan State in India. Data were collected from primary stakeholders pertaining to physical (ground water, soil erosion, runoff reduction, etc.), biological (afforestation, cropping intensity, productivity levels of dryland crops) and socio-economic parameters (additional benefit-cost ratio, additional annuity value, etc; and 'additional employment and reduction in outmigraton of labour, participation of farmers in watershed programmes) in watershed programme areas compared to non-watershed areas.To conduct the study the Digital Satellite Data was procured for pre and post treatment periods having same date of pass. Supervised classification of image with ground verification for Detection of Change in Land Use / Land Cover condition is done to understand the impact of the watershed programme on the crop production. Generation of Normalised Vegetation Index helped in studying Overall Change in Biomass. Estimation of change in land use/ land cover condition during pre and post treatment period. The analysis indicated that there was an increase in all factors in watershed area villages compared to nonwatershed area villages.

Village GIS

Village GIS is a Geoinformatics application framework for a Gram Panchayat, with facilities to capture data, analyse, integrating priorities, planning for development, social and economic infrastructure, household information, sectoral development, LULC, and various decision support parameters.

Geoinformatics application in MGNREGS

Geoinformatics is being used in asset capturing, monitoring of MGNREGS work and evaluation of the completed projects undertaken under MGNREGS and Watershed Development for monitoring the progress and evaluating the programmes.

Geoinformatics application in Road Network

Geoinformatics is extensively used in digital road networks, condition assessment, distance measurement, networks and routing, repair and maintenance, traffic management, road alignment, land procurement, shortest route analysis, traffic control, and is being used at all levels in the country.

The Geoinformatics applications are wide and varied and a summarised applications are presented as under:

Mapping

Mapping of all types in all scales are now digitally available and Widely used for Census, progress monitoring, environmental impact assessment, NRM, social sector analysis, infrastructure, demography, disaster, agriculture and related aspects and revolutionalised the concept of mapping and its use which could be possible through the use of the Geoinformatics.

Telecom and Network

The planning and decision making, are used in communication and telecommunication sector, through Geoinformatics based design, planning, optimisation, maintenance and activities, and posed to develop in engineering application, customer relationship management and location based services.

Road Accident Analysis

Through the use of Geoinformatics, road accidents, are minimized and optimize road safety. Geoinformatics based identifying the accident locations, precautionary measures, and rerouting made a difference in minimising the road accidents.

Smart Cities

The Geoinformatics technology is helping the planning, monitoring, infrastructure development, providing world class facilities in the Smart Cities Programme in the country, usher urban growth, hinterland and periphery development and bring accessibility of rural areas with the urban facilities.

Transportation

Geoinformatics has been internalised in transportation and networking and coming as a robust system for the economy, saving time, cost and efficiency, route planning, development of rail network, waterways, airways etc.

Environmental Impact Analysis

The Geospatial technology is very effective in the analysis of EIA, integrating navigation for positional information, satellite imageries, and ground information, temporally for both anthropogenic and natural phenomena.

Agricultural

Precision Agriculture is brining maximum change in agriculture productivity in an optimum manner, where Geoinformatics technology is playing a critical role. Suitability, soil analysis, productivity analysis and the like can be easily handled by Geoinformatics technology, including the seasonal agriculture production of crops.

Disaster Management and Mitigation

NOMA, ISRO and State Agencies help in disaster management in terms of rescue, rehabilitation, predication, early warning and damage analysis and provide support to national, state, local agencies and Local Elected Bodies to manage the disasters with minimum impact and to develop greater resilience and coping mechanism against the regular disasters.

Landslide

In hilly and inaccessible areas, satellite imageries help landslide hazard zonation, vulnerable areas, damage assessment, rescue and rehabilitation and help plan for protecting the areas against land slides, by integrating a variety of spatial data such as geological, structural, surface cover and slope characteristics of an area.

LULC

The Land Use and Land Cover (LULC) provides significant information on the area utilized for particular uses and natural coverage of land feature. Geoinformatics determine land use/land cover and estimate the changes, in the different areas.

Navigation

The Global Navigation Satellite System (GNSS) like NAVSTAR, GLONASS, GALLILEO, BEDUIN, GAGAN etc provide precise navigation on land, sea, ocean and river routes, location of changes occurring on land, effective management of logistics, cargo, routes, etc.

Natural Resources Management

Geoinformatics help agricultural, water, forest, soil, land resources etc, and help monitor forest condition, crop yield, monitoring crop rotation, water prospecting etc.

Banking Sector

The banking and retail finance sector have started using Geoinformatics for locating their service area, infrastructure, accessibility, growth and expansion, catering to customers, business and industries, link the local economy, primary production, expansion of infrastructure etc.

Land Information System

Geoinformatics help decision support system and taxation system, Digital Land Records, assessment, payments for private land with owner details, tracking of land allotments and possessions identification and timely resolution of land acquisition related issues and help in revenue management.

Surveying

Geoinformatics contribute significantly in surveying, and digital map preparation such as cadastral survey, satellite image analysis with ground truthing, GPS Survey, LIDAR, Drone, GPR Surveys etc.

Industry and Business

Geoinformatics has an essential component in mapping the distribution of products, identifying the shortest route, location of industries, stores, customers, logistics, procurement of input materials, shops, shortest routes, demand and customer area, planning and decision making, etc.

Tourism

Geoinformatics has evolved as a powerful tool for tourism promotion, with information on distance and it's measurement, finding hotels, restaurant and navigate to various places of interest, travel routes, logistics, etc.

Irrigation

Geoinformatics based evapotranspiration, Net Irrigation, Field Irrigation Requirement, Gross Irrigation Requirement, and water require-ment etc are analysed by the application of Geoinformatics.

Fisheries

Daily information on fish concentration is provided by INCOIS for the fisherman community in the coastal areas, in Indian languages through Geoinformatics analysis of Ocean temperature and vegetation information, which has increased the fish catch for the fishing community and their livelihood.

Utilities

The Geoinformation vital for the utilities such as electricity, telecom, gas, etc and help in mapping, inventory, tracking, maintenance, monitoring, distribution, load analysis etc.

Health

Geoinformatics provides the cost effective health delivery system, disease monitoring, disease profiling, vaccination routes, health infrastruc-ture, disease patterns, spatio temporal relationship between environmental pollution and disease, health related environmental hazards, geospatial health data, etc.

Environment

The Geoinformatics applications in environment studies, analysis and protection, monitoring are endless and widely applied across the world, with all facets like GPS, Satellite Imageries and GIS and provides useful data for understanding the environment.

Regional Planning

Geoinformatics is very useful in regional planning, micro planning, sectoral planning and integrated area planning exercise and is used at all levels of planning in the country, by State, Local Bodies, Ministries etc.

Wildlife Management

Wildlife tracking, census, location, migration, monitoring, habitat etc are studied effectively by the use of Geoinformatics.

Ocean Development

Geoinformatics provides information on state of oceans, ocean temperature, waves, currents, pollutions, oil spill etc, which provides vital information for climate change, ocean protection, control of pollution levels, oil spill etc.

A STUDY ON IDENTIFICATION OF LANDSLIDE ZONES ALONG THE RECENT EXPANSION OF BHE MILI BEACH ROAD, VISAKHAPATNAM DISTRICT-AGIS APPROACH

B.Sridhar*.Y. Padmini*'

*Department of Geo-Engineering, College of Engineering (A), Andhra University, Visakhapatnam

*Department of Geo-Sciences, Dr. B. R. Ambedkar University, Etcherla, Srikakulam

sridhar .bendalam@gmail.com gbujji.paddu@gmail.com

Abstract

Roads and Highways are the index of development of any nation. The study area considered covers the recent road expansion in between MVP colony to Bheemili, is a strategic important road which connects Visakhapatnam and Bheemili. Therefore, the work has been taken up to study the areas liable to collapse along the road expansion. The geological vulnerable zones were located using the spatial technology coupled with civil engineering studies. Initially, the drainage pattern of the study area is delineated to study the drainage condition, streams terminating into the sea and its characteristics. The desired location positions are measured using GPS. In the field work, the rock and soil samples are collected and the strike and dip of the rock are measured.

Keywords: Landslides, Remote Sensing, GIS, Geomorphology, Drainage pattern

Introduction

Roads and Highways are the index of development of any nation. India has the longest Highway road network which connects Kashmir to Kanyakuari [I]. It connects Northern border to Southern tip of India has a length of 2535.74 Km. The roads connect different areas varied type of topography and climate conditions etc. India has one of the finest road systems in the world. Delhi, Chandigarh and other major metropolitan cities have good road network [2]. Recently, Government of India has taken up expansion of the existing roads with a view to accommodate increasing road traffic [3].

In the history of road constructions, Romans had taken up the earliest road constructions. Roman army took up construction of roads activities which were as straight as possible. Similarly European countries have also developed road network in their respective countries. Constructions of major roads have come up in a highway during the period of industrial era. America has excellent road network followed by European countries. In Japan 8 tired road systems have been constructed to divert the heavy traffic to different places. Owing to scarce land, underground roads and railway systems being taken up in most parts of the world.

The present Grand Trunk Road had been constructed by Shear-sha-Suri during 17th century. This road connects Bengal in East to Peshawar in Pakistan in west. Present new roads have been following the old existing road system [4]. After independence, India has taken up to improve the road system to cater the needs of industries and public utilities at large.

The present study, recent road expansion in between MVP colony to Bheemili is a strategic important road which connects Visakhapatnam and Bheemili. This road has a length about 23 kilometers and passes along the sea coast of Visakhapatnarn and Bheemili. The Old Dutch settlement of Bhemili is the second oldest municipality in India. The expansion of existing road has consumed remove hill rock masses which are barely exposed onto the road may likely to collapse as slip land slides, etc [5]. Hence, this topic has been taken up to study the areas liable to collapse along the road. The present topic has been taken up with the following objectives.

Objectives of the study

1. To study the existing road conditions in view of present traffic load.
2. To study the existing topographical conditions along the road.
3. To study the rock, hill mass, cut exposures which are liable to collapse, slip, landslides, etc.
4. To study the drainage condition, streams terminating into the sea and its flood characteristics.
5. To study the geological, stratigraphical condition of the area.
6. To study the structural and geomorphological features of the area.
7. To study the tidal condition and erosion pattern of the sea along the road.
8. To study the geotechnical parameters of soil permeability, compressive strength of soil and rock, etc.

Location of Study Area

The area of investigation is located in between 17° 73' and 17' 80 North latitude and 83° 32' and 83° 45' Eastern longitudes. Geographically, the area is covering 236 km^2, out of which approximately half of the area covers under the jurisdiction of GVMC and rest comes under the Bheemili municipality. The study area is a part of Visakhapatnam and Bheemili municipalities of Visakhapatnam district of Andhra Pradesh.

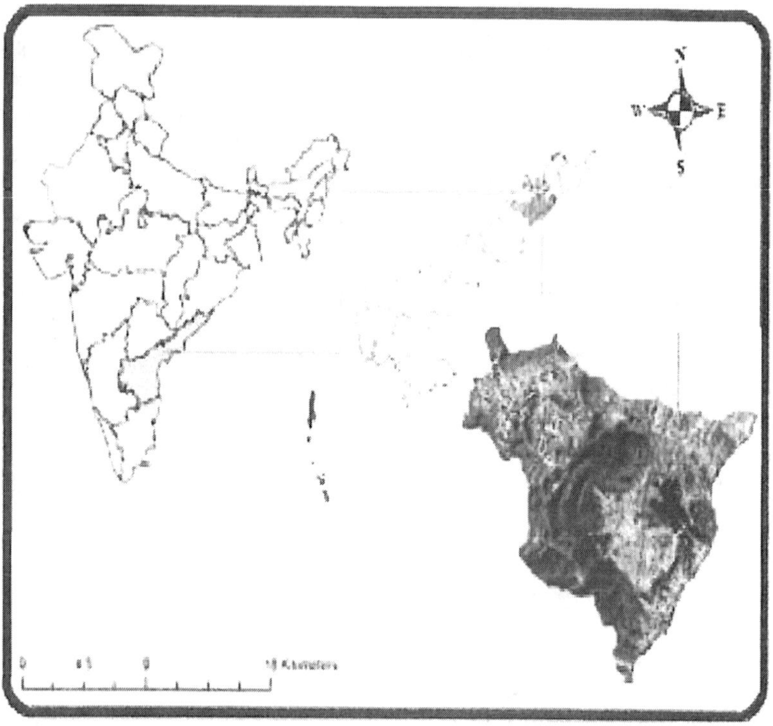

Figure : Location Map of the Study Area

Study area as viewed on IRS ID LISS III, 20I I.

The study is confined to recent expansion of four lane roads connecting between Visakhapatnam to Bheemili. The road laid adjacent to the sea coast of Bay of Bangal, and it is under the natural vagaries of sea coast on one side and land and its natural activities on the other side render the road vulnerable. Recently, IT Parks, Rama Naidu Cinema Studio, several resorts and urban built up come into existence. This anthropogenic activities has altered the topography along the road system. The major important places located enroute of this road are Rushikonda, Bojjannakonda, Erramattidibbalu, etc. Apart from natural and historical importances, INS Kaling as Indian Navy is established adjacent to this road. Traffic load is increasing year after year. In view of the traffic load recent road expansion has been taken up in place of old road network. This activity has led to cutting of hill flanks, foothills, sea sand dunes, culverts, drainages and highly denuded land forms etc. Hence, this topic has been taken up to study the soil creep, rock creep, solifluction, land slips, landslides, tidal action and beach erosion along the Bhimili road.

Methodology

Maps have been used for better administration, revenue collection, etc. for thousands of years. But it is only within the last few decades that the technology has existed to combine maps with computer graphics and databases to create Geographic Information Systems or GIS [6]. The themes in the above graphic are only a small example of the wide array of information that can view or analyze with a GIS.

GIS is used to display and analyze spatial data which are tied to databases. This connection is what gives GIS its power. Maps can be drawn from the database and data can be referenced from the maps. When a database is updated, the associated map can be updated as well. GIS databases include a wide variety of information including; geographic, social, political, environmental, and demographic. It is estimated that approximately 80 percent of all information has a "spatial" or geographic component. So when making decisions about siting new facilities, creating hiking trails, protecting wetlands, directing emergency response vehicles, designating historic neighbourhoods or redrawing legislative districts, geography plays a significant role [7].

Non-spatial (attribute) data

Attribute data have been generated either at the time of digitization of the polygon/polyline/point feature or after the digitization. All the feature attributes for all the layers have been assigned before the GIS analysis is taken up.

Assignment of weights

Weight values have been assigned depending upon the feature parameter and its importance [8] on assessment of landslide vulnerable zones along the Bheemili road. The output maps generated in the intersection were again intersected with the features to obtain the final output of erosion zones in the study area.

Integration of thematic layers

In this study, geology, soil, geomorphology, land use/land cover and slope thematic layers have been used in GIS analysis. Toposheets have been used for digitization of drainage pattern of the area. Onscreen digitization has been carried out and assigned stream orders.

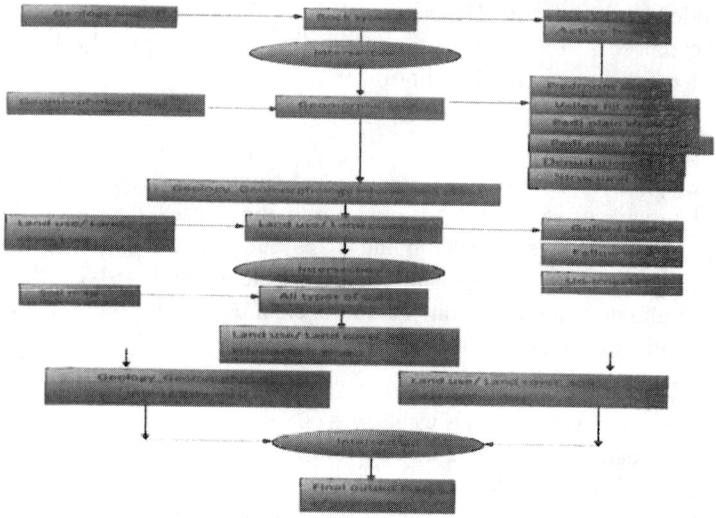

Figure 5.1 : Methodology adopted for landside vulnerable along the Bhemili Road.

Methodology adopted for landslide vulnerable zones along the Bheemili road.

Geology

Geology map has been generated using the GSI Visakhapatnam District map 2001.

Three major rock types are exposed in the area, out of which khondalite is the major rock type followed by Chamockite and quartzite. Chamockite and quartzite occur as intrusive bodies into the country rock. The weight classes were assigned on the basis of rock type which in turn its ease to weathering cohesiveness and erosion. The following weight classes assigned to the rock types in which khondalite country rock is considered in the GIS analysis.

Rock type	Weight class
Khondalite	I
Active beach	2
Chamockite	Restricted
Quartzite	Restricted
Laterite	Restricted
Sandstone	Restricted

Geomorphology

The study is focused light on sediment deposition in the landslide vulnerable zones along the Bheemili road. Geomorphology of the area has been delineated on IRS-ID-LISS-III satellite data. In this 13 fluvial and erosional classes were identified in which six are run-off zones and rest is infiltration zones. Run-off zones contribute sediment to the plains. Thus surface water bodies in the area have been highly silted up [9]. In GIS analysis, six classes have been considered to locate landslide vulnerable zones in the area. The following weight classes assigned to tbe geomorphic classes.

Geomorphic class	Weight class
Piedmont slope	1
Denudational hill	2
Marine sand dunes	3
Wave cut bench	4
Fluvial sand deposits	5
Valley fill shallow	6
Structural hill	7
Pedi plain shallow	8
Pedi plain moderate	9

The thematic layers of geology and geomorphology were intersected in Arc Toolbox in Arc G1S-9.2. Unwanted classes were removed from the output (Fig. 3). In this, khondalite is the base rock on which the erosional feature formed by the fluvial activity.

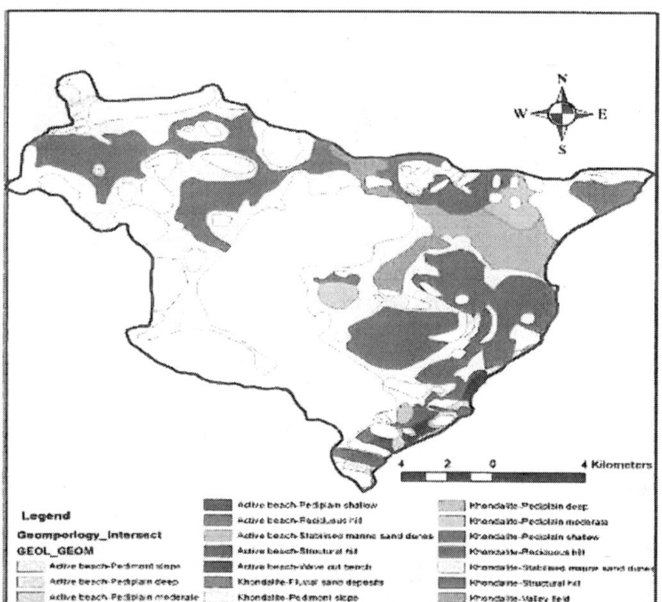

Figure 3: Intersection map of geology and geomorphology.

Soil

Soil is the upper most layers and composed with unconsolidated earth material which is prone to erosion. Besides its natural conditions soil erosion is triggered by anthropogenic activities. All types of soils of the area have been considered in to GIS analysis.

Land use/Land cover

Land use/Land cover of the area reveals the present status natural on and anthropogenic activity of the area. Cultivation is the major land use, followed by plantation and deciduous forest, etc [10]. The land use/land cover of the area has been delineated as per the norms suggested by NRSC, 1990. The analysis was carried out both by visual interpretation and digital interpretation. However, visual interpretation results have been used in GIS analysis [II]. The following weight classes

Assigned to the categories of land use/land cover for the GIS analysis. The soil layer and land use/ land cover were intersected in ArcGIS-9 .2. To arrive the erosion zones, the land use/ land cover features were considered. These features with intersection of different soils are considered rest of the soil zones were removed from the output (Fig. 4).

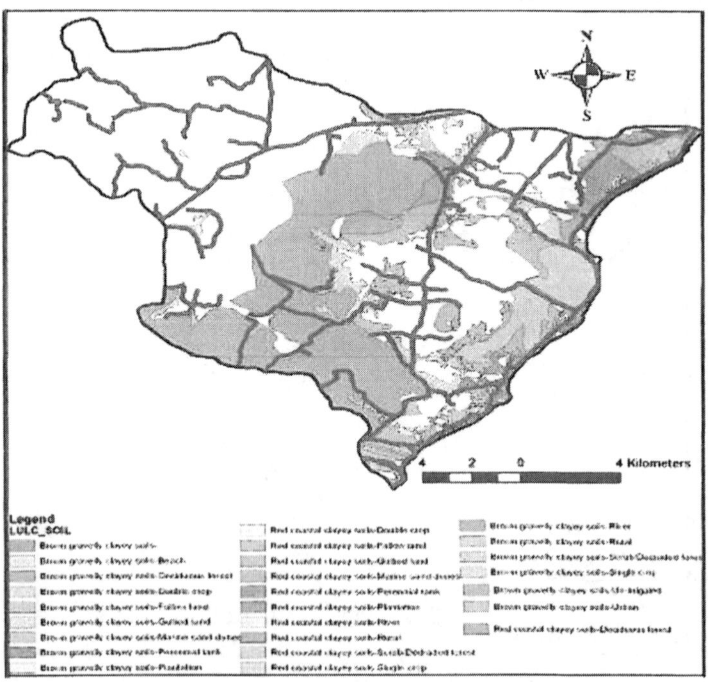

Figure 4: Intersection map of soil and land use/ land cover.

GIS analysis

GIS with its capability of map overlaying, reclassification, proximity analysis, and other mathematical operations is used in carrying out criteria based analysis [12]. Thematic layers are overlayed in GIS environment to locate land slide/soil creep zones. Weights have been assigned to geology, geomorphology, land use/land cover and soil. Using Analysis tool in ArcToolbox, intersection was performed to geology and geomorphology. The combined output is further assigned weightage and intersected with land use/land cover and soil map to locate landslide vulnerable zones along the Bheemili road Fig. 5.

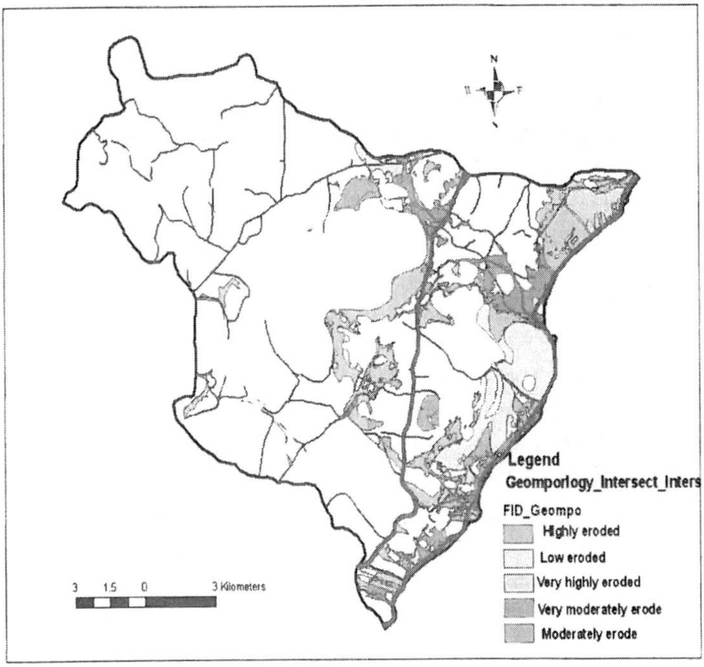

Figure 5: Landslide vulnerable zones along the Bheemili road in the study area

4. Results and Discussions

Thematic maps of geology, soil, geomorphology, landuse/landcover and slope thematic layers have been used in GIS analysis [13]. Toposheets have been used for digitization of drainage pattern of the area.

Geology map has been generated using the GSI map of Visakhapatnam District-2001. Three major rock types are exposed in the area, out of which khondalite is the major rock type followed by Active beach and Quartzite.

The weight classes were assigned on the basis of rock type which in turn its ease to weathering and erosion. In which Khondalite country rock is considered in the GIS analysis.

Soil is the uppermost layers composed of unconsolidated material [14]. Besides its natural conditions soil erosion is triggered by anthropogenic activities. All varieties of soils of the area have been taken in to consideration in GIS analysis.

Geomorphology of the area has been delineated on IRS-ID-LISS-ITI satellite data. In GIS analysis, nine classes of Piedmont slope, Wave cut bench, Fluvial sand deposits, Marine sand dunes, Valley fill shallow, Denudational hill, Structural hill, Pedi plain shallow, Pedi plain moderate, Pedi plain moderate have been considered to locate landslide vulnerable zones along the Bheemili road.

The land use/land cover of the area has been delineated as per the norms suggested by NRSC, 1990. The analysis was carried out by both visual interpretation and digital interpretations. Only, visual interpretation results used in GIS analysis. The weight classes assigned to the categories of land use/land cover for the GIS analysis is Gullied land, Fallow land, Unirrigated.

Thematic layers are overlayed in GIS environment to locate erosion zones. Weights have been assigned to geology, geomorphology, land use/ land cover and soil. Using Analysis tool in Arc Toolbox, intersection was performed to geology and geomorphology. The combined output is further assigned weightage and intersected with land use/land cover and soil map to locate soil erosion zones.

The values of weightage factor ranges from 0 to 10 and these have been assigned on the basis of erosion characteristics. The GIS analysis was carried out in ArcToolbox (Extension of Arc GIS-9.2) environment. The final output is generated after successful execution shows the landslide zones are about 62 km^2 area.

6. References

1. Ghani, E., Goswami, A. G., and Kerr, W. R. (2013). Highway to success in India: the impact of the golden quadrilateral project for the location and performance of manufacturing. The World Bank.
2. Pucher, J., Peng, Z. R., Millal, N., Zhu, Y., and Koratt yswaroopam, N. (2007). Urban transport trends and policies in China and India: impacts of rapid economic growth. Transport reviews, 27(4), 379-410.
3. Tiwari, G. (2002). Urban transport priorities: meeting the challenge of socio-economic diversity in cities, a case study of Delhi, India. Cities, 19(2),95-103.

4. Ranjan, A. (2015). The China-Pakistan economic corridor: India's options. New Delhi.

5. Sridhar, B., Rao, P. J., Rao, G. N. Duvvuru, R. Anusha, C. Naidu, D. S.,...and Padmini, Y. (2019). Identification of Landslide Hazard Zones Along the Bheemili Beach Road, Visakhapatnam District, AP. In Proceedings of International Conference on Remote Sensing for Disaster Management (pp. 515-522). Springer, Cham.

6. Longley, P. A., Goodchild, M. F., Maguire, D. J., and Rhind, D. W. (2005). Geographic information systems and science. John Wiley & Sons.

7. Rustamov, R. B., Salahova, S. E., Hasanova, S. N., and Zeynalova, M. H. (2011). Space Technology as the Tool in Climate Change Monitoring System. In Climate Change-Research and Technology for Adaptation and Mitigation. InTech.

8. Jagadeeswara Rao, P. Brinda, V. Suryaprakasa Rao, B. and Harikrishna, P., (2007). Determination of landfill destinations for strong waste administration in and around Visakhapatnam City-A GIS approach. Asian Jour. of Geoinformatics, VoL7, No. 3, pp. 35-41.

9. Sartor, J. D., and Boyd, G. B. (1972). Water pollution aspects of street surface contaminants (Vol. 81). US Government Printing Office.

10. Lambin, E. F., and Geist, H. J. (Eds.). (2008). Land-use and land-cover change: local processes and global impacts. Springer Science & Business Media.

11. Shalaby, A, and Tateishi, R. (2007). Remote sensing and GIS for mapping and monitoring land cover and land-use changes in the Northwestern coastal zone of Egypt. Applied Geography, 27(1), 28-41.

12. Malczewski, J. (1999). GIS and multicriteria decision analysis. John Wiley & Sons.

13. Srivastava, P. K., and Bhattacharya, A K. (2006). Groundwater assessment through an integrated approach using remote sensing, GIS and resistivity techniques: a case study from a hard rock terrain. International Journal of Remote Sensing, 27(20), 4599-4620.

14. Schoeneberger, P. J., Wysocki, D. A., and Benham, E. C. (Eds.). (2012). Field book for describing and sampling soils. Government Printing Office.

A STUDY ON IDENTIFICATION OF THE SUITABLE SITES FOR WATER HARVESTING STRUCTURES ARE SELECTED ALONG THE RECENT EXPANSION OF GVMC, VISAKHAPATNAM, DISTRICT-AGIS APPROACH

Y. Padmini*· B.Sridhar*.

*Department of Geo-Sciences, Dr. B. R. Ambedkar University, Etcharla, Srikakulam *Department of Geo-Engineering, College of Engineering (A), Andhra University, Visakhapatnam gbujji.paddu@gmail.com, sridhar.bendalam@gmail.com

Abstract : A suitable sites map provides basic data for understanding both past and present-day processes affecting a region of the Earth. This is the key to provide geologic information that can be utilized to reduce death and damage caused by geologic hazards. For the present investigation, thematic maps of geology have been generated from the LANDSAT 8 image, dated on 11th Jan 2016. Standard visual interpretation methods given by NRSA (1996) have been adopted to portray the features on map. From this study of the GVMC area, the result of Review of literature chapter describes about selecting the sites for water harvesting structures and techniques like check dams, percolation ponds, infiltration wells, afforestation, contour trenching etc., previous literature gives us the techniques of image interpretation, concepts of remote sensing which help in identifying different features in the study area.

Keyword : GVMC area, LANDSAT 8 image, Harvesting structures and Suitable sites map

Introduction

Water being one of the most important natural resources need to be conserved and managed properly. As water covers 71 percent of the Earth's surface only three percent is fresh water and the rest 97 percent of the water on the Earth is salt water. 0.687 percent of total water resources are available as ground water by the year 2005. Owing to industrialisation and urbanisation Indian metropolitan cities, were constructed unscientifically leading to irrational urban planning. Unless the need for scientific planning is realised, it is sure to clear up the environment. In coastal cities like Visakhapatnam, another major problem is seawater intrusion. As the seawater moves, inland groundwater aquifers become contaminated with salts, which may cause permanent damage to the aquifer.

The Greater Visakhapatnam Municipal Corporation (GVMC) city forms the area of the study in the present investigation. The population in the city is increasing at a rapid pace due to migration from surrounding areas, with corresponding increase in sub-urban areas also. The extensive growth of residential apartments along the coastal stretch resulted in excess withdrawal of groundwater initiating seawater intrusion in these tracts. All these factors combined, leading to an acute environmental crisis in the area. Forecasting urban water demand can be of use in the management of water utilities (Salvatore Campisi-Pinto, 2012). Hence, it is necessary to manage the available water resources in an efficient manncr. This is done using advanced technologies like Remote Sensing and Geographical Information System.

Location of the Study Area

The study area the Greater Visakhapatnam Municipal Corporation (GVMC) is located between $17^{0}32'30^{1}$" - 17°52'30" northern latitude and 83°04'30"- 83°24'30" eastern longitude. The urban area of GVMC is divided into six zones. These six zones are further divided into 72 municipal wards covering a total area of 545 km^2. The city is bounded by Bay of Bengal on eastern side, Duvvada hills, (Adavivaram hills) on the western side, Yarada -konda on the southern side and Madhurawada dome on the north side. (Fig. 1.1)

The study area is one of the major municipal corporations in the state of Andhra Pradesh. The area is famous for industries and tourism; often it is called as industrial city or city of destiny. The area has the reserved forests within the jurisdiction of GVMC. Due to recent developments such as IT Park and other constructions have come up in thick vegetated hilly area resulted in reduction of reduced forest cover. The area is well connected by rail, road, air and water (sea). According to 2001 census, the area has 1.7 million population. High density of population is located in the vicinity of GVMC area. The fringe area has very low density population where as areas like Chinthala Agraharam, Adavivaram, Gambhiram appears to be rural. Extensive agriculture is the major land use in these villages.

The area has more number of major industries such as Visakha Steel Plant, BHPV, Zinc smelter etc. The GVMC is not able to provide sufficient water to all industries. The situation is more precarious during summer period. Visakha Steel Plant is having its own source of water supply whereas other industries are depending on GVMC water supply. Presently, GVMC is drawing water from Mudasarlova, Meghadrigedda, Gambhiram, Thatipudi and Raiwada reservoirs. Majority reservoirs have been silted up above its dead storage (Jagadheeswara Rao, 2011) capacity resulting in less storage in reservoir. Water demand is increasing year after year which is leading to severe water crisis. To address this problem the present topic has been selected to augment ground water levels by adopting artificial recharge techniques in the study area. The study has been carried out with the following objectives.

Objectives of the study Area

The study has been carried out with the following main objectives for ground water resource management in GVMC are

- To quantify the ground water scenario in GVMC area.
- To study the feasibility for implementation of artificial recharge structures.
- To study the suitable sites for the construction of check dams and percolation tanks.
- To extract automated built-up area from Normalised Differential Building Index (NDBI).
- To study Land Use/ Land Cover pattern for better understanding of the study area.

Data used

In this study, the following data have been used for ground water resources management:

- The study area is covered in 650/ 1,2,4 & 6 of Survey of India toposheets on 1:50,000 scale.
- Google Earth image of the study area is downloaded in the Elshayal Smart Web Online Solutions open source software with an elevation of 500 m.
- LANDSAT 8 image of the study area is downloaded from the website United States Geological Survey.
- Population for the years 2021 and 2031 is calculated.
- Dug and bore well distribution data collected from GVMC.
- Agriculture data collected from Statistical Abstract of Visakhapatnam District, 2012-13.

The study area is one of the major municipal corporations in the state of Andhra Pradesh. The area is famous for industries and tourism; often it is called as industrial city or city of destiny. The area has the reserved forests within the jurisdiction of GVMC. Due to recent developments such as IT Park and other constructions have come up in thick vegetated hilly area resulted in reduction of reduced forest cover. The area is well connected by rail, road, air and water (sea). According to 2001 census, the area has 1.7 million population. High density population is located in the vicinity of GVMC area. The fringe area has very low density population whereas areas

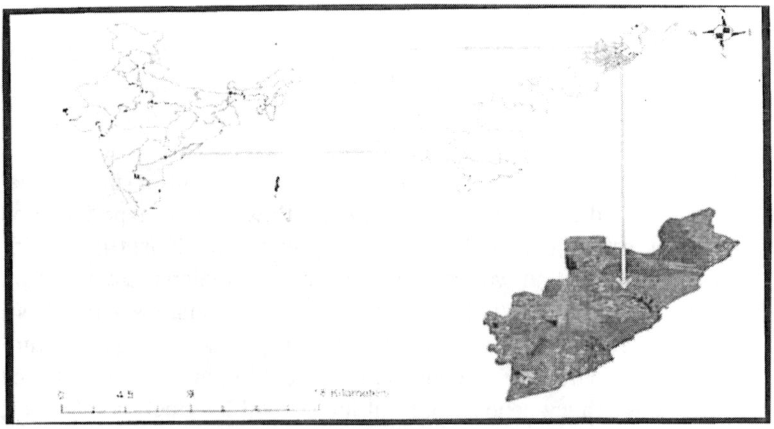

Figure : Location Map of the Study Area

like Chinthala Agraharam, Adavivaram, Gambhiram appears to be rural. Extensive agriculture is the major land use in these villages. The area has more number of major industries such as Visakha Steel Plant, BHPV, Zinc smelter etc. The GVMC is not able to provide sufficient water to all industries. The study area is divided into 6 zones from the administrative point of view (Fig. 1 .1) . Further, these six zones are divided into 72 municipal wards.

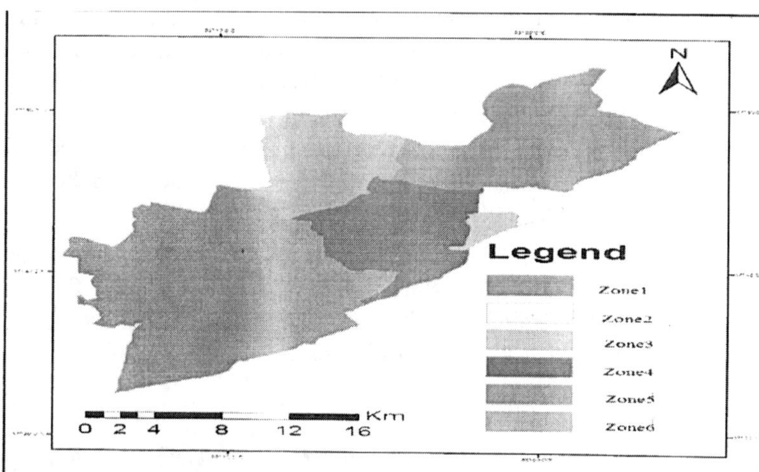

Fig. Zone wise map of GVMC Source GVMC, Visakhapatnam

Review of Literature

Li Xiaoyanl et al., (2002) made a study on "Effects of Rainwater Harvesting on the Regional Development and Environmental Conservation in the Semiarid Loess Region of Northwest China". This study deals with the major environmental issues in the Loess Plateau and evaluates the influence of rainwater harvesting implemented since 1980s on the regional development and environment conservation. Based on the experiment on rainfall harvesting and field investigation, micro catchment model for ecosystem construction was proposed to improve regional environment. The micro catchment rainfall -harvesting model with small watershed as a unit is characterized by incorporation of rainfall harvesting with yard economy and environmental construction. $\geq 25^0$ sloping land is protected as water conservancy zone by prevent human and livestock interference; tree (or shrub) and grass can be planted in the gentle slope by means of micro catchment water harvesting techniques. The natural slope can also be treated as catchment for collecting runoff into the cistern for supplemental irrigation for farmland, which is the main part of the system for supply food to farmer by various water-saving agriculture techniques.

Ranzi, et al., (2002) made a study on "Effects on floods of recent afforestation and urbanisation in the Mella River (italian Alps)". This study involves is to quantify the effects of the urbanisation on the flood volumes and peaks in the Mella river basin, 311 km^2 in size, changes in land use in the past 50 years have been compared using two land use maps. The comparison showed an increase in the forested areas in the upper part of the basin as the use of wood for fuel had declined and an increase in urban development in the valley bottom. Land use has been changing in the Mella River since 1954. Forested areas increased (+15.1 km^2,+9%) as did urban areas (+ 12.1 km^2,+25.2%) while crops and pasture areas decreased and the capabilities of forests to store more water, as interception or in the soils rich in organic matter.

Girish Kumaret al., (2002) made a study on "Delineation of Potential Sites for Water Harvesting Structures Using Remote Sensing and GIS" In the present study, potential sites for construction of rainwater harvesting structures in the Bakhar watershed of Mirzapur District.

Methodology

Maps have been used for better administration, revenue collection, etc. for thousands of years. But it is only within the last few decades that the technology has existed to combine maps with computer graphics and databases to create Geographic Information Systems or GIS. The themes in the above graphic are only a small example of the wide array of information that can view. In this chapter, information about the need of the study, objectives of the study, location of study area, physiography, temperature, rain fall, vegetation, climate, demography, etc., are dealt. The overall process is represented in a flowchart.

Review of Literature chapter describes about papers related to methods for the selection of suitable sites for water harvesting structures and extraction of built-up land. The project related literature both from international and national is summarised in order to strengthen the methodology and other procedure.

Remote Sensing and GIS

Remote Sensing and GIS chapter deals about the basic concepts of remote sensing and GIS. Extraction of study area's LANDSAT-S data and Google Earth's data is explained. Preparation of land use/ land cover data and automated extraction of built-up area using Normalized Differential Built-up Index (NDBI) algorithm for the study area is also explained.

Water Resource Management

Water resource management chapter deals with quantification of ground water. Different methods are suggested for water harvesting and suitable sites are selected for water harvesting structures like contour trenching, check dams, percolation ponds, infiltration wells and afforestation on the basis of different terrain characteristics.

Irrigation and Cropping Pattern

Built-up is the major land use in Greater Visakhapatnam Municipal Corporation, However, a limited cultivation is noticed in the suburban areas. Water supplied for irrigation is from Meghadhrigedda, Gambhiram reservoir. A less is available for agricultural in zones and zone 6 and these agricultural fields are irrigated by nearby water bodies. Paddy is the major food crop during Kharif season. Pulses and vegetables are the major crops in other season.

Majority agricultural lands' are converting into urban layouts. However, cultivating Paddy and Vegetables in Chintala Agraharam, Gambhiram and Pinagadi villages. Agricultural areas were identified on satellite image pale red stone with irregular shape.

Integration of thematic layers

In this study, geology, soil, geomorphology, land use/land cover and slope thematic layers have been used in GIS analysis. Toposheets have been used for digitization of drainage pattern of the area. Onscreen digitization has been carried out and assigned stream orders.

Climate

The area comes under humid to sub-humid climatic conditions, with high humidity all the year round, oppressive summer and good seasonal rainfall. The average annual rainfall of the district is 1201 mm. The rainfall during the monsoon period i.e., June to October amounts to about 79 percent of the total rainfall with October as the rainiest month. The mean maximum and minimum temperatures in the district range from 28.54°C to 33.51°C and 20.34° C to 27.31°C respectively. In general, the area receives 1200 to 1300 mm rainfall in the year. The highest rainfall is recorded in the month of October and the least in the month of December. The rainfall and temperature pattern of Visakhapatnam city (Table 1.1) which is nearest to the study area is shown in Figures 1.2 and 1.3.

Table 1.1: Temperature and Rainfall of Visakhapatnam

Month	*Average Maximum Temperature (°C)*	*Average Minimum Temperature (°C)*	*Precipitation (mm)*
May	33.6	27.9	80.56
June	33.8	28.0	97.32
July	30.5	26.3	137.08
August	31.7	26.8	164.38
September	32.4	26.3	148.72
October	31.7	25.0	226.7
November	30.2	23.7	127.26
December	29.2	21.3	4.86
January	28.3	21.0	10.8
February	29.3	22.1	14.2
March	30.9	25.5	15.44
April	31.9	27.3	25.3
Average	32.5	23.7	87.72

Flora and Fauna

The study area comes under the Eastern Ghats Mobile Belt (EGMB). The Eastern Ghats are known for a variety of flora and fauna. The hilly terrain has a number of wild plant species and fauna. It supports Kharif and Rabi crops and also plantation like coconut, banana, cashew and mango, etc.

About twenty percent of the area is covered by the degraded forests, deciduous forests and evergreen forests. There is diverse flora and fauna in this sanctuary representing the Eastern Ghats. Floral diversity is high and

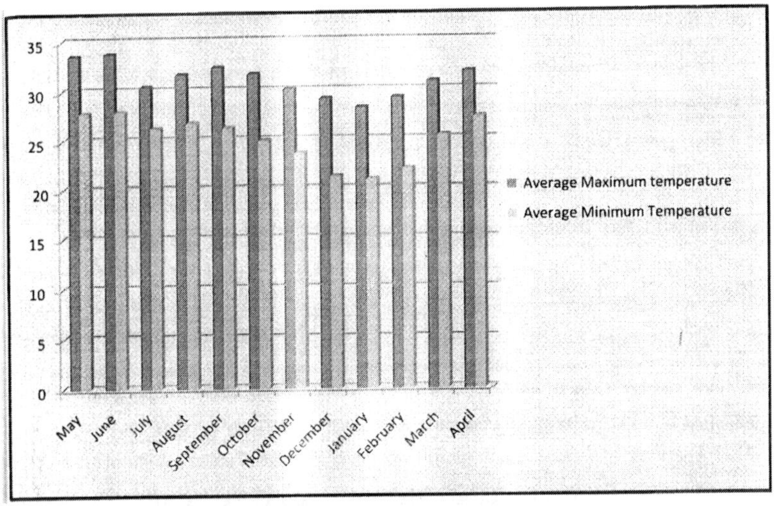

Figure 1.2 : Temperature variation of the study area

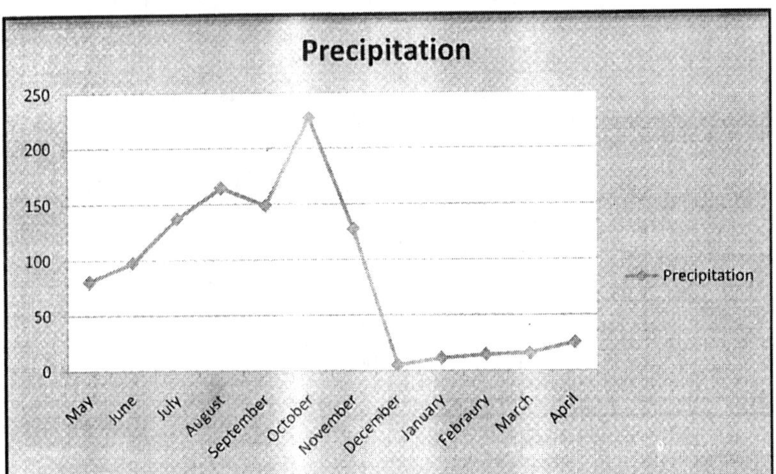

Figure 1.3 : Rainfall pattern of the study area

includes Tectona grandis, Catunaregam spinosa, Grewia tiliaefolia, and Abrus precatorius.

The fauna present in the sanctuary is Russell's Viper (Daboia russelii), Indian Cobra (Najanaja), Chameleon, Treepie, quails, partridges, Indian Leopard (Pantherapardusfusca), Indian Munt jac(Muntiacusmuntjak), Indian Pangolin, Chital (Axis axis), and Indian Jackal (Canis aureus indicus) etc (Hand Book of Statistics, Visakhapatnam District, 2011).

Data Used

The following data have been used in this study. The details of which is given in Table 3.1

- LANDSAT 8 image
- Google Earth image
- SOl Toposheets

Table 3.1: Details of Landsat-8 image

Name of the satellite	*Row*	*Path*	*Sensor*	*Date of acquired*
Landsat-8	48	141	OLI,TIRS	13-3-2015

Landsat 8 image

LANDSAT 8 image for GVMC area is downloaded from the United States Geological Survey website. The path and row of the image are 141 and 48 respectively. The sensors of LANDSAT 8 image are panchromatic, multispectral and thermal with the resolution of 15, 30 and 100 metres. The map projection is UTM and the study area falls under the zone 44. The LANDSAT 8 satellite consists of image has II bands. The list of bands in LANDSAT 8 image is given in Table 3.2.

Table 3.2: Band width and resolution of all the bands of Landsat-8 image

Band Number	***Band width (μm)***	***Resolution(m)***
Band I Coastal	0.433-0.453	30
Band 2 Blue	0.450-0.515	30
Band 3 Green	0.525-0.600	30
Band 4 Red	0.630-0.680	30
Band 5 NIR	0.845-0.885	30
Band 6 SWIRl	1.560-1.660	30
Band 7 SWIR2	2.100-2.300	30
Band 8 Pan	0.500-0.680	15
Band 9 Cirrus	1.360-1.390	30
Band 10 TIRSI	10.6-11.2	100
Band 11 TIRS2	11.5-12.5	100

Composite Bands

A composite band is the process to combine the required bands of the satellite image. The composite band tool is present in a set of raster processing tools in raster tools in data management tools. The following bands are combined for the present study (Table 3.3).

Table 3.3: Bandwidth and resolution of selected bands of LANDSAT-8 image

Band Number	*Band width (μm)*	*Resolution(m)*
Band 1 Blue	0.450-0.515	30
Band 2 Green	0.525-0.600	30
Band 3 Red	0.630-0.680	30
Band 4 NIR	0.845-0.885	30
Band 5 SWIR1	1.560-1 .660	30
Band 6 SWIR2	2.100- 2.300	30

Extraction by mask

The LANDSAT-8 image downloaded and layer stacked consists of whole Visakhapatnam district. To get the image consisting only the Greater Visakhapatnam Municipal Corporation area, that particular area is to be extracted. Extraction should be done by overlaying the boundary of the study area. The following are the steps involved in the process of extraction:

- Open the layer stacked image and boundary of the GVMC area.
- Open Arc tool box.
- Click on spatial analyst tools.
- Click on extraction by mask.
- Give the satellite image and boundary respectively in the window opened.
- Save the output in the required folder.

A single model for atmospheric correction, composite bands and extraction by mask is written in model builder window in Are GIS 10.3.

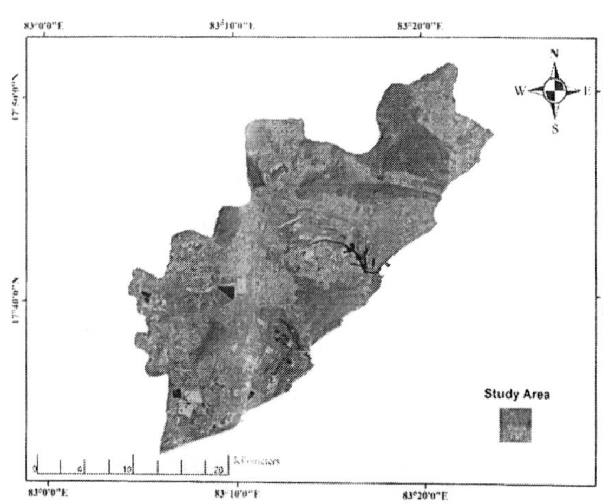

Figure: LANDSAT-8-image

Land Use / Land Cover Studies

Land Use/Land Cover information is the basic requisite for land, water and vegetation resources utilization, conservation and measurement. Land use describes how a piece of land is used, such as for agriculture or industry, whereas land cover describes the materials, such as vegetation, rocks or buildings that are present on the surface. Land use/land cover features to some extent reflect the geological/geomorphological controls.

Interpretation of satellite imagery (GOOGLE EARTH and LANDSAT-8-0Ll, path 141 and row 48 dated 13th March, 2015), coupled with thematic maps has helped in mapping the various land use/land cover features in the (GVMC). A review of the major land use/land cover features of the city area is described below.

Significance of Information on Land Use and Land Cover

Information on existing land use/land cover and pattern of their spatial distribution forms the basis for any development planning. The current land use need to be assessed for its suitability in the light of the land potential before suggestion alternate land use practices. The land cover maps derived by remote sensing are the basis to know the hydrological response units in the area. In order to have a better understanding of the hydrology of the area with little available data, a better insight into the distribution of the physical characteristics of the catchment areas is needed. By image processing techniques, image can be produced which depict some of the characteristics, primarily the cover types such as areas with vegetation, water bodies, areas with bare soils or out crops and settlement areas etc. land use pattern of any watershed influences the runoff and evapotranspiration.

Land Use and Land Cover Categories

Classification of the land use / land cover types as per NRSC specifications is presented in Table 4.3. This is a modified version of the land use / land cover classification suggested by Anderson (1965).

Built up land

It is an area of human habitation developed because of non-agricultural use of the land and it has a cover of buildings, transport and communication utilities in association with water, vegetation and vacant lands. In the present study area, the built-up land cover comprises of mostly GVMC area and other important villages / area are Gopalapatnam, Gajuwaka, Malkapuram, MVP colony, Isakathota, Venkojipalem, Mindhi, Scindia, NAD junction, Industrial area, RTC complex, Jagadamba junction, old post office etc.

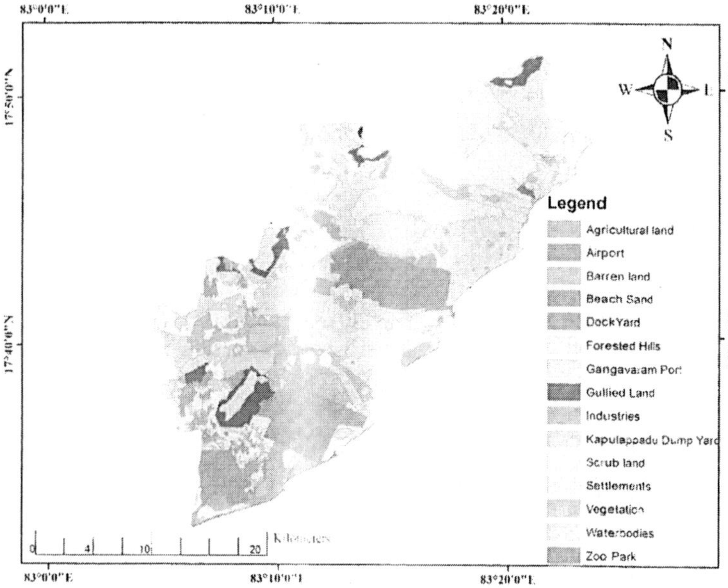

Figure.: Land Use/ Land Cover of the study area

(a) Built-up land (High / Medium density)

This is basically a residential, commercial and Industrial areas under GVMC and come in this category.

(b) Built-up land (planned residential area)

All the recently developed residential areas come under this category.

Examples are M.V. P. colony. Sithammadhara, Muralinagar and Dwarakanagar etc. All these areas were developed by YUDA. The built-up area is identified on the satellite image with the cyan colour and medium texture. All these are connected by road network. MVP colony is one of the biggest residential colony in Asia (Fig. 3.8).

(c) Built-up land with vegetation and sub-urban area

In this category, the areas which are properly planned with plantation cover are considered. It comprises of some parts of the city, rural areas of GVMC such as Narava, Sheelanagar, Pendhurthi, Kommadi, Adavivaram etc. And also areas under construction, upland areas like Waltair uplands, Dasapalla hills, slope areas like Railway yard, Port.

Soil map

Soil map is a geographical representation showing diversity of soil types and soil properties. Soil maps are most commonly used for land evaluation, traditional soil maps typically show only general distribution of soils. Generally soil maps are used to simply identify soils and their properties, but sometimes required for more specific purposes, such as determining the suitability of a soil for particular crops, harvesting structures and land drainage capabilities of an area. Soil map of GVMC area consists of different soils namely Brown clay soil, Brown gravel clay soil, Brown gravel loamy soil, Clay soil, Red clay soil, Red coastal clay soil, Red loamy soil and Sandy soil (Fig.3.17).

Selection of soil type is based on the type of harvesting structure technique is taken. Brown clay soil is covered in mostly Yisakhapatnam rural mandal areas like Madhurwada, Kommadhi and some part in Peddha-gantyada mandal. Similarly Brown gravel clay soils is covered areas like NAD, Narava, Steel Plant and some places in Peddhagantyada mandal.

Brown gravel loamy soil is covered only besides the Meghadrigedda. Clay soil is covering areas of Gopalapatnam, NAD, Sheelanagar. Red loamy soil is covering industrial area and sandy soil is present near Meghadrigedda and some places in Peddhagantyada mandal and Gajuwaka mandal.

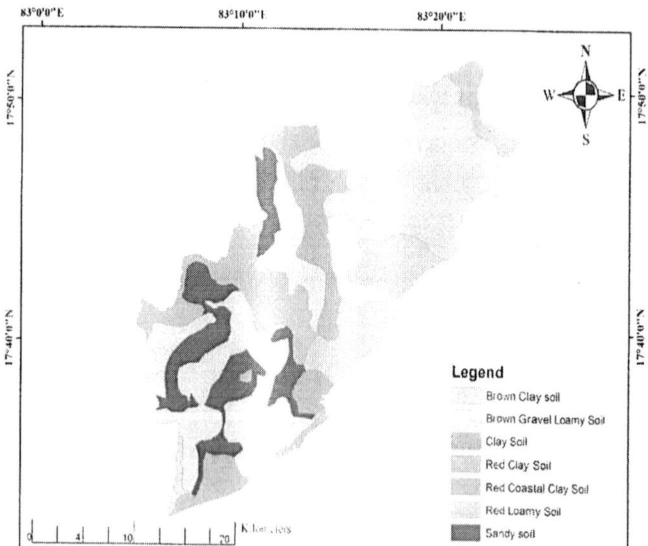

Figure: Soil map

Different artificial recharge techniques have been selected based on soil, slope, drainage and other properties. Mostly loamy type soil has been chosen for artificial recharge techniques. High clay content soils were rejected due to impermeability.

Slope map

Slope map shows the elevation of the particular area. The steepness value is bounded between maximum and minimum values. The slope of elevation can be depicted in two ways one is in degree and another in percent wise. The generation of slope map includes the following procedure.

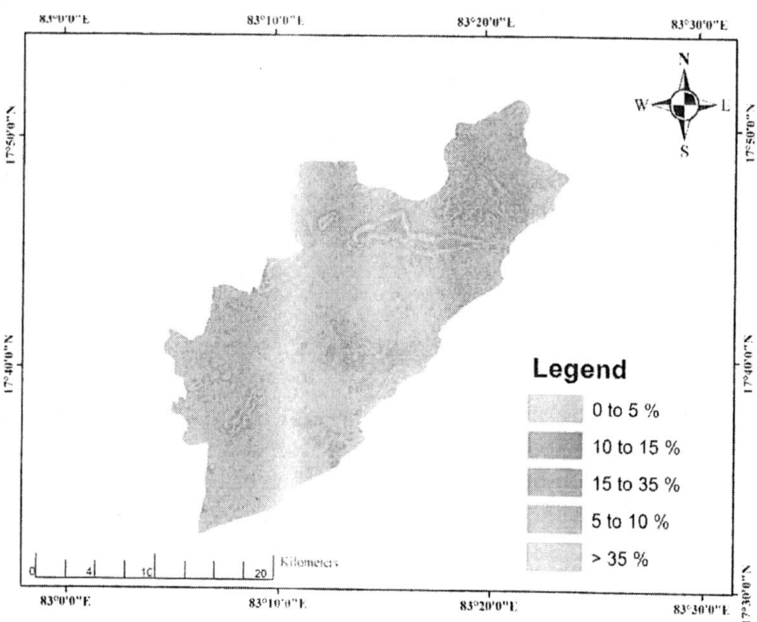

Figure : Stope map

Geomorphology

The study is focused light on sediment deposition in the landslide vulnerable zones along the Bhimili road. Geomorphology of the area has been delineated on LANDSAT-8 satellite data. In this 13 fluvial and erosional classes were identified in which six are run-off zones and rest is infiltration zones. Run-off zones contribute sediment to the plains. Thus surface water bodies in the area have been highly silted up [9]. In GIS analysis, six classes have been considered to locate landslide vulnerable zones in the area. The following weight classes assigned to the geomorphic classes.

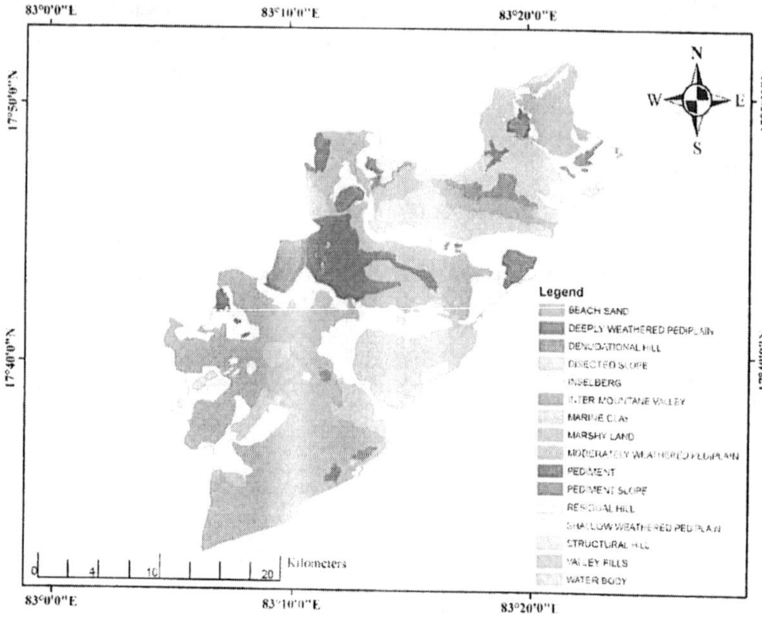

Figure: Geomorphology map

Geology

Geology map has been generated using the GSI Greater Visakhapatnam Municipal Corporation (GVMC) Visakhapatnam District. Three major rock types are exposed in the area, out of which khondalite is the major rock type followed by Chamockite and quartzite. Chamockite and quartzite occur as intrusive bodies into the country rock. The weight classes were assigned on the basis of rock type which in tum its ease to weathering cohesiveness and erosion. The following weight classes assigned to the rock types in which khondalite country rock is considered in the GIS analysis.

Drainage map

Drainage map has been generated using the toposheet, Greater Visakhapatnam Municipal Corporation (GVMC) Visakhapatnam District. Drainage Area. The term "drainage area" is defined as the land area where precipitation falls off into creeks, streams, rivers, lakes, and reservoirs. It is a land feature that can be identified by tracing a line of the highest elevation between two areas on a map, often a ridge. 1 to 5 orders streams.

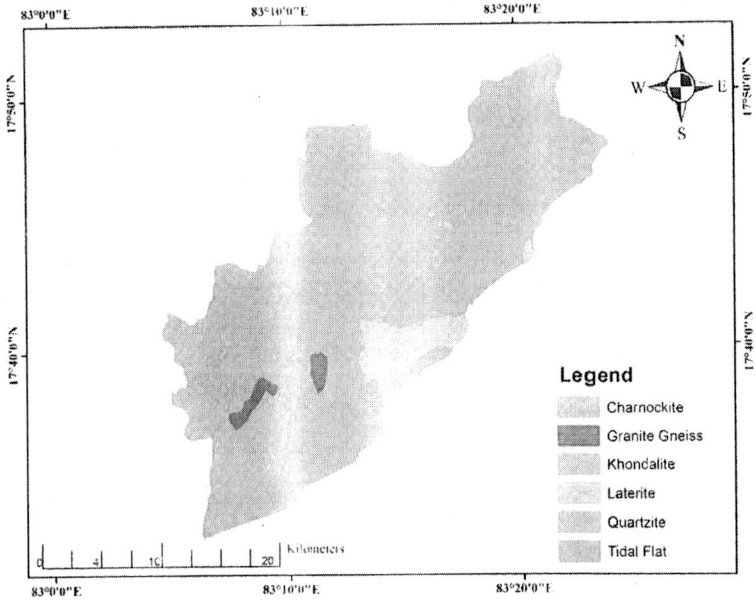

Figure: Geology map

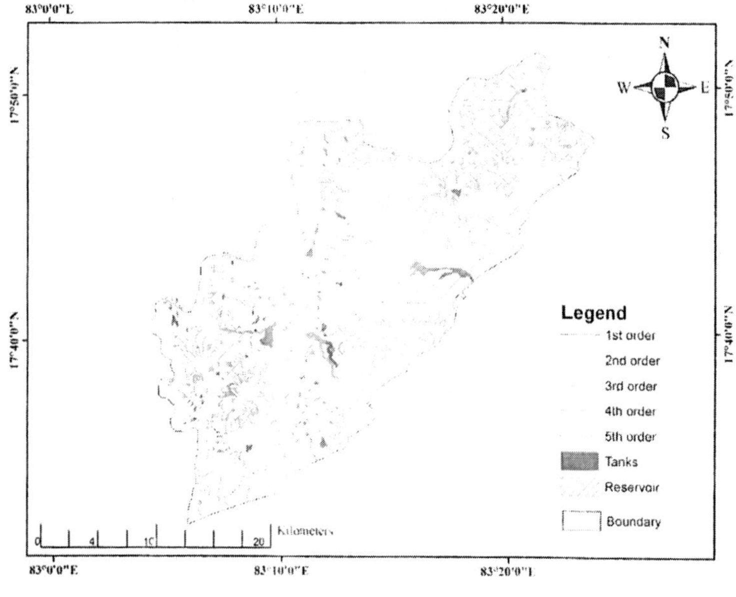

Figure: Drainage map

Summary and Conclusions

This includes the information in earlier chapters like introduction, review of literature, remote sensing and GIS and methodology (calculation of water demand for present population and industrial, water demand in future for years 2021 and 2031, selecting appropriate sites for harvesting structures to meet the demand of water for the Greater Visakhapatnam Municipal Corporation study area.

Review of literature chapter describes about selecting the sites for water harvesting structures and techniques like check dams, percolation ponds, infiltration wells, afforestation, contour trenching etc., previous literature gives us the techniques of image interpretation, concepts of remote sensing which help in identifying different features in the study area. Papers related to Geographic Information System tell us about the concepts of GIS which help in overlaying different layers for selecting the harvesting structures.

In this chapter the supply and demand of water details are discussed and the deficit is calculated. Also the suitable sites for water harvesting structures are selected. They are listed below.

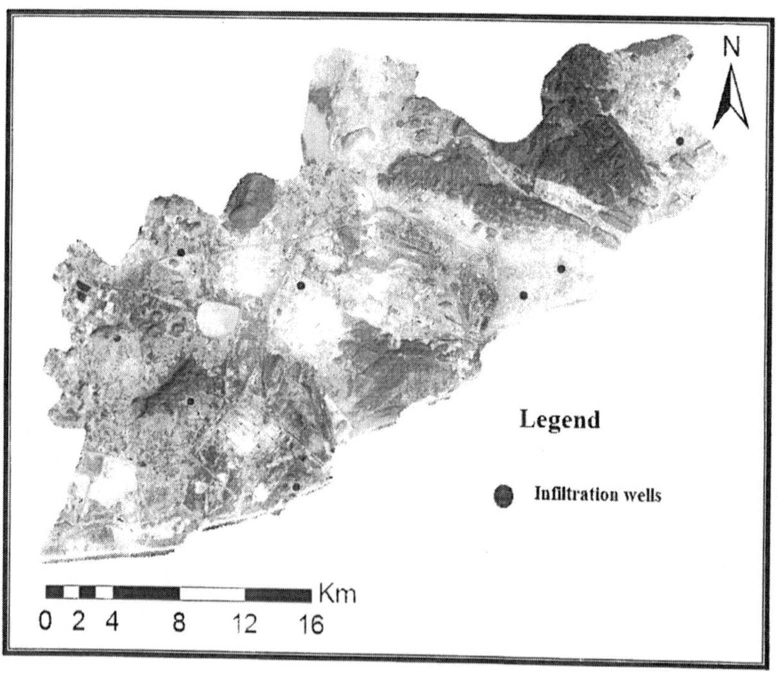

Figure: Infiltration wells

- The demand of water in study area is 57.09 MGD.
- Water supply for the domestic purpose is 49.46 MGD.
- Deficit of water for domestic purpose is 7.632 MGD.
- Water supplied for industrial purpose is 17.97 MGD.
- Demand for industrial purpose is 19.16 MGD.
- Deficit of water for industrial purpose is 1.98 MGD.
- Total deficit is 8.822 MGD.
- The demand of water will be 91.86 MGD for population 2784 171 in year 2021.
- The demand of water will be 151.154 MGD for population 4581075 in year 2031.
- Importance and need of water harvesting methods is discussed. Rain water harvesting structures are suggested to store water and increase the water levels in GVMC area.
- Desiltation of tanks are suggested for main tanks like KBR and Mudasarlova tanks. Sites for check dams are suggested. 4 check dams are suggested.
- 2 sites for percolation of ponds are suggested.
- 10 infiltration wells are also bc suggested all over thc study area.
- Contour trenching technique is also suggested for the hill forests in GVMC area.
- Afforestation is suggested in some areas of study area and the total area suggested for afforestation is 2479.88 ha.

References

Ratnakar Dhakate and Gurunadha Rao, V. V. S,. Anandagajapathi Raju.B, Mahesh J, Mallikharjuna Rao. S. T and Sankaran, S.2012. Integrated Approach for Identifying Suitable Sites for Rainwater Harvesting Structures for Groundwater Augmen-tation in Basaltic Terrain.

Yogesh BamneI, Patil 2, Dr. K. A, Vikhe,S. 2014. Selection of Appropriate Sites for Structures of Water Harvesting in a Watershed using Remote Sensing and Geographical Information System International Journal of Emerging Technology and Advanced Engineering. ISSN 2250-2459, ISO 9001:2008 Certified Journal, Volume 4.

Singh,PJ, Darshdeep Singh, Litoria, P.K. 2009. Selection of suitable sites for water harvesting structures in soankhad watershed, punjab using Remote sensing and Geographical information system (RS & GIS) Approach- a case study Research article.

Harish Chand Prasad, Parul Bhalla and Sarvesh Palria 2014. Site Suitability Analysis of Water Harvesting Structures Using Remote Sensing and GIS - A Case Study of Pisangan Watershed, Ajmer District, Rajasthan. The International Archives of the Photogrammetry, Remote Sensing and Spatial Information Sciences, Volume XL-8.

Deivalatha, A, Senthikumaran, P and K. Ambujam, N. 2014. Impact of desilting of irrigation tanks on productivity of crop yield and profitability of farm income African journal of Agricultural Research.

Jasroti A. A. S. (2008). Water Balance Approach for Rainwater Harvesting using Remote Sensing and GIS Techniques, Jammu Himalaya. India.

Hanqiu Xu., 2007. Extraction of Urban Built-up Land Features from Landsat Imagery Using a Thematic-oriented Index Combination Technique Photogrammetric Engineering & Remote Sensing Vol. 73, No. 12, pp. 1381-1391.

Hordur, V. Haraldsson, Harald U. Sverdrup, Salim Belyazid, Bjarni D. Sigurdsson and Guomundur Halldorsson 2007. Assessment of effects of afforestation on soil properties in Iceland, using Systems Analysis and System Dynamic methods.

Li Xiaoyan, Zhang Ruiling, Gong Jiadong and Xie Zhongkui 2002. Effects of Rainwater Harvesting on thc Regional Development and Environmental Conservation in the Semiarid Loess Region of Northwest China.

Ranzi, R, Bochicchioo M and Bacchi. B 2002. Effects on floods of recent afforestation and urbanisation in the Mella River (Italian Alps) Hydrology and Earth System Sciences.

Girish Kumar. M, K. Agarwal. A. Rameshwar Bali 2008. Delineation of potential sites for water harvesting structures using Remote Sensing and Geographical Information System, Journal of the Indian Society of Remote Sensing.

B. Balakrishna. H, C. Jayaramu, K 2014. Identification of Potential Sites for Rainwater

Harvesting using Remote Sensing and Geographical Information System.

Lejiang Guo, Lei Xiao Lejiang Guo, Lei Xiao Hu 2010. Application of GIS and Remote Sensing Techniques for Water Resources Management, 2nd Conference on Environmental Science and Information Application Technology.

GEOSPATIAL EVALUATION OF WATERSHED

Dr V Madhava Rao, Dr P Kesava Rao and Dr NSR Prasad

Introduction

Watershed-based development has been the strategy for growth and sustainability of agriculture in the vast semi-arid and dry sub-humid regions popularly called rain-fed regions. Watershed Development Projects have been undertaken to enhance agricultural production, conserve natural resources base, ensure rural livelihood, soil and water conservation. Geospatial technology analysis of the terrain, socio-economic appraisal of the stake holders and knowledge about local practices provide scientific insights of the soils, hydro-geomorphology, land use/land cover pattern, surface and ground water potential, which play a vital role in the implementation of appropriate soil and moisture conservation measures, water harvesting, land development, vegetation development and oveall ecosystem development of the region.

Black stated a watershed is a natural unit of land where water is accumulated from direct precipitation, snowmelt and other storage collects in a channel and flows downhill to a common outlet at which the water enters another water body such as stream, river, wetland, lake or the ocean. According to Frank, watershed management is the analysis, protection, repair, utilisation and maintenance of drainage basin for optimum control and conservation of water with due regard to other resources. Watershed development aims at rehabilitating the watershed through proper land use and conservation measures in order to minimize erosion; reduce the damage caused by sedimentation to the multipurpose reservoir; develop the watershed's crop, livestock, forestry, fish culture and recreational activities: ensure that the watershed provides water of the highest quality for municipal uses; and manage the watershed in order to minimize natural disasters such as floods, drought and landslides, etc.

Geospatial Technology Application

Hydrologic units like river basin and watersheds, are independent of political and jurisdictional boundaries, and relates to the water resources of the region, basin and watershed levels. The assessment of condition of vegetation is one of the indicators of environment. Vegetative cover discriminated from the other feature using near infrared bands. Natural resources like soil, surface and groundwater, landforms have their relevance but best results for assessment and management of natural resource are achieved by integrating various themes and assessing their potentiall in ideal geographical unit; i.e., a watershed under the subsystem of land, air, and water, with socioeconomic back drop by multidisciplinary approach. The emphasis on watershed development responses that rainfed areas need to be developed and managed in a sustainable manner.

Study Area

The study area for evaluating the watershed development was choosen in Bhilwara district of Rajastan State to understand the impact of the watershed development programmes and to come out with measures to optimise the benefits of the watershed development programmes implemented in the study region.

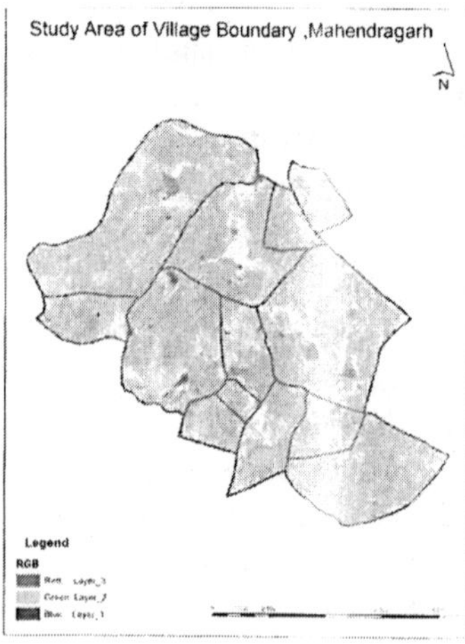

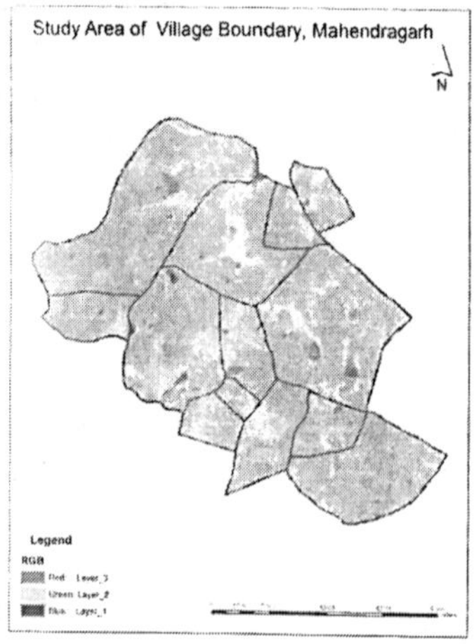

The satellite imagery of the study area is procured for different years. The analysis of the Satellite Imagery for the year 2000 was done using the Digital classification system. The study area was divided into four major land use/land cover classes using the digital classification and the aerial extent under each class is given in the listed in the table given below:

Areal extents of various Land Use/Land cover classes derived from the 2000 satellite imagery:

Land Use Class	*Area in Hectares*
Waterbody	130.2
Cropland	7076.1
Fallowland	2155.3
Scrub	1381.5
Total	10743.1

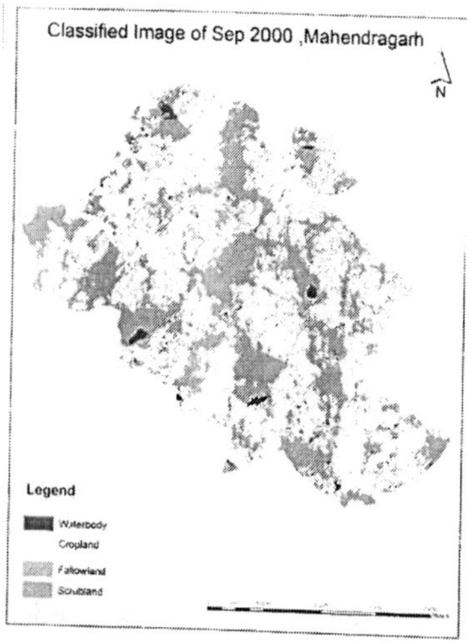

The total crop and in the study area occupied is around 7076. 17 ha, which constitutes nearly 65.8 percent of total study area. The total fallow in the study area occupied is 2155.3 ha, which constitute 20.1 percent of total study area. The water body in the study area occupied is 130.2 ha, which constitute 1.21 percent of total study area. The Scrub in the study area occupied is 1381.5 ha, which constitute 12.8 percent of total study area.

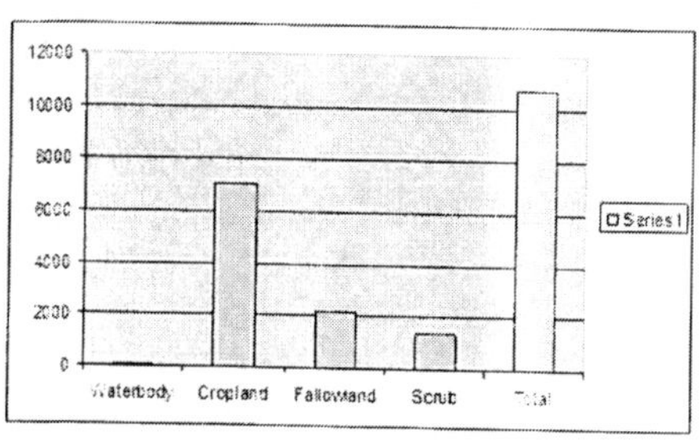

Digital Analysis and Findings

The evaluation of watershed development programmes of 3 temporal periods in Bhilwara district of Rajasthan State were analysed using satellite imageries, field survey and geopositional analysis, for the years 2005, 2007 and 2008, to observe the changes through its impact of watershed development programmes and identify the need to take measures to optimise the watershed development programmes in land, water, soil, productivity and socio-economic benefits of the local communities.

Digital Analysis of the 2005 Satellite Imagery: The analysis of the Satellite Imagery for the year 2005 was done using the supervised classification. The study area was divided into 4 classes and the aerial extent under each class is given in the table below:

Land Use Class	Area in Hectare
Waterbody	327.8
Cropland	7341.6
Fallowland	2435.9
Scrub	637.8
Total	10743.1

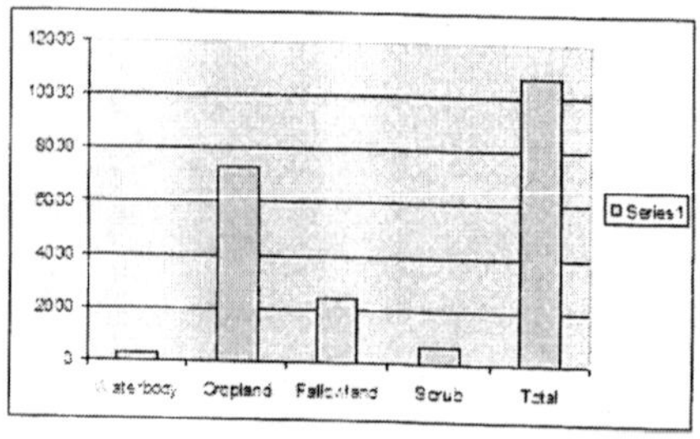

The total crop and in the study area occupied is around 7341.6 ha, which constitutes nearly 68.3 percent of total study area. The total fallow in the study area occupied is 2435.9 ha, which constitute 22.6 percent of total study area. The water body in the study area occupied is 327.8 ha, which constitute 3.05 percent of total study area. The Scrub in the study area occupied is 637.8 ha, which constitute 5.93 percent of total study area.

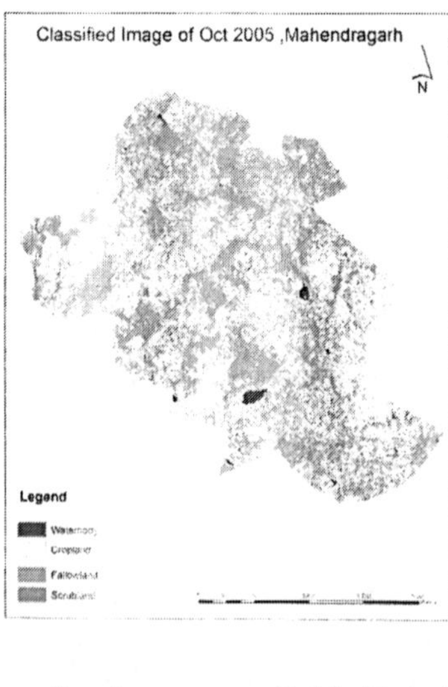

The Comparison of study area was divided into 4 classes and the aerial extent under each class is given in the table below:

Land Use Classes	***September*** 2000	***October*** 2005	***Change in*** Area
Water body	130.2	327.8	197.6
Crop land	7076.1	7341.6	265.5
Fallow land	2155.3	2435.9	280.6
Scrub	1381.5	637.8	-743.7
Total	10743.1	10743.1	

From the digital analysis it was observed that there was an increase of 265.5 hectares in crop land from 2000 to 2005.The fallow lands have increased by 280.6 hectares after the implementation of the watershed project in between 2000 to 2005 whereas the land with scrub has decreased by 743.7 hectares from 2000 to 2005.

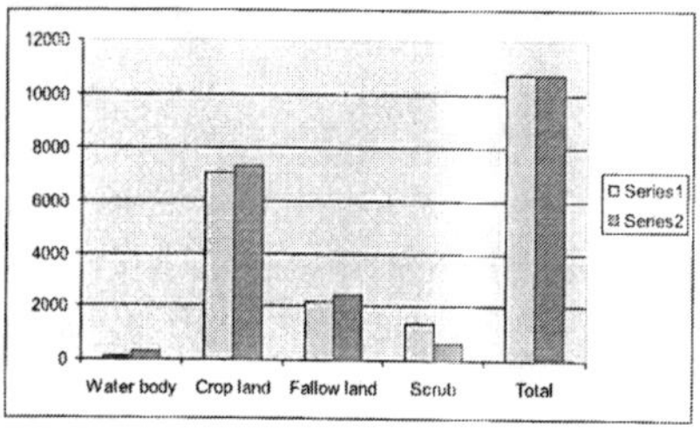

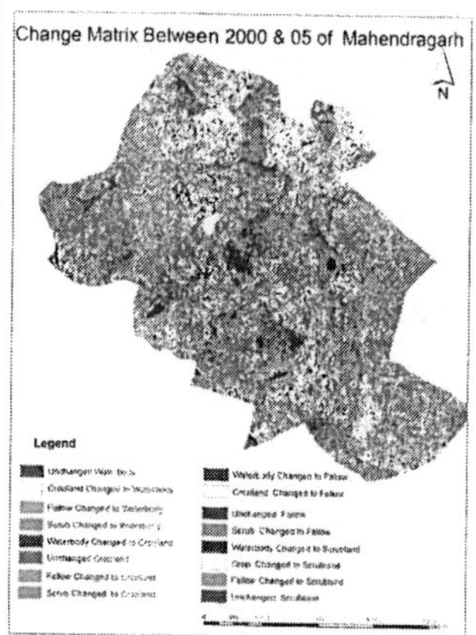

Change Matrix Between 2000 and 2005

2000/2005	*Water body*	*Cropland*	*Fallowland*	*Scrubland*
Water body	26.68	42.9	29.7	2.62
Crop land	12.54	4320.8	2397.9	90.6
Fallow land	18.67	930.6	1322.3	172.9
Scrub land	6.93	321.2	693.2	330.7

From the change matrix it is observed that the diagonal represented in the red font indicates area which have not changed from the year 2000 to 2005. The total unchanged area of the water bodies is 26.68 ha, crop land is 4320.8 ha, fallow land 1322.3 and scrub land is 330.7 ha.

Change Matrix Between 2000 and 2005

Changed related to the water bodies : From the analysis it is observed that the unchanged water body is 26.68 ha, the area under crop land which changed to water body is 12.54 ha, the fallow lands which changed to water body is 18.67 ha and 6.93 ha of scrub land has changed to water bodies from 2000 to 2005.

Changed related to the Crop Land: From the analysis it is observed that the unchanged Crop land is 44320.8 ha, the area under fallow lands which changed to crop land is 930.6 ha, 321.2 ha of scrub land has changed to crop land and 42.9 ha of water bodies has changed to crop land from 2000 to 2005.

Changes related to Fallow Lands: From the analysis it is observed that the unchanged Fallow land is 1322.3 ha, the area under Crop lands which changed to fallow land is 2397.9 ha, 693.2 ha of scrub land has changed to fallow land and 29.7 ha of water bodies has changed to fallow lands from 2000 to 2005.

Changes related to Scrub Lands: From the analysis it is observed that the unchanged Scrub Lands is 330.7 ha, the area under water bodies that changed to Scrub Land is 2.62 ha, 172.9 ha of fallow lands has changed to scrub lands and 90.6 ha of crop land has changed to scrub lands from 2000 to 2005.

Change Matrix between 2000 and 2005

Classes	Areas in Hectreas
Unchanged Waterbody	26.68
Crop changed to Waterbody	12.54
Fallow changed to Waterbody	18.67
Scrub changed to Waterbody	6.93
waterbody changed to Crop	42.9
Unchanged to Cropland	4320.8
Fallow changed to Crop	930.6
Scrub changed to Crop	321.2
Waterbody changed to Fallow	29.7
crop changed to Fallow	2397.9
Unchanged to Fallowland	1322.3
Scrub changed to Fallow	693.2
Waterbody changed to Scrub	2.62
Crop changed to Scrub	90.6
Fallow changed to Scrub	172.9
Unchanged Scrubland	330.7

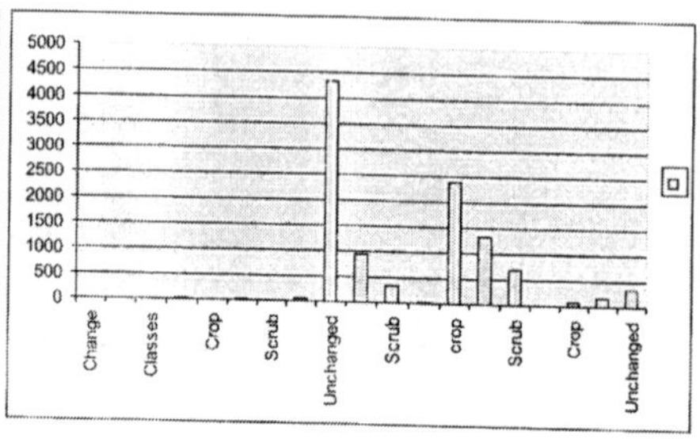

Digital Analysis of the 2007 satellite Imagery: The analysis of the Satellite Imagery for the year 2007 was done using the supervised classification. The study area was divided into 4 classes and the aerial extent under each class is given in the table below :

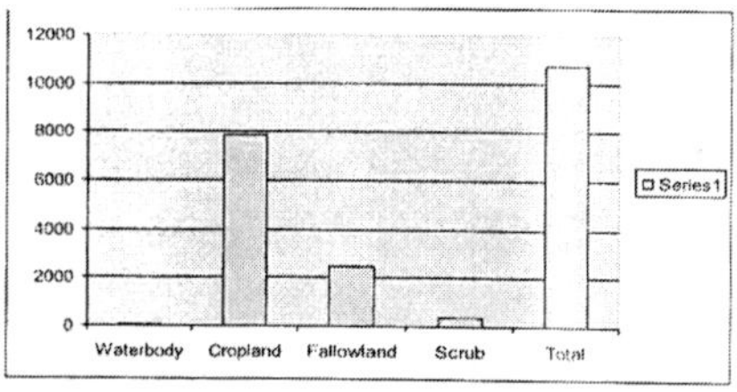

Land Use Class	Area in Hectares
Waterbody	52.9
Cropland	7832.9
Fallowland	2464.8
Scrub	392.5
Total	10743.1

The total crop and in the study area occupied is around 7832.9 ha, which constitutes nearly 72.9 percent of total study area. The total fallow in the study area occupied is 2464.8 ha, which constitute 22.9 percent of total study area. The water body in the study area occupied is 52.9 ha, which constitute 0.49 percent of total study area. The Scrub in the study area occupied is 392.5 ha, which constitute 5.93 percent of total study area.

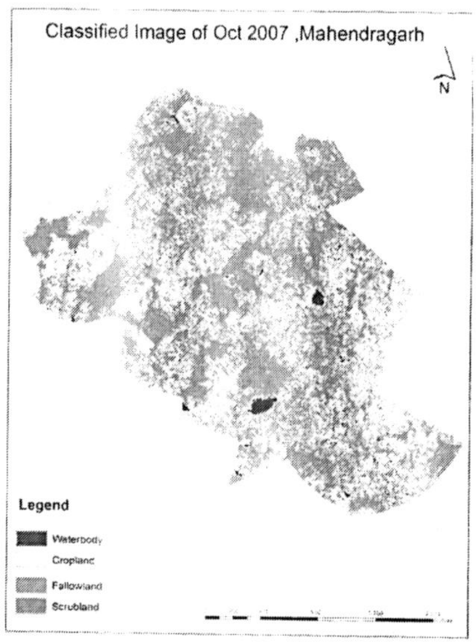

The comparison of study area was divided into 4 classes and the aerial extent under eaeh class is given in the table below:

Land Use Classes	***September 2000***	***October-2007***	***Change in Area***
Water body	130.2	52.9	-77.3
Crop land	7076.1	7832.9	756.8
Fallow land	2155.3	2464.8	309.5
Scrub	1381.5	392.5	989
Total	10743.1	10743.1	

From the digital analysis it was observed that there was an increase of 756.8 hectares in crop land from 2000 to 2007.The fallow lands have increased by 309.5 hectares after the implementation of the watershed project in between 2000 to 2007 whereas the land with scrub has decreased by 989 hectares from 2000 to 2007.

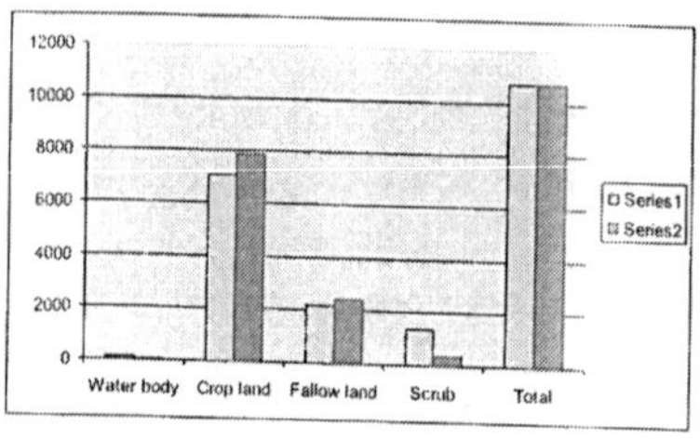

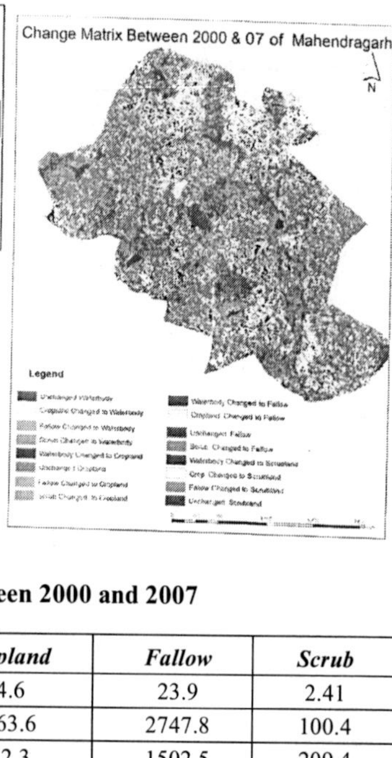

Change Matrix Between 2000 and 2007

2000/2007	*Water body*	*Cropland*	*Fallow*	*Scrub*
Water body	30.9	44.6	23.9	2.41
Cropland	10.9	3963.6	2747.8	100.4
Fallow	20.2	712.3	1502.5	209.4
Scrub	5.54	179.6	692.4	474.5

From the change matrix it is observed that the diagonal represented in the red font indicates area which have not changed from the year 2000 to 2007. The total unchanged area of the water bodies is 30.9 ha, crop land is 3963.6 ha, fallow land 1502.5 and scrub land is 474.5 ha.

Change Matrix between 2000 and 2007

Changed related to the water bodies: From the analysis it is observed that the unchanged water body is 30.9 ha, the area under crop land which changed to water body is 10.9 ha, the fallow lands which changed to water body is 20.2 ha and 5.54 ha of scrub land has changed to water bodies from 2000 to 2007.

Changed related to the Crop Land: From the analysis it is observed that the unchanged Crop land is 3963.6 ha, the area under fallow lands which changed to crop land is 712.3 ha, 179.6 ha of scrub land has changed to crop land and 44.6 ha of waterbodies has changed to crop land from 2000 to 2007.

Changes related to Fallow Lands: From the analysis it is observed that the unchanged Fallow land is 1502.5 ha, the area under Crop lands which changed to fallow land is 2747.8 ha, 692.4 ha of scrub land has changed to fallow land and 23.9 ha of water bodies has changed to fallow lands and from 2000 to 2007.

Changcs related to Scrub Lands: From the analysis it is observed that the unchanged Scrub Lands is 474.5 ha, the area under water bodies that changed to Scrub Land is 2.41 ha, 209.4 ha of fallow lands has changed to scrub lands and 100.4 ha of crop land has changcd to scrub lands from 2000 to 2007.

Change Matrix Between 2000 and 2007

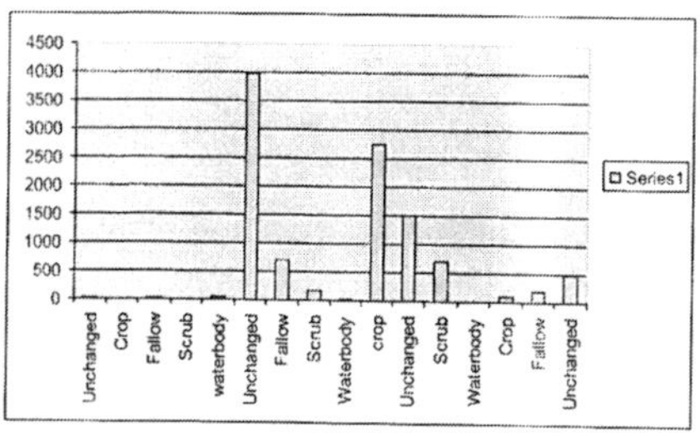

Classes	Areas in Hectreas
Unchanged Waterbody	30.9
Crop changed to Waterbody	10.9
Fallow changed to Waterbody	20.2
Scrub changed to Waterbody	5.54
waterbody changed to Crop	44.6
Unchanged to Cropland	3963.6
Fallow changed to Crop	712.3
Scrub changed to Crop	179.6
Waterbody changed to Fallow	23.9
crop changed to Fallow	2747.8
Unchanged to Fallowland	1502.5
Scrub changed to Fallow	692.4
Waterbody changed to Scrub	2.41
Crop changed to Scrub	100.4
Fallow changed to Scrub	209.4
Unchanged Scrubland	474.5

<u>Digital Analysis of the 2008 satellite Imagery:</u> The analysis of the Satellite Imagery for the year 2008 was done using the supervised classification. The study area was divided into 4 classes and the aerial extent under each class is given in the table below:

Land Use Class	Area in Hectares
Waterbody	15.9
Cropland	5896.9
Fallowland	3189.1
Scrub	1634.5
Total	10743.1

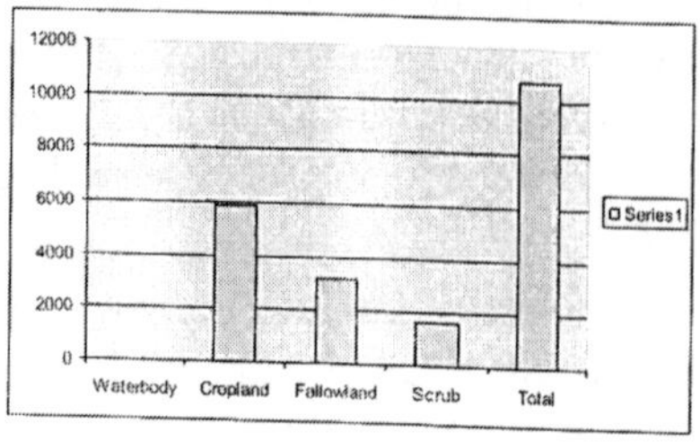

The total crop and in the study area occupied is around 5896.9 ha, which constitutes nearly 54.8 percent of total study area. The total fallow in the study area occupied is 3189.1 ha, which constitute 29.6 percent of total study area. The water body in the study area occupied is 15.9 ha, which constitute 0.14 percent of total study area . The Scrub in the study area occupied is 1634.5 ha, which constitute 15.2 percent of total study area.

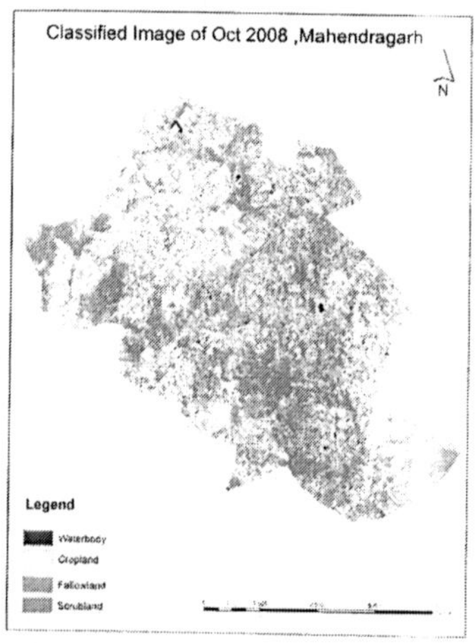

The comparison of study area was divided into 4 classes and the aerial extent under each class is given in the table below:

Land Use Classes	***September 2000***	***October 2008***	***Change in Area***
Water body	130.2	15.9	-114.3
Crop land	7076.1	5896.9	-1179.2
Fallow land	2155.3	3189.1	1033.8
Scrub	1381.5	1634.5	253
Total	10743.1	10743.1	

From the digital analysis it was observed that there was an decrease of 1179.2 hectares in crop land from 2000 to 2008. The fallow lands have increased by 1033.8 hectares after the implementation of the watershed project in between 2000 to 2008 whereas the land with scrub has increased by 253 hectares from 2000 to 2008.

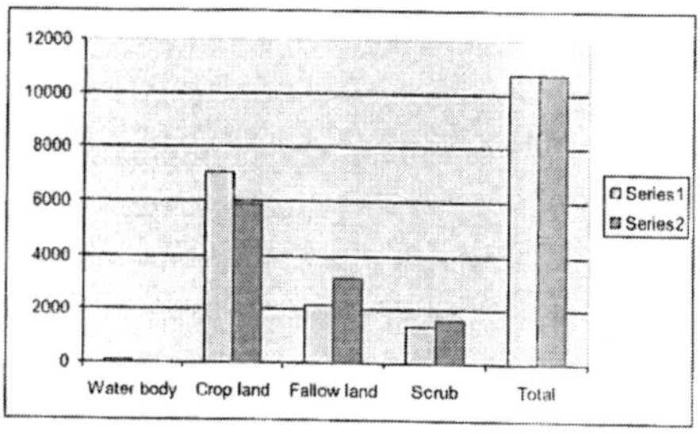

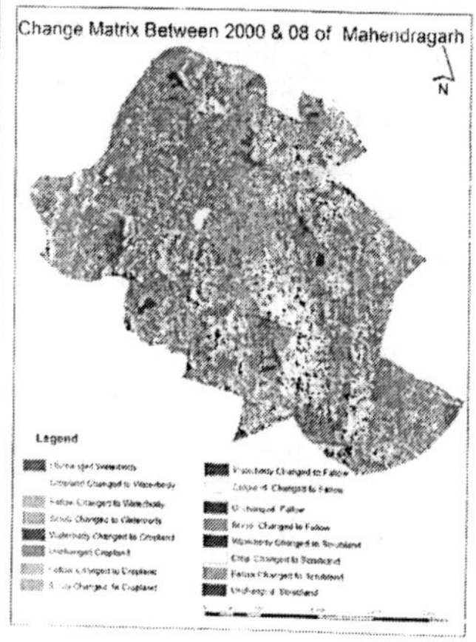

Change Matrix Between 2000 and 2008

2000 /2008	*Waterbody*	*Cropland*	*Fallow*	*Scrub*
Waterbody	3.46	47.1	27.6	24.8
Cropland	4.32	4231.1	2048.8	538.8
Fallow	4.21	111 7.1	744.9	569.4
Scrub	4.9	492.9	364.03	494.3

From the change matrix it is observed that the diagonal represented in the red font indicates area which have not changed from the year 2000 to 2008. The total unchanged area of the water bodies is 3.46 ha, crop land is 4231.1 ha, fallow land 744.9 and scrub land is 494.3 ha.

Change Matrix between 2000 and 2008

Changed related to the water bodies: From the analysis it is observed that the unchanged water body is 3.46 ha, the area under crop land which changed to water body is 4.32 ha, the fallow lands which changed to water body is 4.21 ha and 4.9 ha of scrub land has changed to water bodies from 2000 to 2008.

Changed related to the Crop Land: From the analysis it is observed that the unchanged Crop land is 4231.1 ha, the area under fallow lands which changed to crop land is 1117.1 ha, 492.9 ha of scrub land has changed to crop land and 47.1 ha of waterbodies has changed to crop land from 2000 to 2008.

Changes related to Fallow Lands: From the analysis it is observed that the unchanged Fallow land is 744.9 ha, the area under Crop lands which changed to fallow land is 2048.8 ha, 3643.03 ha of scrub land has changed to fallow land and 27.6 ha of water bodies has changed to fallow lands from 2000 to 2008.

Changes related to Scrub Lands : From the analysis it is observed that the unchanged Scrub Lands is 494.3 ha, the area under water bodies that changed to Scrub Land is 24.8 ha, 569.4 ha of fallow lands has changed to scrub lands and 538.8 ha of crop land has changed to scrub lands from 2000 to 2008.

Change Matrix Between 2000 and 2008

Classes	*Areas in Hectares*
Unchanged Waterbody	3.46
Crop changed to Waterbody	4.32
Fallow changed to Waterbody	4.21
Scrub changed to Waterbody	4.9
Waterbody changed to Crop	47.1
Unchanged to Cropland	4231.1
Fallow changed to Crop	111 7.1
Scrub changed to Crop	492.9
Waterbody changed to Fallow	27.6
Crop changed to Fallow	2048.8
Unchanged to Fallowland	744.9
Scrub changed to Fallow	364.03
Waterbody changed to Scrub	24.8
Crop changed to Scrub	538.8
Fallow changed to Scrub	569.4
Unchanged Scrubland	494.3

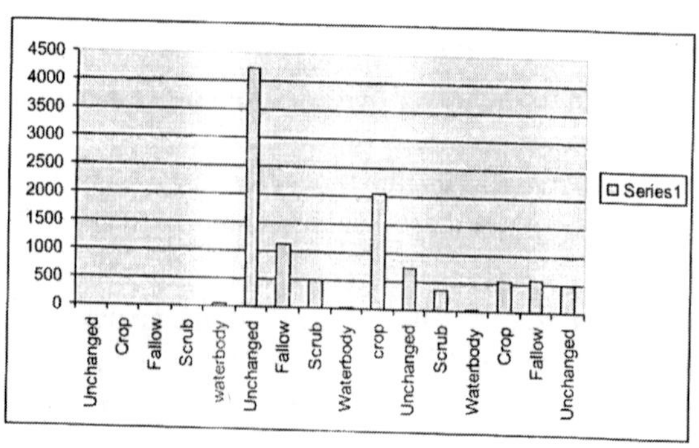

The Comparison of study area was divided into 4 classes and the aerial extent under each class is given in the table below:

Land Usc Classes	***October 2005***	***October 2007***	***Change in Area***
Water body	327.8	52.9	-274.9
Crop land	7341.6	7832.9	491.3
Fallow land	2435.9	2464.8	28.9
Scrub	637.8	392.5	-245.3
Total	10743.1	10743.1	

From the digital analysis it was observed that there was an increase of 28.9 hectares in Fallow land from 2005 to 2007. The Crop lands have increased by 491.3 ha after the implementation of the watershed project in between 2005 to 2007 whereas the land with scrub has decreased to 245.3 hectares from 2005 to 2007.

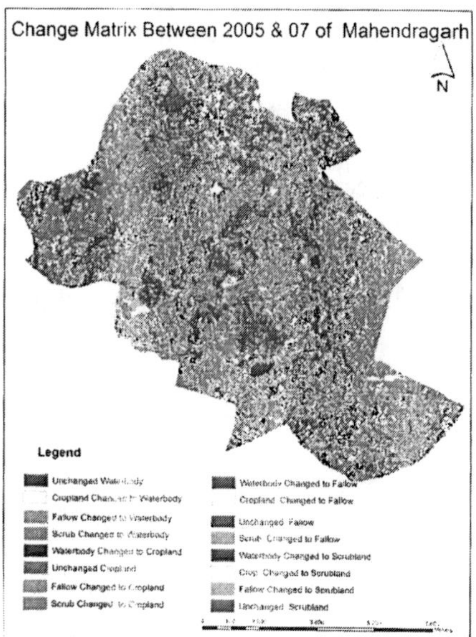

Change Matrix Between 2005 and 2007

2005/2007	***Waterbody***	***Cropland***	***Fallow***	***Scrub***
Waterbody	53.6	8.14	2.36	0.16
Cropland	10.1	3928.2	1568.6	102.4
Fallow	3.03	939.9	3264.6	255.2
Scrub	0.084	23.4	143.4	441.1

From the change matrix it is observed that the diagonal represented in the red font indicates area which have not changed from the year 2005 to 2007. The total unchanged area of the water bodies is 53.6 ha, crop land is 3928.2 ha, fallow land 3264.6ha hand scrub land is 441.1 ha.

Change Matrix between 2005 and 2007

Changed related to the water bodies: From the analysis it is observed that the unchanged water body is 53.6 ha, the area under crop land which changed to water body is 10.1 ha, the fallow lands which changed to water body is 3.03 ha and 0.084 of scrub land has changed to water bodies from 2005 to 2007.

Changed related to the Crop Land: From the analysis it is observed that the unchanged Crop land is 3928.2 ha, the area under fallow lands which changed to crop land is 939.9 ha, 23.4 ha of scrub land has changed to crop land and 8.14 ha of water bodies has changed to crop land from 2005 to 2007.

Changes related to Fallow Lands : From the analysis it is observed that the unchanged Fallow land is 3264.6 ha, the area under Crop lands which changed to fallow land is 1568.6 ha, 143.4 ha of scrub land has changed to fallow land and 2.36 ha of water bodies has changed to fallow lands from 2005 to 2007.

Changes related to Scrub Lands : From the analysis it is observed that the unchanged Scrub Lands is 441.1 ha, the area under water bodies that changed to Scrub Land is 0.16 ha, 255.2 ha of fallow lands has changed to scrub lands and 102.4 ha of crop land has changed to scrub lands from 2005 to 2007.

Change Matrix Between 2005 and 2007

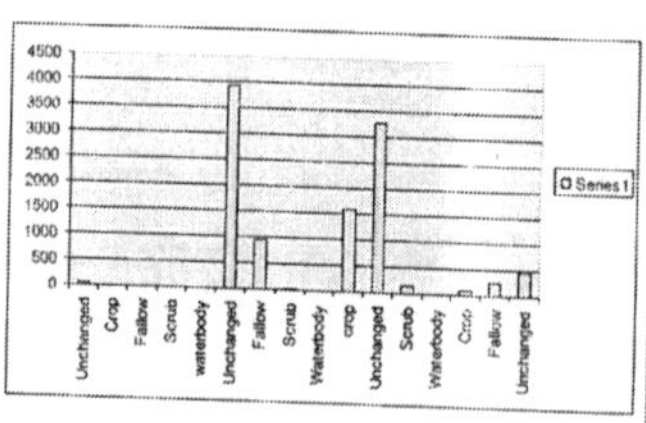

Classes	Areas in Hectreas
Unchanged Waterbody	53.6
Crop changed to Waterbody	10.1
Fallow changed to Waterbody	3.03
Scrub changed to Waterbody	0.084
waterbody changed to Crop	8.14
Unchanged to Cropland	3928.2
Fallow changed to Crop	939.9
Scrub changed to Crop	23.4
Waterbody changed to Fallow	2.36
crop changed to Fallow	1568.6
Unchanged to Fallowland	3264.6
Scrub changed to Fallow	143.4
Waterbody changed to Scrub	0.16
Crop changed to Scrub	102.4
Fallow changed to Scrub	255.2
Unchanged Scrubland	441.1

The Comparison of study area was divided into 4 classes and the aerial extent under each class is given in the table below:

Land Use Classes	***October 2005***	***October 2008***	***Change in Area***
Water body	327.8	15.9	-311.9
Crop land	7341.6	5896.9	-1444.7
Fallow land	2435.9	3189.1	753.2
Scrub	637.8	1634.5	996.7
Total	14023.6	14023.6	

From the digital analysis it was observed that there was an increased of 753.2 hectares in Fallow land from 2005 to 2008. The Crop lands have decreased by 1444.7 ha after the implementation of the watershed project in between 2005 to 2008 whereas the land with scrub has increased to 996.7 hectares from 2005 to 2008.

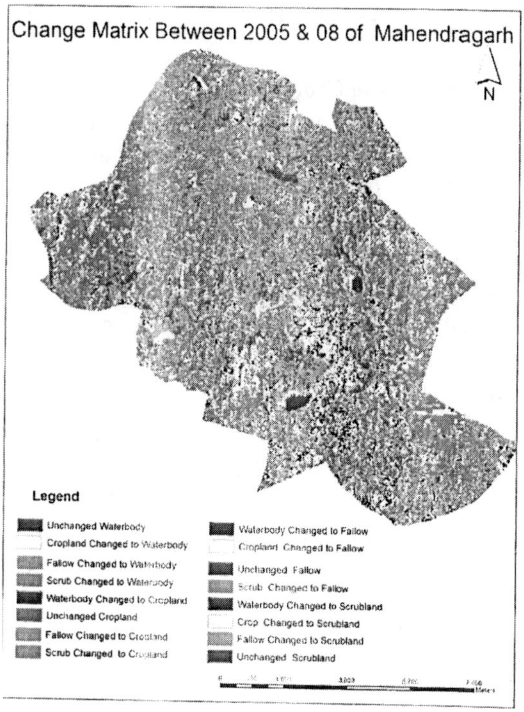

Change Matrix Between 2005 and 2008

2005/2008	*Waterbody*	*Cropland*	*Fallow*	*Scrub*
Waterbody	3.1	18.8	28.9	12.6
Cropland	6.5	3507.2	1598.6	482.6
Fallow	5.8	2 173.6	1425.6	847.5
Scrub	1.5	190.1	131.9	283.7

From the change matrix it is observed that the diagonal represented in the red font indicates area which have not changed from the year 2005 to 2008. The total unchanged area of the water bodies is 3.1 ha, crop land is 3507.2 ha, fallow land 1425.6 and scrub land is 283.7 ha.

Change Matrix between 2005 and 2008

Changed related to the water bodies: From the analysis it is observed that the unchanged water body is 3.1 ha, the area under crop land which changed to water body is 6.5 ha, the fallow lands which changed to water body is 5.8 ha and 1.5 ha of scrub land has changed to water bodies from 2005 to 2008.

Changed related to the Crop Land: From the analysis it is observed that the unchanged Crop land is 3507.2 ha, the area under fallow lands which changed to crop land is 2173.6 ha, 190.1 ha of scrub land has changed to crop land and 18.8 ha of water bodies has changed to crop land from 2005 to 2008 .

Changes related to Fallow Lands: From the analysis it is observed that the unchanged Fallow land is 1425.6 ha, the area under Crop lands which changed to fallow land is 1598.6 ha, 131.9 ha of srub land has changed to fallow land and 28.9 ha of water bodies has changed to fallow lands from 2005 to 2008.

Changes related to Scrub Lands: From the analysis it is observed that the unchanged Scrub Lands is 283.7 ha, the area under water bodies that changed to Scrub Land is 12.6 ha, 847.5 ha of fallow lands has Changed to scrub lands and 482.6 ha of crop land has changed to scrub lands from 2005 to 2008.

Change Matrix Between 2005 and 2008

Classes	*Areas in Hectares*
Unchanged Waterbody	3.1
Crop changed to Waterbody	6.5
Fallow changed to Waterbody	5.8

(Contd...)

Scrub changed to Waterbody	1.5
Waterbody changed to Crop	18.8
Unchanged to Cropland	3507.2
Fallow changed to Crop	2 173.6
Scrub changed to Croo	190.1
Waterbody changed to Fallow	28.9
Crop changed to Fallow	1598.6
Unchanged to Fallowland	1425.6
Scrub changed to Fallow	131.9
Waterbody changed to Scrub	12.6
Crop changed to Scrub	482.6
Fallow changed to Scrub	847.5
Unchanged Scrubland	283.7

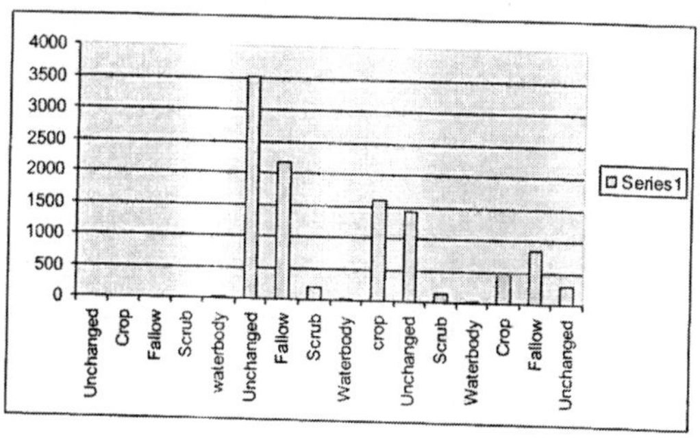

The comparison of study area was divided into 4 classes and the aerial extent under each class is given in the table below:

Land Use Classes	***October 2007***	***October 2008***	***Change in Area***
Water body	52.9	15.9	-37
Crop land	7832.9	5896.9	- 1936
Fallow land	2464.8	3189.1	724.3
Scrub	392.5	1634.5	1242
Total	10743.1	10743.1	

From the digital analysis it was observed that there was an decreased of 724.3 hectares in Fallow land from 2007 to 2008.The Crop lands have decreased by 1936 ha after the implementation of the watershed project in between 2007 to 2008 whereas the land with scrub has increased to 1242 hectares from 2007 to 2008.

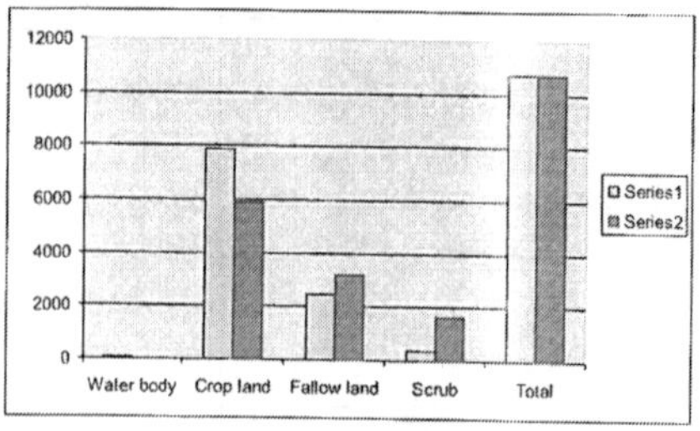

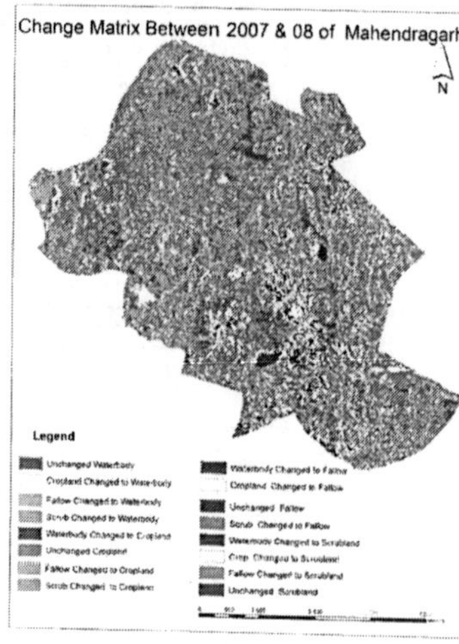

Change Matrix Between 2007 and 2008

2007/2008	*Waterbody*	*Cropland*	*Fallow*	*Scrub*
Waterbody	3.3	19.4	31.3	12.6
Cropland	5.9	2858.4	1386.4	383.7
Fallow	5.6	2757.9	1584.7	885.9
Scrub	2.7	257.8	182.8	344.3

From the change matrix it is observed that the diagonal represented in the red font indicates area which have not changed from the year 2007 to 2008. The total unchanged area of the water bodies is 3.3 ha, crop land is 2858.4 ha, fallow land 1584.7 and scrub land is 344.3 ha.

Change Matrix between 2007 and 2008

Changed related to the water bodies : From the analysis it is observed that the unchanged water body is 3.3 ha, the area under crop land which changed to water body is 5.9 ha, the fallow lands which changed to water body is 5.6 ha and 2.7 ha of scrub land has changed to water bodies from 2007 to 2008.

Changed related to the Crop Land: From the analysis it is observed that the unchanged Crop land is 2858.4 ha, the area under fallow lands which changed to crop land is 2757.9 ha, 257.8 ha of scrub land has changed to crop land and 19.4 ha of water bodies has changed to crop and from 2007 to 2008.

Changes related to Fallow Lands: From the analysis it is observed that the unchanged Fallow land is 1584.7 ha, the area under Crop lands which changed to fallow land is 1386.4 ha, 182.8 ha of scrub land has changed to fallow land and 31.3 ha of water bodies has changed to fallow lands from 2007 to 2008.

Changes related to Scrub Lands: From the analysis it is observed that the unchanged Scrub Lands is 344.3 ha, the area under water bodies that changed to Scrub Land is 12.6 ha, 885.9 ha of fallow lands has changed to scrub lands and 383.7 ha of crop land has changed to scrub lands from 2007 to 2008.

Change Matrix Between 2007 and 2008

Classes	*Areas in Hectares*
Unchanged Waterbody	3.3
Crop changed to Waterbody	5.9
Fallow changed to Watcrbody	5.6
Scrub changed to Waterbody	2.7
Waterbody changed to Crop	19.4
Unchanged to Cropland	2858.4
Fallow changed to Crop	2757.9
Scrub changed to Crop	257.8
Waterbody changed to Fallow	31.3
Crop changed to Fallow	1386.4
Unchanged to Fallowland	1584.7
Scrub changed to Fallow	182.8
Waterbody changed to Scrub	12.6
Crop changed to Scrub	383.7
Fallow changed to Scrub	885.9
Unchanged Scrubland	344.3

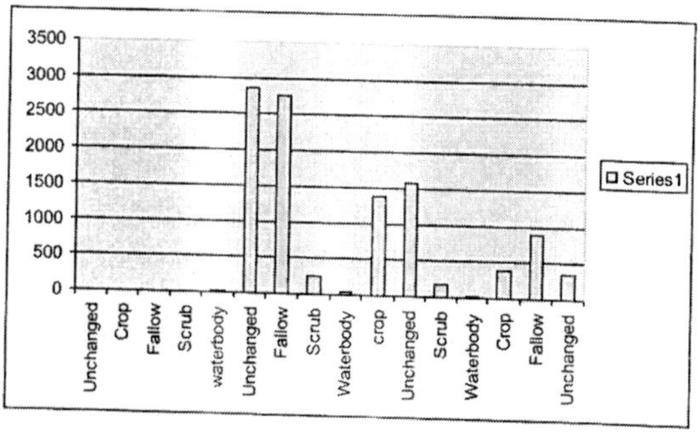

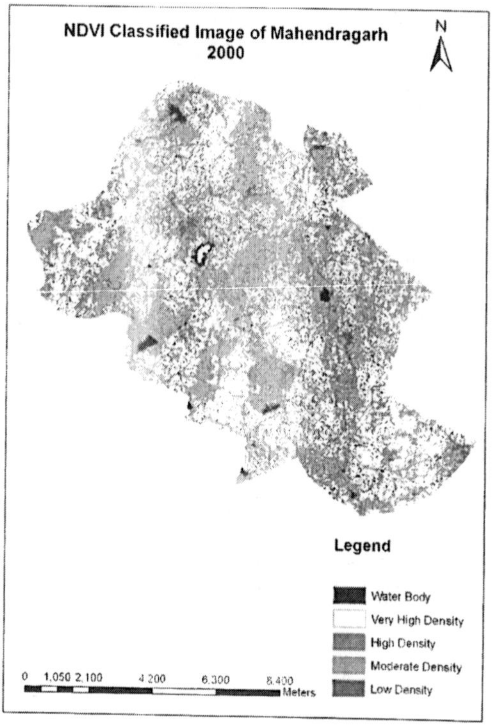

The analysis of the Satellite Imagery for the year 2000 was done using the NDVI classification.

NDVI Class	*Area in Hectares*
Waterbody	90.8
Cropland	7347.9
Fallowland	2827.5
Scrub	469.9
Total	10735.9

The total study area is 10735.9 Hectares. The water bodies in the study area occupied is 90.8 Hect, which constitute 0.84 percent of total study area. The Cropland in the study area occupied is 7347.9 Hect, which constitute 68.4 percent of total study area. The Fallow in the study area occupied is 2827.5 Hect, which constitute 26.3 percent of total study area. The Scrub in the study area occupied is 469.9 Hect, which constitute 4.37 percent of total study area.

The analysis of the Satellite Imagery for the year 2005 was done using the NDVI classification.

NDVI Class	*Area in Hectares*
Waterbody	270.7
Cropland	7360.5
Fallowland	2369.9
Scrub	734.9
Total	10735.9

The total study area is 10735.9 Hectares. The water bodies in the study area occupied is 270.7 Hect, which constitute 2.52 percent of total study area. The Cropland in the study area occupied is 7360.5 Hect, which constitute 68.5 percent of total study area. The Fallow in the study area occupied is 2369.9 Hect, which constitute 22.1 percent of total study area. The Scrub in the study area occupied is 734.9 Hect, which constitute 6.84 percent oftotal study area.

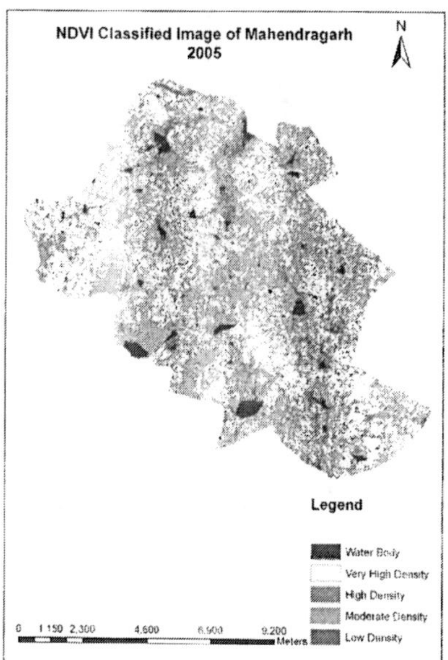

The analysis of the Satellite Imagery for the year 2007 was done using the NDVI classification.

The total study area is 10735.9 Hectares. The water bodies in the study area occupied is 60.6 Hect, which constitute 0.56 percent of total study area. The Cropland in the study area occupied is 7170.8 Hect, which constitute 66.7 percent of total study area. The Fallow in the study area occupied is 3253.8 Hect, whieh constitute 30.3 percent of total study area. The Scrub in the study area occupied is 250.7. Hect, which constitute 2.33 percent of total study area.

NDVI Class	*Area in Hectares*
Waterbody	60.6
Cropland	7170.8
Fallowland	3253.8
Scrub	250.7
Total	10735.9

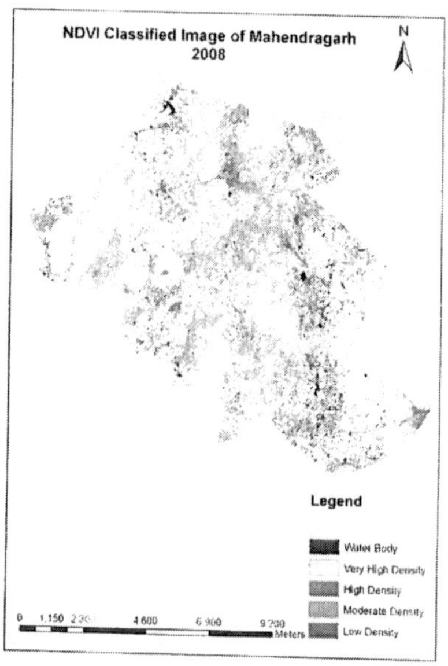

The analysis of the Satellite Imagery for the year 2008 was done using the NDVI classification.

NDVI Class	*Area in Hectares*
Waterbody	46.4
Cropland	8758.1
Fallowland	1364.9
Scrub	566.6
Total	10735.9

The total study area is 10735.9 Hectares. The water bodies in the study area occupied is 46.4 Hect, which constitute 0.43 percent of total study area. The Cropland in the study area occupied is 8758.1 Hect, which constitute 81.5 percent of total study area. The Fallow in the study area occupied is 1364.9 Hect, which constitute 12.7 percent of total study area. The Scrub in the study area occupied is 566.6 Hect, which constitute 5.27 percent of total study area .

The Comparison of the aerial extent under each class is given in the table below:

Classes	*September 2000*	*October 2005*	*October 2007*	*October 2008*
Waterbody	90.8	270.7	60.6	46.4
Cropland	7347.9	7360.5	7170.8	8758.1
Fallowland	2827.5	2369.9	3253 .8	1364.9
Scrub	469.9	734.9	250.7	566.6
Total	10735.9	10735.9	10735.9	10735.9

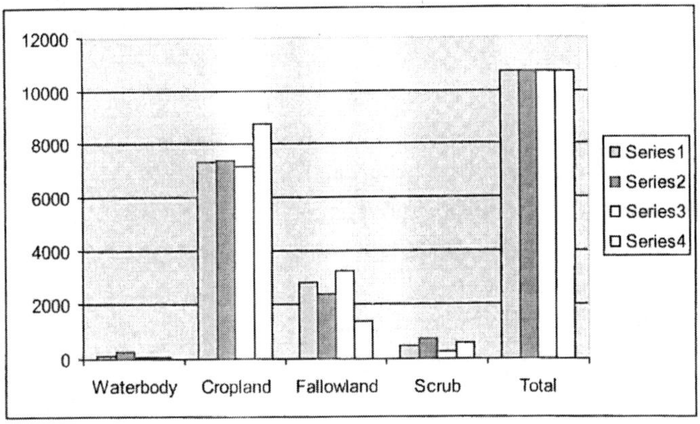

Recommendations

The following recommendations could be suggested for effective watershed development in the districts of Bhilwara in Rajasthan State:

1. From the rain fall patterns of last decade, it is observed that sudden flash floods emanated from heavy rainfall are rare and rainfall pattern is consistent or below average. Hence it is being suggested that appropriate rain water harvesting structures with requisite height should be constructed.
2. Plantation should be implemented in areas where soil condition is good and water sources are there to take care of initial months of the plantation, for their survival.

3. Too many Checkdams and Khadins should be avoided on the same drainage basin.
4. Appropriate cropping pattern suitable to the soil conditions and rainfall pattern should be promoted rather than conventional agriculture practice, which is posing non-sustainable.
5. As drinking need is very acute. Tonkas need to be promoted for water storage for human and animals.
6. Development of bore wells and tube wells where ground water is not saline and water resources are available, may be considered.
7. Agro forestry for fuel wood and pasture development for fodder in suitable agri lands, needs immediate attention.
8. Stabilisation of sand dunes need to be immediately taken up in Jaisalmer and Barmer Districts.
9. Dairy has lot of promise in the region and has proved to be a good economical and livelihood support activity and needs extensive promotion.
10. Sprinkler and Drip irrigation need to be promoted wherever there is agriculture activities by ground water utilisation. Under innovative practices, additional subsidies may be considered for solar systems, biogas, sprinkler and drip irrigation etc, for integrated development of watershed.
11. Selection of watersheds should be purely on the basis of scientific basis with GP wise prioritization.
12. DPRs to be generated with Geospatial technology application with the consideration of slope, aspect, drainage, land usc and land cover factors.
13. For promoting scientific inputs in the watershed planning, monitoring and evaluation, value added satellite data could be used from State Remote Sensing Centres and Bhuvan Platform of NRSC ISRO.
14. Inventory and mapping of all existing structures before the start of work, by a GPS to be mandatory in DPR Generation, and these GPS generated GIS maps to be superimposed on the base maps and satellite images as pre-project scenario.
15. Open source software like Quantum GIS and customised maps from NRSCI State Remote Sensing Centres to be utilised at Block level and District level which are user friendly.

16. As desert areas are very difficult areas for selection of proper sites for water harvesting structures and as structures like Khadin, Dhora and Tonka etc require huge investments, cost norms for desert areas, should be considered appropriately.
17. In most of the present structures, additional deepening may cause break of base layer which causes more seepage of water to downwards which nobody knows which aquifer is going to be recharged by that water. This can in turn cause negative impact of activity.
18. Lack of Proper rates for new and innovative activities, frequent revision of rates is required. Districts in Rajasthan are having separate BSR for each district which is based on various prevailing BSR rates of forest, Irrigation and PWD etc. The rates remained constant for a longer duration than the change in the market rates of material. BSR rates should be revised and changed frequently keeping the pace with materials market.

    Absence of this encourages malpractices and false record maintenance, to fit the vouchers in the estimated labour and material cost.
19. Region specific standardisation of items in estimate preparation, namely number of rows of a seed or grass required per running meter length, vegetation is required and type of structure, ratio proportion concrete or masonry appropriate and type of WHS or building structures, number of items to be included in the estimates, Agencies like KVKs, forest, Irrigation, PWD departments, CAZRl, AFRI to help develop region specific standards for a particular activity. Standardisation of estimate preparation to be published as manual as a base for the preparation of estimates.
20. GPS entries along with Khasara number to be made mandatory. GPS entries in the measurement books, and generated shape files may be superimposed time to time on the existing various layers of various watersheds at GP level.
21. Plantation activity is observed to be not so successful in desert areas executed by Watershed Department and post project management is also under the hand of Gram Panchayats which again is not being followed properly, and after the utilisation of all WDF funds, no fund is there for sustaining the watershed development works. In case of Plantation Works, these should be handled by the Forest Department.

22. Timing of plantation and species selection in consonance with biodiversity, agroclimatic conditions, local species, weather cycles in case of plantation improves the survival rate and sustainability.

Concluding Remarks

The reasons attributed are climate change, human activities, vegetal erosion, salinity, rocky and barren process, are the major components of desertification and land degradation. The Geospatial technology evaluation of watersheds implemented in the district of Bhilwara of Rajasthan State analysis was validated with field survey of each structure and GPS coordinate data, with extensive field surveys of the watersheds, validated by temporal satellite data, by assessing the extent and density and type of vegetation and anlysc the deforestation, land use and land cover, geomorphological aspects, and present land conditions, by extensive use of GIS, Remote Sensing and Digital Image Processing techniques, carried out specifically for the years, 1992, 1997, 2000, 2001, 2005 and 2007. The Data Products Used for this study are satellite imageries, GPS/DGPD readings, SOl Maps, field data from Watershed Departments to reach the implementation point and information gathered from beneficiaries and local people. The themes generated were land use and land cover, Normalised Differential Vegetative Index (NDVI), Ratio of Vegetative Index (RVI), Square root of Vegetative Index (SQRT) and Transformed Normalised Vegetative Index (TNDl). Digital image processing is carried for the extracting information from satellite imagery by importing the image, georeferncing, subsetting study area, image enhancement, land use and land cover classification, supervised and unsupervised classification, Accuracy Assessment, Determination of Vegetation Density, estimation of Vegetation Indices and finally estimation of Change Detection.

Soil, water, flora and fauna are the important land resources, which together influence in the survival of human beings by supporting food production and providing a congenial living environment. Land resources are being exploited faster than they are renewed, as a result ecosystems are degraded, life support processes are threatened and biodiversity, being the key factor in maintaining biospheric resilience is decreasing at an alarming rate. Geospatial technology Watershed evaluation has given many lessons to learn to develop innovations and strategies for the formulation of programmes and policies for watershed development and reversing the impact of desertification and improving the ecological balance of the region.

References

1. National Remote Sensing Centre Satellite Data (2005-2009).

2. District Watershed Department DPR Reports
3. Survey of India
4. State Remote Sensing Application Centre, Jodhpur
5. Zilla Parishad Watershed Progress Reports

GIS APPLI CATION FOR GRAM PANCHAYAT PLANNING AT MICROLEVEL

VASALA MADHAVA RAO*, P KESAVA RAO*, NSR PRASAD***

*(Ex. Prof & Head, **Head, ***Assistant Professor, CGARD, NIRDPR, Hyderabad)*

Introduction

The advent of space technology all pervading and the pace of ICT facilitating the data acquisition on almost real-time mode gives opportunity for judicious decision making at all levels of governance for the developing world for reduction of redundancy and time and for optimum utilisation of the scarce resources. The planning process has undergone a drastic change in recent years where decentralized participatory decision-making is resorted to ensure sustainability. However for this participatory decision-making, accessibility to a comprehensive data base which is easy to access and understand of land records, topography, resources, settlement patterns and infrastructure new methodology and technology are needed. This is an area where spatial technologies playa key role in generating timely and reliable information for planning and decision-making at all levels.

The use of GIS for a micro administrative unit for planning and implementation was tested in an Action Research Project in one of the panchayats in India, where the knowledge base is developed up to cadastral level (land parcel level) and the household socio-economic data is embedded on this layer on a GIS platform, with all graphic features of house type and household linked, to enable stake holders take decisions in a dynamic mode.

Even though it is widely recognized that the Geographic Information System (GIS) has the capacity to analyze both spatial and temporal data on a cost effective manner for effective planning and management, its application at the micro level for participatory planning and management has not reached the desired level. In this context an Action Research Project was taken up at the Panchayat level by the National Institute of Rural Development where efforts were made to develop an interactive package for participatory management at the panchayat level.

Planning requires association and integration of various activities with spatial (georeferenced) and non-spatial characteristics. Facility planning and management is one such an important area. Geomatics-based approaches to facility planning and management have, of late, gained prominence as they offer rational, efficient and effective solutions. Further, the rapid advances in the hardware and software technologies coupled with a growing competition among the related vendors have brought down the cost of Geomatics/GIS technology by manifold, making it affordable for deployment on a large scale for use in decentralised planning.

Several attempts were made by the various National Organisations, Universities, Institutes, Govt Departments, NGOs, National and international Organisations, but these could not address the exact needs of local self governments for local applications. Even web based applications were developed for wider applications in States like Kerala, Andhra Pradesh, Madhya Pradesh and West Bengal but only helped the Administration monitoring agency of both State and Central Government.

In view of this scenario, an attempt has been made to actually apply the GIS in a simple, user friendly, customised, local need based, interactive basis and can be handled by the local youth and Gram Panchayat functionaries, which helps taking various decisions at the Gram Panchayat level integrating layers of information both spatial and attribute pertaining to the Gram Panchayat.

Premise

The primary objective of evolving a simple GIS applications are to devise a GIS based Action Plan for the Gram Panchayat Level Planning on an Interactive Mode and to test the interactive GIS based Gram Panchayat Plan on a Pilot Basis with the help of Local Self Government, Government Functionaries, NGO, and the Local People.

Study Area

The study area chosen was the Villivalam Gram Panchayat of Wallijabad Block of Kanchipuram District, Tamil Nadu State, a Southern State in India. The study area consists of entire Villivalam Gram Panchayat. It is created using the geographical extents of the Gram Panchayat and true origin (74 N 21°E) of the Walijabad Block of Kanchipuram District of the State of Tamilnadu. The Gram Panchayat has three (3) villages namely Villiva lam, Koyambakam and Pandyan, The purpose was to give appropriate development initiatives in planning, monitoring and projectisation by the local people of Villivalam Gram Panchayat and the local bodies, for developing a reliable database and take decisions based on the same.

Methodology and Analytical Framework

The base data forms the attribute database and the maps, satellite imagery, Ariel photographs etc spatial database. These databases are integrated in a GIS platform and an information system is developed. The developed information system is embedded with query facilities so as to make it interactive, to adopt to new situations and environments. A group of youth are specially trained at SIRD, Tamil Nadu in computer skills, who are enthusiastic in operating and maintaining the same. It showcases the household level data, infrastructure, schemes and programmes, plans and proposals, Government, NGO and Local Bodies for their daily activities, reporting, decision makin g, data needs and other allied activities. Integrated resource surveys (Natural resources and Human resources) and mapping at the panchayat level involving local volunteers, panchayat officials etc, surveys relating to basic infrastructure of the panchayat roads, drinking water resources, schools etc, household information, housing structure, type of material used in house construction, basic amenities like electricity, water, telephone etc, photograph of the house and its members, household wise collection of data relating to house tax, water tax etc, cadastral map in the scale of 1: 5000. Plot wise information were captured and integrated in GIS platform.

A Participatory Rural Appraisal (PRA) exercise was carried on to understand the priorities and needs of the people of Villivalam Gram Panchayat, with the PRA Resource Map showing good understanding of people about their Gram Panchayat, spatial spread, resources, infrastructure, Governmental programmes and projects and their neighbourhood. The database on the same was built up from existing database of the Gram Panchayat, Walijabad Block and Kanchipuram District information base, with further consolidated with Tamilnadu Sate making accessible for youth, students, Panchayat Fuctionaries and others. Topo Sheet of the district and cadastre map of Villivalam including that of Koyanbakam and Pandyan was geo-coded along with satellite imagery.Various relational database of the Gram Panchayat were integrated with the base vector layer and analysis based on the Gram Panchayat day to day decision requirements were attempted for use by the Panchayat for local level application.

Data sets related to status on village-level basic amenities, population census, special requirements as identified by the gram panchayat were embedded for consideration for facility planning at village level. The database on village level basic amenities under provided the status on the schools, hospitals/dispensaries, Gram Panchayat Building, Anganwadi, etc., and accessibility to post offices, telephones, road and rail connectivity, amongst others, population census provided the demographic profile for the village, while the special requirements for Gram Panchayat were related to Gram Panchayat administration and management, besides data related to weekly market places *(haat bazars*).

Output

An iterative method is inbuilt into the system for identification of a suitable location (optimized) for creation of a facility based on certain predetermined norms with the optimized location for the creation of facilities, accessibility, infrastructure, norms, gap analysis, present Schemes and Programmes, fund analysis and the like help the GP functionaries to present in Gram Sabha and take actions for development activities.

Village GIS has been customized for facility planning and management for the Villivalam Gram Panchayat in Walijabad Block of Kanchipuram District of Tamilnadu State. Although Village GIS can support a wide range of applications due to its open-ended design, it is presently being contemplated for use for the applications such as facility planning (Identification of suitable locations for creation of new facilities such as primary schools, middle schools etc.), monitoring the functional status of various village amenities such as transformers, hand pumps, schools, hospitals etc, monitoring and evaluation of the implementation of various rural development and poverty alleviation programmes/schemes (Mid-day meals scheme for school children, housing and employment guarantee schemes etc.), management of road network, village connectivity to Panchayat Headquarters, Land Holding Analysis, House Type Analysis, Income Analysis, Occupation Analysis, Eligibility Analysis and Age Group Analysis for education infrastructure.

Observations and Findings

The striking revelations in this study is the fact that local people are greatly enthusiastic in adapting to new technology and new way of working together and takes lot of interest in knowing new ways of doing things. Secondly, the people at the local level raise above political, economic and social affiliations, and express their solidarity in effecting the new tools and technology in their day to day work. The women participation was quite encouraging and they come forward for propagating the use and adoptability to new way of doing things.

The younger mass feel social upheaval and increase in their social status in exposure and use of new IT Tools at the local level. The people' s representatives give all encouragement and support and stand by the people in introduction of new technology and in new ways of doing things. irrespective of their political affiliations. The district and local administration takes great interest in introducing new IT Tools and request development of these tools with in built functionality of day to day administrative use at all level, in improving their performance and effectiveness and express their support and cooperation in any attempt in this regards.

Concluding Remarks

The user friendly interactive GIS for a micro administrative unit has helped in ensuring better participation of the stakeholders in decision making. The variation in the level of education of the community was bridged by pictorial representation of data and help in empowerment of the community and generated land literacy.

User friendly interactive GIS data base generated at a micro administrative unit (panchayat) can improve the efficiency of administration, improve resource mobilization and help in informed decision making. The GIS facilitation is simple and customized and open for modifications and hold lot of promise for local level applications and has capabilities of liking wide graphic aspects, like photographs, audios, videos, imageries and analyzed maps etc, which project field realities and help taking appropriate decision making, by people themselves.

Village GIS is a GIS based Gram Panehayat Planning system, which has all the data formats to build up data inventory. link graphics, identify locational features, generate various graphic analysis for decision making and shows information both horizontal and vertical.

Village GIS is expected to usher in the desired transparency and easeness in the Gram Panchayat planning and enable a faster response to the changing ground realities in the development planning, owing to its in-built scientific approach and demonstrate cost effective solutions for local level planning in rural areas, and help bring the benefits of geospatial technology applications for the rural masses.

GIS could become a tool for empowerment, decision alternatives, scenarios, modeling, what if analysis, locational and spatial spread analysis and an integrating tool for interfacing all information for synthesis, which can be a very potential tool for Gram Panchayat Planning, monitoring and evaluation process and can be an integral part of our life, administration, policies and programmes.

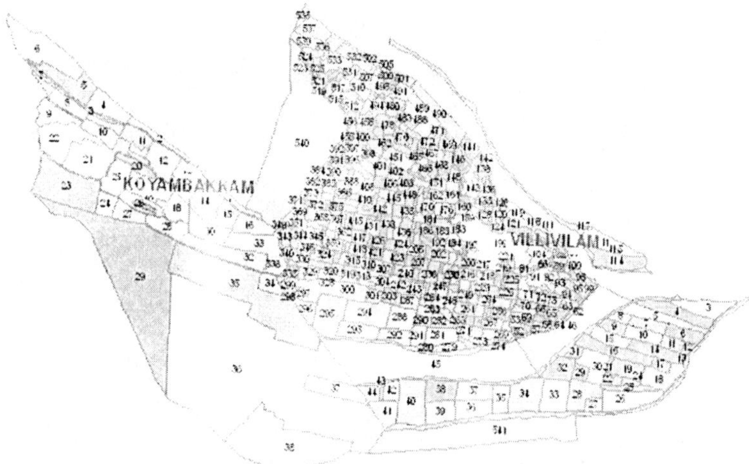

Survey numbers of land parcel integrated with household and house numbers for a integrated information system at local level.

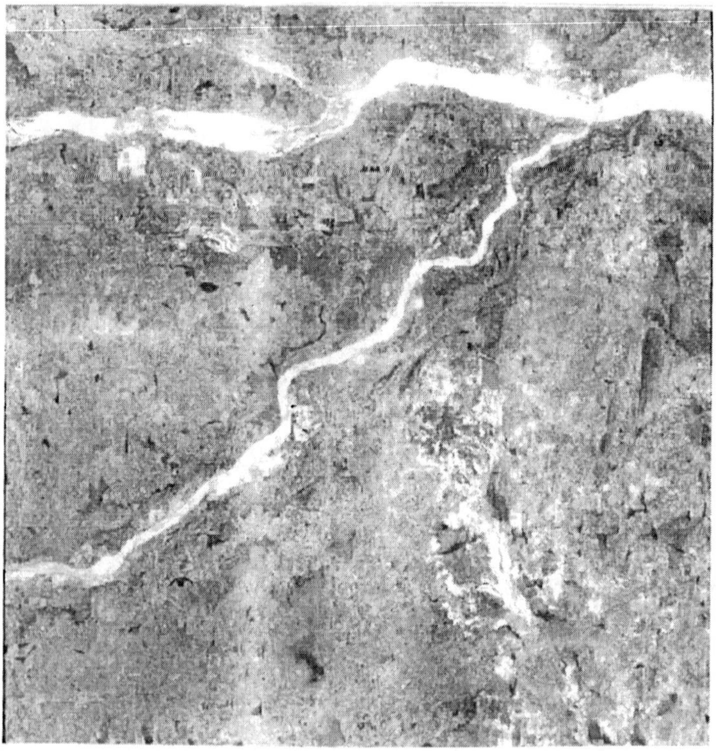

Satellite imagery of the study area showing land use and land cover and river basin.

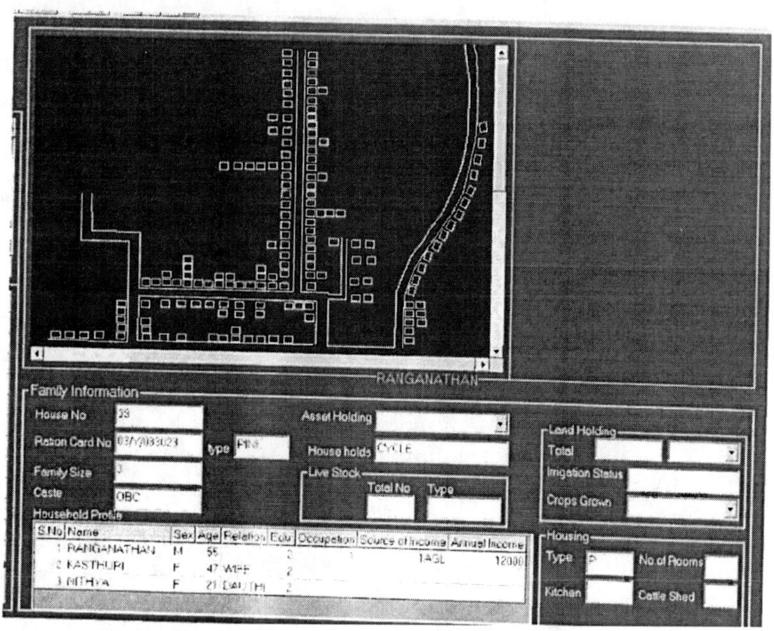

Villivalam Gram Panchayat Layout and PRA interface for interactivity

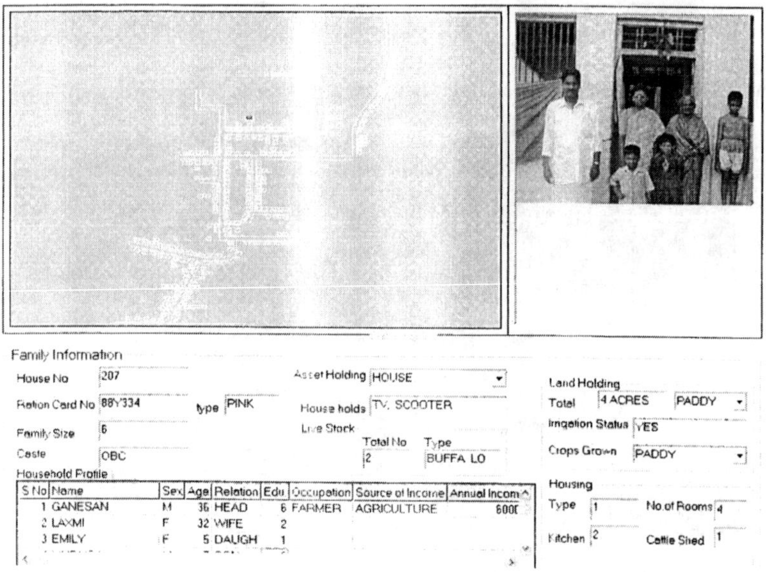

Household information

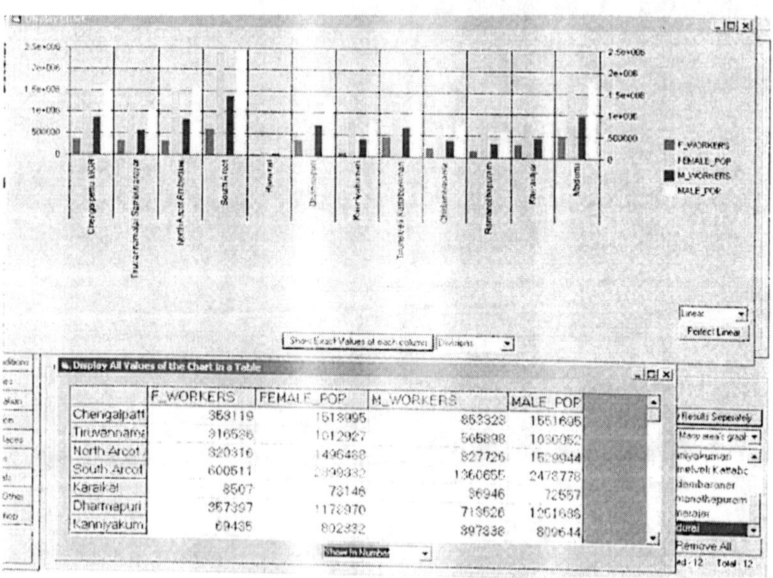

Data Analysis for decision making

Typological Research:

A Systematic Survey

In this chapter, an intensive attempt has been made over an extensive area to present the typological research trends at three points of time with four phases. Phase-1 deals with unidiscipline; Phase-II deals with interdisciplinary one and phase-III deals with Multidisciplinary perspectives on one topic (i.e.) "suicide" besides the future areas of research.

Phase - I: During this period (1960-1980), researcher as well as research supervisors themselves were confined exclusively to their own discipline for example: the Ph.D. theses were of this nature.

1. Land utilisation and occupational structure of people around Kolleru Lake (1970).
2. Hyderabad and Secunderabad: A study in Urban Geography (1965).

It is observed that the presentation of the thesis was on the track of the subject without having any deviation and interaction with the other subjects (other disciplines), The methodologies that have been applied for analysis was confined only to their own disciplie. It is further examined that subject experts were also more confined to their own discipline.

Phase-II: During this period (1960-2000), the Social Sciences research has been wide spread and much confined to statistical methods besides their own discipline. During this period, researchers were much concerned and contracted to analysis with statistical methods. During this period both the researchers and supervisors were much interactive with people of different disciplines besides their own discipline. Research institutions as well as funding agencies were very particular about the interdisciplinary nature of the topic. The researcher may belong to different subject to that of the research supervisor. For example: Agro Economic study of Godavari districts. A case study from Andhra Pradesh.

In the above process of research, many investigators were recruited for the collection of data at the primary level. Later, the collected data has been analysed through statistical methods as well. Computerized data processing was the order of that time and it was also has been encouraged by the funding agencies such as ICSSR, New Delhi and University Grants Commission, New Delhi.

Phase-III: Daring this period (2000-2008), both the researchers and the supervisors themselves were very much interactive and conversant with the latest technological methods and innovations. It has been identified and examined that some subjects were exclusively included in the subject of Geography with GIS and remote sensing methodologies. The present thesis in geography are very much prove to the attachment of GIS and ₹ For example: to study the landslides one has to depend upon geomorphology, top-sheet, Aerial photography and satellite imageries are used to interpret the data for analysis. In the same way, the above methods are also quite useful to study urban geography, settlement geography, regional planning and development besides social and spatial pattern of a society whether it is rural, urban, rurban, For urban studies, economics, history, geography and sociology are quite helpful for collection of the data as well as analysis.

Phase-IV: The present day research since 2009, besides inter-disciplinary typological research, a new and innovative methods of research have been used for example. inter-national seminar on multi-disciplinary perspectives on suicide experience of SAARC countries, 9-10 January, 2009 organized by centre for economic and social studies, Hyderabad, Andhra Pradesh, India is an important contribution by social Scientists in India.

The inaugural session was by professor R. Radhakrishna (Economics discipline); Background paper was presented by Prof. S. Galab, Prof. U. Vindhya and Dr. E. Revathi (CECS) Economics and statistics disciplines; Dr. Daya Sana Sundaram, Department Psychiatry University of Adelaide, Australia, Prof. Lakshmi Vijayakumar, Head of the Department of Psychiatry voluntary Heath services, Chennai were the prominent speakers of the session.

Professor P. Radha Krishnan, Department of Sociology, Madras Institute of Development Studies Chennai has given lecture on "Social context of the rise in suicide". Professor D. Narasimha Reddy visiting professor, Institute for Human Development, New Delhi has given lecture on, "Economists perspectives on suicide, later, discussion has taken place for 20 minutes.

Professor B.D. Lahoti, Department of Philosophy, Osmania University, Hyderabad has given lecture on, "Philosophical Reslections on the problem of suicide and murder" and later lecture, entitled, "Regime politics and Rural crisis: contexteralizing suicides in Rural AP by professor K. Srinivasulu, Department of Political Science, Osmania University, Hyderabad.

Professor G.N. Rao, Centre for Development Studies, Thiruvantha-puram has achieved and Dr. Srijit Mishra, Associate Professor, I.G.I.D.R., Mumbai have presented an excellent paper, "Farmers suicides in India: save trends and patterns" followed by Dr. Lenim Raghuvanshi's, Director, People's Vigilance Committee on Human Rights, Uttar Pradesh. Paper on suicides and malnutrition among weavers in Varanasi".

Later, Prof. Galab, Dr. E. Revathi, P. Prudhvikar Reddy and Mr. P. Dharma Raju, CESS, Hyderabad have presented a paper "Distress and suicides among weavers in Andhra Pradesh" followed by Prof. Rama Melkote, Prof. M. Kodandaram, Osmani University, Hyderabad's paper on "Starvation Deaths in Rural Andhra Pradesh". Further followed by a lengthy discussion on the above papers.

Professor Vikram Patel, Department of International Mental Health, London School of Hygiene & Topical Medicine, London delivered a lecture on, "The Social Determinants of suicidal behaviour: Lessons from Goa." Later Professor Michael Philips' Executive Director, Beijing Suicide Research and Prevention center, Beijing Huilonguan Hospital, China has delivered a lecture on, "Cument status and future direction for suicide research and prevention on in China" in the session 3, predictors, prevention and policy measure, was chaired by Professor K.C. Suri, Department of Political Science, University of Hyderabad, Hyderabad.

Fourth Session, "Socio-Political Restabilization of Society and suicides" chaired by Professor G. Haragopal, Department of Political Science, University of Hyderabad, Hyderabad. In this sessions Dr. Daya Somasundaram, clinical Associate Professor, Department of Psychiatry, University of Adalaide, Australia has presented an excellent paper, "Suicide in Times of Civil conflicts case study of North Lanka". Later Mr. P.O. George Social Scientist, Maithrikochi, Kochi, Kerala has presented an important theme, "Socio-cultural Factors influencing suicidal behaviour, with special reference to Kerala". Discussion torch place about the interlinking factors with suicides.

Dr. Kapil Ahmed, Epidemiologist, St. George's University of London, London spoke on, "Violent Deaths among Women in Reproductive Age in Rural Bangladesh, followed by Dr. A.H.M. Zehadul Karik, Professor of Anthropology, Comilla University, Bangladesh, Paper on, "Suicide among Women in Bangladesh: An Anthropological investigation of the empirical level". The sixth session and final session was civil society/ NGO initiatives in suicide prevention, achived by Prof. P. Radhakrishnan, Professor of Sociology, Madras Institute of Development Studies, Chennai where in MS Lakshmi Ratnayaka, Director, Sumanthrayo Rural Programme, Srilanka spoke on, "Crisis intervention and suicide prevention in Rural communities in Srilanka (Grass-root level experiences", Dr. Krishnan Giresh, clinical psychologist, Government Mental Health Centre, Thiruvanthapuram gave a lecture on, "Bias in the Design of Intervention - A Challenge to suicide prevention in Kerala".

Mr. Akheel Siddique, Roshini, Hyderabad has presented a paper on, "Suicide Across life span - Elderly and Youth" which it has been identified as an important paper for the session.

FUTURE ARAS OF RESEARCH

2.1 Geography

1. Agricultural Geography of Telangana State using G.I.S. and R.S. Technologies.

2.2(2) Regional Planning with special reference to newly formed state of Telangana 29th State of Indian Union.

2.4(5) Disaster Management: A case study of Andhra Pradesh.

2.3(4) Land form and landuse: using GIS & ₹ : A case study of Nothern Telangana State, India.

0.3 Commerce, Management, Economics and Statistics:

1. Commercial activity in Telangana State (from local to Global).
2. Management of Small Scale Industries (Problems & Prospectus).
3. Human Resource Managements: A case study of Telangana State, India.
4. Human Research Management: A case study of Andhra Pradesh, India.
5. H.R.D. - A case study of Coastal Andhra Pradesh.
6. Mineral Resource Management - A case study of Rayalaseema Region of Andhra Pradesh.
7. Agro Economic Study of Andhra Pradesh.
8. Agro Industries : A case study of Andhra Pradesh.
9. Rural electrification and Benefication through Planning and Development (Location, structure, growth and development).
10. Changing demographic structure and occupational patterns of People: A case study of Andhra Pradesh (Polavaram Project, migration of people and environs).
11. Stochastic process in Statistical Research - Methodology.
12. Role of Dependent, independent and Dummy variables- A statistical Appraisal - A Study in Methodology.

4.1 History, Political Sciences and Public Administration

1. Cultural History of Telangana Region.
2. Economic history of Andhra Pradesh.

4.2.3. Sri K. Chandra Sekhara Rao - A Political Study.

4. Political ideology of governance of Telangana.
5. B.J.P's Role in National Development.

4.3.6.Health Programmes of Telangana State.

7. Poverty Alletiction Programmes and its impac on Human society.
8. Education and Health Programmes of A.P. Governance.
9. Nutritional deficiency deseases among the Tribal people - A case of Adilabad district.
10. Polavaram Project - Multidisciplinary and Interdisciplinaray approach.
    (Strategies and status of government programmes.)
11. Riverwaters a tribute and tribunal punishments -An enquiry.
12. Appraisal of watershed Development: A Geopolitical and Administrative Reforms and sharing of river waters of the Godavari and the river Krishna.

5.1. Library and Information Science and Urban Sociology

1. Digitalization of Library from the grass roots level -A study.
2. Computerization and digitization of Library at University level.
3. Impact of Technology on storing, maintenance of Librarians in India (Grass Roots Approach).
4. Research Trends in Library and Information Science in Andhra Pradesh and Telangana State, India.
5. Mapping of the Publication of National Level.
6. Applied Bibliometric Methodology - Current trends in Library Science Research.
7. Schemes of Potential for Excellence Status - A study.
8. Electronic Theses and Dissertations (ETDS) at University level / State level / National level.

5.2.9. A.P. Housing Programmes of State Government / Government of India during plan periods - A background paper.

10. Education programmes to SC /ST and visually handicapped.

Conclusion

1. It is observed that social science research programmes should be interlinked with two or more than disciplines so that the equipmentments of research could be identified UGC and IGSS of funded research programmes related to refresher courses should be planned to cater to the needs of the people and areas - (Spatio-temporal base).
2. Further observed that international seminar on multi disciplinary perspectives of suicide experience of SAARC countries has really

gained the momentum during and after 2009 and has created a platform for multi-disciplinary research.

3. Research scholars are advised to visualize the web sites which helps to understand the current scenerio of research of different levels in various subjects of funding agencies such as ICSSR, UGC, IHR, CSIR and inter-disciplinary nature of research than unidiscipline.

Suming up

1. "Research in Social Sciences : A Survey" has been designed into Seven chapters and each chapter indicates in its entirety with a new innovation at large.

The first chapter deals with an introduction, wherein the chapter wise content has been presented into segmented pattern with subject number in order to identify and recognize the conent trends in social science research. The background material has also been stated to enable the reader to understand easily the process and development of the theme with lucid language.

2. The Second chapter has been designed into different components of subjects. The second chapter (2.1) starts with Agricultural Geography, 2.2 Integrated Area Development plan for a delta taluk, Tanuku of West Godavari District, Andhra Pradesh, India. In 2.3, small scale industries in Telangana Region of Andhra Pradesh has been presented with location, structure, problems and prospects by S. Ramakrishna under the supervision of Dr. K. Vithal Reddy, Professor & Head Department of Geography Osmania University during the year 1988. It is an important study to understand the growth process of small scale industries and their component to economy.

Chapter two deals and represents the cylcone prove areas and the author has presented the economic planning and development. Agro-Economic studies has been present in 2nd chapter.

3. The Third chapter deals with, Commerce, Economics and Statistics carries the 3.1, 3.2, 3.3 and 3.4 subscripts, Management and commerce having been playing an important and pivotal role in any economy at the three levels, such as Nation/State/District or at the microest level Dr.V. Madhava Rao has presented the Rural Electrification in Medak District of Telangana State, where in has identified activities of Rural electrification Corporation, State Electricity Board and rural electric co-operatives operating in the region, assessed the problems that have accruing and the associated factors in the promotion of rural electrification and also suggested technological alternatives in light of the problems being falled in the region and growing need of electricity for various potentialactivities in Medak region, besides Investigating the situation through primary survey of the actual beneficiaries of the schemes and the grassroot panchayat raj institutions. It has been observed that, "eventually energy planning and audit should be an integral part of any sector planning or area planning and rural electrification to be reflected prominently, as base infrastructure for development".

CVS SRL Hanumantha Rao has presented the operations research in Statistics faculty and operations research has an important role in statistical research in the present century and opined that "the major constituent processes of the queuing model are arrival and service processes. Many of the queueing models to consider that arrival and service processes are independent and homogeneous. But this assumption is meaningful only, when we develop and analyse the models in a single environment".

4. Entitled asttistons and The Fourth chapter it has three sub disciplines such as History (4.1); 4.2 political science and 4.3, public administration S. Abdul Khadar has identified the impact of Tribal Policy on the select tribes of Andhra Pradesh and assessed the developmental programmes for the tribal during the plan periods with special emphasis on the fifth five year plan and also examined the extent of suitability of programmes for the different tribal areas vis-a-vis the social, economic and cultural values. He has identified that, "the granting of scheduled tribe status to the lambodies has unleased the process of large scale population migration into the Adilabad district from the neighbouring Maharashtra state. This population growth increased pressure on the forests causing dwindling of minor forest produce and encroachment of Gond land" (Most important research point).

4.2 In this section, political science relating to applied constitution with sectional interpretation at large includes centre - state relation in particular. 'federation in India win the context of Administrative relations between centre and states' by R. Gangadhara Sastry. Sastry opined, that, "their wisdon and foresight in developing a unique federal system can best be appreciated today when forces of disintegration are threatening the very existance of the republic".

4.3 "Implementation of Jawaharlal Nehru National Urban Renewal Mission : In the Mission city of Hyderabad" has been presented by V. Gangaiah, under the supervision of professor S. Bhoopathi Row (R), Department of Public Administration, Osmania University, Hyderabad, Telangana State, India. The author opined that, "it is hoped that the new programmes like the SMART City will continue the urban development momentun pickedup with JNNURM but with more focus, determination and funding".

5. The 5th Chapter deals with Digital Library as peets and content in 5.1 related to worldwide web. Hypermedia is used as a logical extension of the term hypertext in which graphics, audio, video, plain text and hyper links interlink to create a generally non-lined medium of information. She opined that "the duties of librarians are changing; librarians are, indeed inseded more than ever to assist in these new endeavours. No longer are librarians just keepers of the books. Librarians must be professionals who are knowledgeable and proactive in reaching out to their patrons in a

responsible way. Library and information professionals need to be well-versed with the on the information world and its view technologies".

B.M.K. Mohan has presented, the thesis entitled, "Housing policy and programmes in Urban Bhopal : A study in Social and Environmental change" under the supervision of Dr. I.S. Chauhan, Professor & Head, Department of Sociology, Barakatullah University, Bhopal (1992). Mohan opined that, between 40 to 50 percent of the population of Bhopal is living in Jhuggies in the new city and slum areas in the old city". The present work is a modest attempt in this direction to deal with this aspect in the 4th chapter of the entitled Volume. The author narrates the environmental changes due to Housing problems in Urban Bhopal.

6. In the 6th Chapter, analysis (core chapters) part has been presented cumulative content of core chapters took them as core components, which decides the performance appraisal related to research in social sciences : A survey 'stands as an exemplary study and paves, the way for future researchers and Practitisness of social sciences.

7. Four important and thought provoking papers related to GIS and ₹ applicable to physical environ-ment in the over all framework of environmental studies the interdisciplinary and multi-disciplinary nature of current research has been reviewed, which helps the future generation of researchers to adopt and design new innovative methodologies besides quantitative and qualitative methodologies including geographical carto-graphic technique not only help the geographers but also help, the non-geographers, such as social scientific related researchers. A new way of change is indispensible to adopt in their researches in the 21st century. summing up of the entire material has been Presented for a comprehensive and complete 100 to understand the social science Research process totally.

in 7th chapter broasly entitle.

" Role of Remote Sensing and GIS in

Social Science Research," where in,

Annexure - I

List of Theses

1. Regional Agricultural Geography of Andhra Pradesh - Y.V. Ramanayya.
2. Planning for Integrated Area Development - K.L. Narasimha Murthy.
3. Location, Structure, Problems and Prospects of Small Scale, Industries in Telangana - S. Ramakrishna.
4. Impact of Cyclone on development - A case study of Yanam - Kameswari, Varanasi.
5. Human Resource Accounting - K Anjaneyulu.
6. Planning and Management of Rural Electrification:

   A case study of Medak Region of Andhra Pradesh - V. Madhava Rao.
7. Heterogeneous queues and queues with independent Arrivals and services processes - CVSSRL Hanumantha Rao.
8. Impact of Tribal Policy of the select Tribes of Andhra Pradesh - S. Abdul Khader.
9. Federalison in India in the context of Administrative Relations between centre and states - R. Gangadhar Sastry.
10. Implementation of Jawaharlal Nehru National Urban Renewal Mission: In the Mission city of Hyderabad-V. Gangaiah.
11. Information Technology - Digital Liberary - Kandimalla Bharathi.
12. Housing Policy & Programmes in Urban Bhopal: A study in Social and Environmental Change - B.M.K. Mohan.

Annexure - II

C. V. of Dr. K.L. Narasimha Murthy

1. Name : Dr. K.L NARASIMHA MURTHY
2. Father's Name : Late Sri K.R.B. Chaynulu
3. D.O.B. : 2nd September, 1949.

4. Educational Qualifications:

- M.A., (Geography), specialization on Agricultural Geography, Second Class, Osmania University, Hyderabad 1971-73.
- Ph.D., (Regional Planning), Andhra University, Vishakhapatnam, 1985.
- Life Member of the National Association of Geographers, India, New Delhi.

5. Awards:

- A.P. Best - Teacher's Award 5th September, 1995.

6. Designations Held:

- Principal, Government UG & PG College (Men), Srikakulam - 532001
- APHES, Hyderabad (1976-2007) Govt. College, Rajahmundry and Government (Women) College, Srikakulam.

7. Publications:

- "Planning for Integrated Area Development" BRPC, New Delhi (1986) Ph. D. Thesis
- Ecology, Environment and Development, Mangal Deep Publications, Jaipur (2003)
- Applied Geo Informatics, Mangal Deep Publications, Jaipur (2007).

- Computerization and Digitization of Land Records - CGARD - Concept Publications, New Delhi (Communicated)

8. Edited Volumes

- Applied Geo-environmental Studies, Volume 1 (2008), Mangal Deep Publishers, Jaipur (2008).
- Applied Geo-environmental Studies, Volume 2 (2009), Mangal Deep Publishers, Jaipur.

9. Research Methodology and Indian Social Sciences Research

- Research in Geography, Published by Ashish Publishers, New Delhi (1992)
- Geographical Research, Concept Publishers, New Delhi (1999)
- Indian Social Science Research, Teja Publishers, Hyderabad (2012)
- Research Methodology in Geography, Concept Publishing Company, New Delhi (2014)

10. Texbooks and Practical Geography

- World geography, Published by Telugu Academy, A.P., Hyderabad (2003).
- I BA/B.Sc, Practical Geography, Telugu Academy, A.P. Hyderabad (2010).
- M.A/M.Sc, Economic Geography (under preparation) Concept Publishing Company Pvt Ltd., New Delhi.

11. Research Papers in Edited Volumes and Books

- Environment and Agriculture by H. Ramchandran, New Delhi (1990).
- Readings in Environmental challenges, sustainable Development, Remote Sensing and GIS by Vijay Bhole, A. Kamalakar Reddy and S. Padmaja, Osmania University, Hyderabad Published by Universal Scientific Publishers, Jaipur (2005).
- Readings in development studies, Rupa Books and Publishers, Jaipur (1995).

12. Research Papers Published in Peer Journals and Referred Journals

- Land Utilization in Vegeswarapuram, Deccan Geographer, Hyderabad (1976)

- Identification of Central Places, IIT Kharagpur (1985)
- Central Place Theory, A Survey, Deccan Geographer, Hyderabad (1987)
- Animal Husbandry Resources, ACARSH, Belgaum (1995)

13. Library and Information Science

- Scientometric Study, Indian Journal of Library and Information Science, (IGLIS), Vol. 24, No.1-2, January-June, 2011 Cuttak, Orissa, India.
- Evolution and Evaluation of Research Methods in Library and formation studies - Bibliometric study. A survey (2005-2009) Indian Journal library and information Science (CIGLIS) Vol. 26, No. 384, July - December, 2013.

14. Review of Books

- Geography of Marketing and Rural Development, by professor, V.K. Shrivastav, Published in Review Projector, Coimbatore (1987).

15. Research Guideship for M.Phil / Ph.D. in Geography

- Vinayaka Institute of Research, Salem (2006)

16. Research Projects

Research Projects Completed so far @ cess, Hyderabad, NIRD Hyderabad and RCPES, Osmania University, Hyderabad.

Four Research Projects - 2008 to 2011, 4 years period @ Centre for Economic & Social Studies, Begumpet, Hyderabad under Dr. P. Padmanabha Rao.

17. One Research Project @ C-GARD National Institute of Rural Development, Rajendra Nagar, Hyderabad under Prof. V. Madhava Rao, Head, C-GARD, NIRD, Rajendra Nagar, Hyderabad.
18. Urban Poverty Alleviation-One Research Project-2013 (one year) @ Regional Centre for Urban and Environmental Studies, Osmania University, Hyderabad - 500 061.
19. NULM. Project-2014 (10th February, 2015) @ Regional Centre for Urban and Environmental Studies, Osmania University, Hyderabad-500061.
20. Urban & Environmental studies - An Assessment (2014 - 2015) @ Regional Centre for Urban & Environmental Studies, Osmania University, Hyderabad - 500 061 (T.S.).

21. Present Research Work

- Writing a text book on Economic Geography for M.A./M.Sc, Geography Students MOU with concept publishing company, New Delhi,

22. Research in Library and Information Science

- Bibliometric Survey 2006 - 2015 under preparation.
- Scientometric study, 2006 - 2015 under preparation.

23. Innovative and Interactive Research - Collaboration with

- Prof. S. Ramakrishna,
  Department of Geography,
  Osmania University, Hyderabad.

24. References

- **Prof. N. Nagabhushanam,**
  Department of Geography, S.V. University, Tirupati, A.P.
- **Prop. M. Sambasiva Rao,**
  Department of Geography, S.K. University, Anantapur, A.P.
- **Prof. P.V. Sarma (Retd.),**
  Department of Economics,
  Andhra University, Visakhapatnam, A.P.

25. Address for Communication

#305, Manikanta Saisudha Apartments,

Meena Cafe Lane, Warasigua, Secunderabad - 500 061, T.S. Cell No.7207337962.

Station : Hyderabad.

Date: 7th February 2019.

Index

F

G

H

I

J

K

N

O

T